A **new christian** READER

A **new christian** READER

Edited by *Timothy Beaumont of Whitley*

SCM PRESS LTD

For Peter, friend and colleague

334 01120 5

First published 1974 by S.C.M. Press Ltd
56 Bloomsbury Street, London

© S.C.M. Press Ltd 1974

Type set by Gloucester Typesetting Co Ltd
and printed in Great Britain by
Fletcher & Son Ltd, Norwich

Contents

A Solitary Grain
Timothy Beaumont of Whitley

When I came back from Hong Kong in 1959 I was aware of two reciprocal gaps in the relationship of religion to journalism in the UK.

The first was a shortage of responsible reporting of church and religious news in the secular press, the second a shortage of self-criticism in the church's own press.

It is difficult today to remember those days before the Vatican Council, the Archbishop of Canterbury's journey to the Holy Land and *Honest to God* when there was so little reporting of religious events and views. The place of religion in the public life of the nation was represented in the press only by a weekly anodyne sermonette in the heavies and the ardent pursuit of any scandal involving a parson in the populars.

Although I felt that there were things which could be done about that situation, in fact it corrected itself fairly soon.

The other problem, although more manageable in size, was tougher in texture. The churches of England were declining in numbers and influence. A hopeful revival of religious interest at the universities had withered away, Christian stewardship had brought some churches to life but with hardly any lasting effect and Christians faced the prospect of a declining ministry devoting more of its time to raising more money to keep open even emptier mediaeval buildings.

But to judge from the religious, and in particular the Anglican, press everything in the garden was lovely. It was true that things would be even better if there were a few more high church bishops (*Church Times*) or low church bishops (*Church of England Newspaper*), but it is an imperfect world and you cannot have everything. Meanwhile, 'The Church is in Good Heart' (Archbishop Fisher).

Obviously what was needed was to blast a hole in this complacency. And a small magazine under the patronage of the Society of the Faith and edited by Christopher Martin and Nicholas Mosley was beginning to do just that. Its name was *Prism* and my next five years with it were great fun.

Eventually we had a circulation of 5000 (which must have been every educated radical Anglican in the country) and we broke even (by not paying our contributors).

But by 1965 it was clear that we had outlived our usefulness and that unless we were to do what we had condemned so fiercely in others and continue to exist for the mere sake of existing we had to change. The value of *Prism* was simple. As we said in our last editorial:

> Our faults have been manifest but at least we have never failed to give space to our critics. Our minor virtues may be in dispute but are not worth disputing. Our major virtue was that we helped in transforming a scattered number of individuals who felt unhappy about the traditional structures of the church and its position *vis-à-vis* the world into a confident and informed body of opinion.
>
> Unlikely archdeacons quietly turning their archdeaconry upside down in response to the obvious needs of the local community, timorous curates knowing that things were wrong but brainwashed into asking forgiveness in their prayers daily for rebelling against 'God's will for his church', and academics following unorthodox thoughts to their logical conclusions, all these needed to know of each other's existence and in the pages of *Prism* they suddenly found there were many others who felt and thought as they did.

But two things in particular were lacking. We were in favour of the ecumenical movement but we were not ourselves ecumenical. We preached involvement in the world but could not get our readers to write about anything except church affairs.

So *New Christian* was born. I leave it to its one very successful editor to recount its life. But before that, a word about its death. From the beginning it was clear that the infant would do well to survive more than the five years for which I could guarantee its losses. Clergy and students are poor. They cannot afford to pay a realistic price for a magazine, nor are they ideal targets for advertisers. And how many radical Christians are there in Britain anyway? Sure enough, the time came when we could carry on no longer.

But I believe we were right to start *New Christian* and we fought hard for what we thought was the right. And although reading this volume and then looking at the state of the churches, it is hard to claim a single victory, nevertheless I believe it was all worthwhile.

> In truth, in very truth I tell you, a grain of wheat remains a solitary grain unless it falls into the ground and dies; but if it dies, it bears a rich harvest.

Foreword

TREVOR BEESON

There is a widespread myth – not discouraged by journalists – that the editing of a newspaper or a magazine calls for rare skills. Nothing could be further from the truth. Hence the postcard from Timothy Beaumont which dropped through the letterbox of my Northern vicarage at the beginning of 1965 and conveyed an invitation to edit his proposed radical/ecumenical fortnightly.

Considered in terms of the prevailing mythology, the invitation was an outrageous one. It is true that I had been known to put pen to paper, but there had been no Fleet Street apprenticeship and no experience of dealing with the problems and pressures that inevitably go with a topical publication scheduled to appear every fourteen days.

Professional journalists whose opinions were sought during the planning stage shook their heads and prophesied disaster. Yet, for the whole of its five-year life, *New Christian* was produced by an editorial staff of three (sometimes four) people, all of whom were quite devoid of previous journalistic experience and who were frequently called away from their editorial duties in order to lend a hand with administrative chores. The basic requirements were catholicity, adaptability, commitment and, not least, good health – for the staff was too small to cover absences of more than a couple of weeks.

A far more serious criticism of the project was the evident lack of research into the size of the potential market for the proposed magazine and the serious lack of resources for reaching this market. It is one thing to produce a magazine; it is quite another to sell it in numbers large enough for the printing bills and other essential expenses to be met. This is not commonly recognized. There is a theory that if a product is of a sufficiently high quality it will sell itself, mainly through the personal recommendation of satisfied customers. This is true up to a certain threshold – in the case of a religious journal somewhere in the region of 4,000–5,000 subscriptions. Beyond this point the accountants and marketing men become more important than the editors.

In the case of *New Christian* these factors were almost totally neglected. Had they been taken seriously the magazine would probably have never been launched. The whole enterprise was, from one point of view, a gigantic folly; from another, it was a remarkable act of faith. From every angle it demanded immense generosity on the part of its proprietor. In the end the editorial staff and the readers had good reason to be grateful for the folly, the faith and the generosity.

From the earliest stages of planning, *New Christian* was modelled on the secular weeklies and in due course shared their printers. In this way it was hoped to present an image far removed from that of the traditional church press and, at the same time, offer a Christian journal which would bear comparison with the *New Statesman*, *New Society* and the *Spectator*. As long ago as 1945 the authors of the report *Towards the Conversion of England* had called for a magazine of this kind, and throughout the brief life of *New Christian* the high standards of its secular contemporaries (achieved, needless to say, with far greater resources of manpower and money) provided a constant challenge to the editorial staff which was stimulating and, in my view, extremely helpful.

Equally helpful was the editorial board which consisted of distinguished members of the mainstream churches who served in a private capacity but, naturally, contributed from within the ethos and outlook of their own traditions. The concept of a magazine edited by a committee is always unattractive. In fact, *New Christian* was not edited by its editorial board. The functions of the board were clearly understood: it had no authority to determine the contents of the magazine and it carried no responsibility for them. This left members of the board entirely free to make suggestions and criticism – and to register disagreements. At the same time, the editor was also free to accept or reject suggestions and criticism, and carried sole responsibility for everything published.

The main editorial in the first number of *New Christian* suggested that the success of the venture would depend on the degree to which readers, writers and editorial staff saw themselves involved in a joint enterprise. In the event, the contribution from readers was considerable. About half the feature articles were commissioned, and the rest simply turned up without prompting and usually in very large numbers. It was never possible to publish more than one in ten of the articles submitted for consideration. Of each ten received, it was plain that seven should not have been published in any journal anywhere, while two of the remaining three we would probably have been ready to publish had the space been available; the one accepted generally presented a new angle on something or other.

Over the course of five years we were able to publish the work of most of the best theological writers in Britain, together with some of the 'big names' in Europe and North America. It was rare for anyone to decline an invitation to write for *New Christian* and we liked to believe that this was not simply because we paid professional writers at the current professional rates. At two levels, however, we failed badly and, although the reasons for these failures were largely beyond our control, they were of much greater significance than we appreciated at the time.

It had always been my hope that *New Christian* would not only provide an outlet for the work of established writers but also offer a nursery for new writers. While we insisted on good standards, we always paid special attention to articles submitted by unknown writers and we tried to be particularly sensitive to work which might contain the germ of new approaches or indicate a talented writer. But we made no significant discoveries, which was a great disappointment. In retrospect it appears that *New Christian* came on to the scene at the end of a decade of considerable creativity in the field of theological literature. This reached its high point with the publication and phenomenal success of *Honest to God* in 1963, but from then onwards the decline was quite rapid. The late 1950s and early 1960s were a time of new hope in most of the British churches. Parish and People, the Keble Conference Group, the Renewal Group in Methodism and similar bodies attracted into their membership large numbers of the most able clergy and there was an abundance of ideas about the reform of the church and the reinterpretation of traditional theology. Some of this found expression in the explosion of paperback theology, and it was within this creative atmosphere that *New Christian* was planned and launched. But by the time the magazine was established the situation was changing: hope was giving way to despair, and it was being suggested that the institutional life of the church was beyond reform. Had *New Christian* continued for a further five years it would certainly have become increasingly difficult to fill its pages with stimulating and useful material. In some ways we were fortunate to meet sudden death while still in our prime and before we were overtaken by arthritis or starvation.

Our second failure, not unrelated to the first, lay in our inability to build a substantial bridge between reflective theology and the political, social and economic issues of the day. From the outset we aimed to be a journal with a secular orientation in which theology and anthropology might establish some common ground. But, although we published a good deal of comment on secular matters, and plenty of theology which attempted to relate Christian insights to matters of current concern, the two rarely met. This was due partly to editorial inadequacy, but chiefly to the fact that it was quite impossible to find politicians, economists and sociologists who could reflect deeply and widely on their work, and theologians who could sit down with representatives of secular disciplines and discover the ways of God within the contemporary world.

In spite of these serious deficiencies, *New Christian* succeeded in attracting to its readership a fair number of laypeople; in fact, they accounted for half of its 10,000 subscribers. Among them were many men and women holding positions of some responsibility within the nation and seeking nourishment not readily available to them in their local churches. Among our clerical readers we numbered the majority of the leaders of the British churches, but most of them were ordinary priests and ministers who were looking, and sometimes working, for the reform of the church and found in *New Christian* a forum for the expression of their ideas and hopes. Perhaps most important of all, a subscription to *New Christian* provided entry to a 'lonely hearts club for radicals' in which an isolated minister or a frustrated curate felt he belonged to a significant movement within the community of faith and had a certain kinship with others of his kind who were fighting similar battles. When the time came for *New Christian* to close it soon became apparent that this spin-off element in our work would be the most serious loss.

Four years after the closure of the magazine the gap left by its demise remains. Several groups of people have met to consider the possibility of launching a replacement, but so far the financial problems have proved insuperable. Yet the massive subsidy which Timothy Beaumont provided from his own pocket during *New Christian*'s five years of life was quite small in relation to what was being attempted. In the broad field of magazine publishing it was trivial, as indeed it was when viewed in the light of the total income and expenditure of the British churches. Thus it is necessary to raise – yet again – the question of how seriously the churches take their business of communication and how much money they might be prepared to devote to publications which stand no chance of paying their own way but might conceivably have an important function within the church and in the church's attempts to share Christian insights with those outside its institutional life.

For some of us, *New Christian* had a proleptic character. It provided a fleeting glimpse of what we hope may be a more abiding future reality. For this we can only be grateful, but it has left us mightily impatient and not a little frustrated.

Honest Interpretation

The first front page article, 7 October 1965

New Christian is published to-day in order to meet an obvious need. At a time of ferment and reformation in the church there is need for a channel of communication which transcends denominational boundaries and which is open to new thought and action coming from many different quarters. The purpose and policy of *New Christian* may be summed up in the word *interpretation*, and we see our interpretive role expressed in three different, yet interrelated ways.

First, the interpretation of world affairs in ways which help Christians and others to discover the kingship of Christ over the whole created order. The pages of *New Christian* will contain information and comment on matters political and sociological, and we shall not feel confined to the traditional 'moral issues' which normally bring a handful of Anglican bishops to their appointed places in the House of Lords. Neither shall we feel constrained to embrace the heresy that Christians are neutral in political matters. There will be regular expressions of opinion in our columns and these will be offered without fear or favour. *New Christian* is not tied to any political party and we shall oppose the forces of reaction wherever they are to be found.

Secondly, the interpretation of the Christian faith in language and ideas which are appropriate to the twentieth century. Since we shall in the days to come be accused of propagating 'heresy and schism', it may be as well at the outset to affirm our belief in the fundamental truth of the Christian gospel. *New Christian* is not designed to be an organ of secular humanism. Yet, having made this affirmation, we must hasten to add that we feel under no necessary obligation to spread those interpretations of the Christian faith which were undoubtedly of enormous value to people of other ages and other places, but which speak no longer to the Europe of the 1960s. It seems to us to be of the greatest importance that the ultimate truth of the Christian religion must be distinguished from human interpretations of that truth, and it will be our aim to present readers with a creative theology appropriate to life in the world today.

Thirdly, the interpretation of the different parts of the church to each other. If the resolutions of the recent Nottingham Faith and Order Conference are taken seriously, the next fifteen years must inevitably see a great increase in discussion amongst church leaders and academic theologians. But, without in any way wishing to demote the diplomat and the don, we venture to suggest that the real enemy of reunion is not theological division but sheer ignorance and misunderstanding. It will be the aim of *New Christian* to provide information about significant thought and action in all the churches, and, although we do not believe that unity and truth may be separated, we are prepared to begin with the assertion that many of the so-called 'barriers to unity' are, in fact, irrelevancies which are hardly worth debating.

In this task of interpretation we shall aim to be honest. We shall be honest about our certainties and not hesitate to parade them before the eyes of our readers. We shall try to be equally honest about our uncertainties and resist the temptation to wrap them up in pious clap-trap. When offence is caused on these counts we shall find comfort and encouragement in the words of Gregory the Great – 'If scandal is taken at the truth, then it is better to allow scandal to arise than to abandon the truth.'

But honesty is not the same thing as infallibility and no claim will be made on this second count. We hope that readers will not hesitate to point out our errors and omissions. The columns of *New Christian* will always be open to those who have a contribution to make to this journal's interpretive role, and we begin by prophesying that the success of *New Christian* will largely depend on the extent to which readers, writers and editorial staff see themselves as engaged on a joint enterprise.

95 Theses for the New Reformation

Out of love for truth and the desire to bring it to light, the following propositions are offered for discussion at the time of the 450th anniversary of the nailing by Martin Luther of 95 theses to the door of the church in Wittenberg. Wherefore it is requested that those who desire to share in the discussion should do so by letter and it is to be noted that thesis 95 may be propounded by any who are aware of notable omissions in this list.

1   God is to be known only in history and in the common ways of men.

2   The hidden is not revealed by speculation, but only by life.

3   Language about God is meant to interpret the meaning of life. Where it fails to do this we have magic, not true religion.

4   The study of theology in isolation from the life of the contemporary world serves no useful purpose and has greatly retarded the spread of the gospel.

5   God is always the beyond in the midst of time and thus the kingdom of God is within men and community.

6   Faith is not synonymous with certainty. Certainty may arise from a refusal to face difficulties, while faith may embrace the acknowledgment of doubt.

7   Theology is part of man's search for God. God is beyond the limits of human reason, so when theology claims to present the truth it is making gods of men.

8   A man will go astray from the way of truth and the quest of the kingdom if he regards as true, merely on the grounds that he has been told they are true, such propositions as cannot be validated.

9   Unthinking orthodoxy is more dangerous than blatant heresy.

10   If a man attempts to believe what he believes to be incredible he is avoiding the truth and destroying his own integrity.

11 Infallibility is no more an attribute of a professor than it is of a Pope and all claims to infallibility in the realm of religion must be dismissed as monstrous.

12 All who profess knowledge of what happens to a man after death are deluded.

13 The promise of happiness after death as compensation for sorrow in this life is immoral.

14 The substitution of religion for faith is an ever-present danger.

15 The abolition of religion is therefore a task laid upon Christians in every generation.

16 God in Christ is in every man and all things cohere in him.

17 There is therefore no such being as a godless person.

18 The true Christian yearns to follow his Master in darkness. He does not rely upon any security that ecclesiastical institutions promise him. He sees the sure way to the kingdom of God in present tribulations.

19 The assertion (Philippians 2) that Jesus made himself nothing, assuming the nature of a slave, is not just a theological statement about the person of Christ, but the principle on which all true greatness is built.

20 The significance of the ministry of Jesus is to be seen in his unwillingness to provide his followers with a body of doctrine or a code of ethics.

21 The statement that God loves the world is only true insofar as Christians become channels of God's love to their fellow men.

22 There is no service of Christ, however pious, which ignores the needs of people.

23 Repentance is not a demand but a gift.

24 Preoccupation with sin is to be explained in psychological rather than theological terms.

25 Preachers and moralizers feed on men's guilt.

26 The 'spiritual man' is not at war with the 'natural man'. He is the man who is at enmity with all that is superficial.

27 Since the Holy Spirit has little room for manoeuvre in the life of the contemporary church, it is to be expected that his activities will be mainly discernible in the life of the world.

28 The creeds belong essentially to the period in which they were written and are to be seen primarily as historical documents.

29 Christian orthodoxy is not, therefore, to be defined by adherence to the letter of credal statements.

30 There is no more misleading statement than an assertion that the Bible is the Word of God.

31 Effective Christian witness is commonly prevented by the unconscious reversal of St John's saying into: 'We know that we love the brethren, because we have passed from death to life.' In this form, the first half of the statement is untrue, and the second arrogant presumption.

32 Man does well to recognize the provisional nature of his interpretation of truth. His unity with other seekers for truth consists rightly not only in agreement on the content of truth, but also in the common concern for truth.

33 The true radical is one who has no fear of the future and can therefore afford to be radical.

34 The moral ideal is not a law or a standard but a relationship.

35 The function of the church in the realm of morality is not to lay down the law but to make clear why there needs to be a law at all.

36 Christian ethics is not concerned with the definition of absolute good and absolute evil, but with the best possible course of action in particular circumstances.

37 Total dependence on rules brings a man no closer to the gospel than total dependence on his own desires.

38 The only valid test of the reality and depth of Christian faith is the ethical test: the questions to be put to believers facing judgment are political, social and economic questions.

39 Elimination of politics from the pulpit is one of the surest ways of muting the gospel.

40 And acceptance of the status quo is itself a profound political act.

41 The Christian doctrine of 'the just war' can never be used to justify the use of nuclear weapons.

42 No man can witness to the Christian way from a superior position.

43 The familiar assertion that we talk far too much about sex is, from the Christian point of view, the greatest nonsense. The Bible starts talking about this in its first chapter, so there is no need to be squeamish.

44 Equally nonsensical is the view that much pornographic literature is too sexy. It isn't sexy enough, for it ignores one vast dimension of human sexuality: its power to create and deepen true relationship.

45 Views on marriage propounded by celibate clerics should always be treated with the greatest reserve.

46 The suggestion that abstention and the 'safe period' are the most natural forms of birth control springs from an inadequate knowledge of nature.

47 The church of Christ is the promise of mankind's future, not the preservation of its past.

48 The purpose of the church is to offer man in its fellowship a foretaste of salvation; in its present state of division it cannot fulfil this purpose.

49 The church, being divided, cannot be identified exclusively with any contemporary human organization.

50 It is therefore in the interests of integrity and truth that any organization calling itself a church should regard itself as a sect.

51 To try to define the boundaries and membership of the church is to engage in a fruitless exercise.

52 The association of the Christian faith with respectability rather than revolution is a clear indication of the extent to which the gospel has been forsaken by the institutional church.

53 Ecclesiastical authority, operating according to the patterns of secular power, while claiming to be 'humble service', is more corrosive of Christ's church than the naked exercise of tyranny.

54 The authority of Christ, being a moral ascendancy, not a forcible subjugation, and exercised only as a person responds to person, cannot be delegated.

55 The church must not try to provide for those people who seek religious security in total submission to an ecclesiastical authority.

56 When the church makes absolute demands, whether for assent to dogma or for obedience to discipline, it exceeds its commission.

57 The church is always disobedient to its calling while it allows its own organization to preclude effective witness and service in the city.

58 A church that confines its ministry to the residential and domestic areas of life cannot serve the whole man.

59 Such a church's own life becomes seriously impoverished.

60 Clinging to tradition for its own sake is the most common form of idolatry.

61 The real enemy of church renewal is not the unrepentant reactionary but the moderate reformer.

62 Flexibility is as essential to the church as is unity and holiness.

63 Christian sacraments are not magical, but are too frequently regarded as such by those who receive them.

64 Worship is too important to be entrusted to the liturgists.

65 Few things are more inimical to true worship than the quest for liturgical uniformity.

66 Liturgical rites should not continue unrevised for more than twenty years.

67 The true purpose of the liturgy is to show the connection between a table in church and all those other tables in life where meals are eaten, counsel is taken and work is done.

68 If the denial of a glass of water to our brethren is to deny it to Christ, it is far worse to refuse to share the eucharist with them.

69 The church's task is to encourage free enquiry, not to defend orthodoxy.

70 Since Jesus offers to men the gift of freedom, all attempts by the church to impose censorship or to restrict freedom of thought and speech are in direct opposition to the task to which the church is called.

71 Christians who speak of the church as the Body of Christ should remember what happened to that body.

72 If it is hard for a rich man to find entry to the kingdom of God it is not unlikely that a rich church will encounter some difficulties.

73 The orthodoxy of a congregation is to be measured more by its annual statement of accounts than by its weekly statement of belief.

74 A church which tolerates segregation – racial, social or economic – has ceased to be the church.

75 To care more for the validity of orders than for the world God loves is a common but unrecognized heresy.

76 Those who build new churches and cathedrals should reflect on the fact that the great church-building eras have invariably been periods of religious decline.

77 In a rapidly changing society the erection of monumental buildings indicates lack of faith.

78 What the world needs to be shown by any body of Christians to-day is not so much a united front as a broad back, different sides, and a blown top.

79 There are no distinctions of ministry apart from service, and all ministry is the continuing ministry of Christ.

80 Ecclesiastical titles are to indicate role, not status, for there is only one status in the church, that of the baptized.

81 There is no evidence that particular groups within the church are given greater insight or better guidance than the rest of the Christian community.

82 The view that women cannot be ordained to the church's ministry since Christ was a man is a denial of Christ's full humanity.

83 It also implies that women cannot be admitted to membership of the church.

84 The image of the minister as a shepherd is false unless accompanied by the image of the minister as a servant.

85 It is therefore important that those who carry a shepherd's crook should also display a symbol of servanthood.

86 Any suggestion that the laity are the church's sheep should be firmly resisted.

87 The task of the Christian layman is to discern the activities of God in the places where he lives and works and to resist all attempts to lure him into the ecclesiastical machine.

88 The call to serve as a church official – full or part-time, ordained or lay – is a special vocation given to a tiny minority of the Christian body.

89 A church official is mistaken if he believes that his work is of greater importance in the kingdom of God than that of his brother who is occupied in the life of the world.

90 The statement 'A house-going parson makes a church-going people' is fortunately untrue.

91 The cleric who demands legal protection to safeguard his freedom of speech is unlikely to have any speech worth safeguarding.

92 A preacher whose concern is with the saving of souls from hell is himself in the gravest peril.

93 Reformation is always a regrettable necessity.

94 Any ascription of infallibility to these theses is contrary to the desires of their compilers.

95 . . . .
. . . .

Sex and Sensibility

MONICA FURLONG

This article originally appeared as a review of four books: E. Schillebeeckx,
Marriage: Secular Reality and Saving History, *Sheed and Ward; Stuart
Barton Babbage*, Sex and Sanity – A Christian View of Sexual Morality,
Hodder and Stoughton; A. Morgan Derham, A Christian's Guide to Love,
Sex and Marriage, *Hodder and Stoughton; Robert Grimm*, Love and
Sexuality, *Hodder and Stoughton. It was published in February 1966.*

An angry lady once wrote to me after I had written an article in a newspaper supporting Lord Arran's Bill, and finished her letter with the words
'I suppose what you would like is a society in which everyone is either
heterosexual or homosexual'.

Unwittingly, she had hit upon exactly the sort of society which I would
like, one in which people lived at peace with their own sexual natures and
so could allow others to live at peace with theirs; a society in which health
and normality were measured by people's ability to love and care for
others, and in which the word 'perverted' was reserved for those who
showed no love at all; a society in which marriage was a happier and more
truthful state than we have yet begun to imagine; in which children did
not learn about love and conception from dirty jokes in the playground
(see Schofield's *The Sexual Behaviour of Young People*, in which he
demonstrates that this is the usual method).

It is with this hope that I turn to Christian books about sex, and the
dusty answer I find there makes me feel that a blasphemy is being uttered
against the gospel. Reading these fear-ridden pages, full of second-hand
ideas, unwarranted optimism and a total ignorance of the real sexual and
psychological wounds with which men and women limp desolately through
life, I find myself remembering some of those splendid old Jewish patriarchs
and their superb zest for the sexual act. On page after page of the Old
Testament (so it seems if you read the Bible continuously) they were going
in to women and uncovering them, apparently with considerable enthu-

siasm for the task. Since then a cloud has blown across the spirit of Western man, wiping out many of the weeds of paganism, no doubt, but destroying many a marvellous blossom in the process.

Why did this happen? I don't pretend to know the answer, but I have been trying to trace clues through Professor Schillebeeckx's books. The professor is a historian – of the pleasant, modest type which is mainly content to recount facts, though there is an understandable Roman Catholic bias – and he has unearthed more interesting facts about the history of marriage than I can remember reading anywhere else. The essentially secular nature of marriage in the early Christian centuries (it was celebrated without benefit of clergy) gave men a great deal of 'room to manoeuvre' within their own particular psychological problems. From then on thinking became ever more rigid, more idealistic and, consequently, more intolerant, towards those who fell short of the ideals.

It may be that this sort of painstaking going over the historical ground is the only kind of constructive writing about sex which Christians are at the moment able to produce. The three other books I read, like many another Christian book on the subject before them, seemed to me to be very, very frightened books indeed. How frightened is perhaps indicated by the way they both try to eat their cake and have it, to pay tribute to progressive psychological thinking, but not to say anything which might give conventional Christians a momentary tremor. Thus, masturbation 'is not a sin', but 'we should certainly pray for strength to deal with the habit', though 'we must be careful lest our very praying should suggest the thought to us and open the way to further trouble'. On the other hand masturbation is 'a rather childish practice which normal people grow out of'. But 'we should not dismiss it lightly'. The book offers no advice to the many lonely men and women to whom masturbation seems the only way of dispersing intolerable tension. I suppose they console themselves (in the intervals of furious prayer, though not about masturbation) with the thought that they are childish and abnormal, but not actually sinners.

Homosexuals, on the other hand, are sinners, or rather they are not because they are perfectly splendid people sublimating their energies in work for the community, or rather they are sinners when they don't succeed in sublimating. They are ever so creative, and Christ died for them, and they are marvellous with young people, except that they do corrupt them, of course. Having followed these mental gymnastics with some difficulty, we end up on the old saluting base. 'The Christians must take a firm stand against even a tacit recognition or acceptance of homosexual practices; having said that we must urge anyone who has any responsibility towards such people to think and act with care and compassion.' I don't happen to be homosexual, but I became so angry when I read this passage ('We do well to remember the beam in our own eye when we think of the splinter in another's') that I threw the book across the room and had to retrieve it later from under the sofa. Such patronizing, insensitive, ignorant stuff has not been put between covers since the report of the Arran debate was bound up in Hansard. If we cannot enter the problems of the homosexual situation at a deeper level than this (and it is a very, very complex issue), then for God's sake let us keep quiet on the subject.

Nor does heterosex fare much better. There is an extraordinary quotation from the Bishop of Exeter about sex outside marriage: 'It is like using a razor to sharpen a pencil – you can do it, but you can't use the razor blade to have a shave with afterwards', which gives me a frisson, no doubt, for all sorts of excellent Freudian reasons. And there is a great deal of shallow nonsense about marital difficulties; church-going and prayer are not universal panaceas – a fact which is painfully obvious to anyone who has had to minister to practising Christians.

In the course of my job, I read many books about sex, and what I can no longer deny is that the non-Christians write about it with infinitely more good sense and loving care than do most Christians. When my daughter reaches adolescence, I shall not select one of these dim little books for her further instruction. More probably I shall go for *An ABZ of Love*, by Inge and Sten Hegler, which buzzes with joy at the fun and wonder of it all. If I wanted to help an unmarried woman friend going through a bad patch I should give her *The Single Woman*, by Laura Hutton, which goes truthfully and bravely into every problem, and does not, as the Christian books do, pretend that Christ is the answer to the menopause. Nor do the unbelieving books bring prayer galloping in like the US Cavalry whenever they are stuck for an answer to something.

The trouble with the Christians is not that they have strict morals, but that they don't seem to care very much. They don't care about the agonies of unhappy marriage, about the loneliness of the unmarried, about the dilemmas of the homosexual. All they care about is the rules, and about not producing (in a phrase one of these writers uses about Harry Williams and John Robinson) 'an unhappy shock'. Thus is the Son of Man betrayed, dishonoured and crucified afresh.

Letters to the Editor

From Mr Alan Overell

Saying 'yes' to life in general and sex in particular would no doubt open up 'the fun and wonder of it all'. But that's not the whole story. It would also open up the pity, the terror and destructiveness of it all. If we say 'yes' to it all, we must take it all, and I wonder if we really mean that, or whether we'd be tough enough?

It's one thing to want a world where people 'live at peace with their own sexual natures and so could allow others to live at peace with their', etc., etc. We can see the ideal. But isn't Utopia as inherently impossible in this field as in others? Isn't Miss Furlong saying, 'Everything would be all right if only people were good'?

From Canon Hugh Montefiore, Vicar of Great St Mary's, Cambridge

Dear Miss Furlong,

I think that you have a genius for words and for many years I have read your writings, usually with a chuckle, often with a cheer. Most unfortunately for me, however, I read your review in today's issue of *New Christian* in bed on my day off. I found that my reaction was such that I had inadvertently leapt out of bed.

I had thought of writing you a letter earlier when I read your recent fulminations on abortion in the *Daily Mail*, as a result of the Church of England report. I've read this report too, and I've listened to the panel who composed it when they discussed this agonizing problem at a meeting of the Institute of Religion and Medicine. They may be wrong; but I don't see how you think them lacking in compassion because they try to think clearly about a matter where emotion may cloud the real issues.

You seem to think that a woman ought to do whatever she feels like doing, so far as what is happening in her body is concerned. They think that the well-being of a mother is paramount, but that even a foetus has some rights and that therefore justice (which is the attempt to regulate rights) is involved. Now, as I say,

they may be wrong, but do you really think that they are fit objects of scorn? I know that I daren't myself resolve morality into what I feel like doing at the time, because my feelings are so changeable. And I know a child, an 'afterthought', who is happy and loved, but his mother was in a terrible state when she was carrying him. It would be ridiculous to suggest to either of them that it would be better if he hadn't been born.

I had to get all this off my chest, but it was really your review in *New Christian* which has been the occasion of this letter. There you review four books on sex. You lump three of them together and you describe them as 'dim little books' and 'very, very frightened books indeed'. Two of these books I haven't read, and you may be quite right in your assessment of them. But it so happens that one of them, *Love and Sexuality* by Robert Grimm, was sent to me for review, and I've read it quite carefully three times.

Now what puzzles me is how you can possibly describe Grimm's book in these terms. (I suppose you have read it!) I find your description so utterly misleading that I hardly know where to begin. I am left with the impression (I hope it's quite a wrong impression) that as this is a book on sex by a Christian, it must be bad and so there is no need for anyone, even a reviewer, to read it. I don't myself agree with everything that Grimm has written. But it does seem to me fresh and fearless and positive and honest, and the author is prepared to think (in fact it seems to me to be too heavily theological to become as popular as it deserves). Please, Miss Furlong, could you do me a favour? Could you spare time to read it again and tell me if you want to change your opinion? Perhaps I could even ask you either to withdraw your damning remarks or to substantiate them (by a responsible critique, of course, not by tearing sentences out of context)?

One last point, I detect in your review an attitude which I can only describe as 'sexier than thou'. Whenever a Christian discusses with venom the lack of love among fellow-Christians, I see a yellow light ahead. Of your fellow Christians (other than yourself, Harry Williams and John Robinson) you write in connection with sex: 'all they care for is the rules'. Now I wonder if you would be willing to withdraw that remark too? Or at least modify it to 'some Christians I have met' or 'some Christians whose books I have read' or something like that? We know, Miss Furlong, that you receive many deeply moving letters from people suffering from great anxiety or torment as a result of unhappy sexual experience or frustration. But some of us actually meet these people almost daily as part of our pastoral jobs; they still come to us, some of them, in their devastating need to ask for help in the agonizing decisions which confront them. 'All they care for is the rules' has not been my experience of Christians. It has been my experience, however, that most people are helped not by emotional outbursts of sympathy but by quiet listening and by a detached and sober clarification of the issues.

From Monica Furlong

Dear Editor,

I am replying as if Canon Montefiore's letter had been sent to you, since I am old-fashioned enough to regard letters addressed to me as private affairs.

May I begin with the Canon's last point, the point about my being sexier-than-thou? Alas, I am rapidly growing too old to be sexier than anybody, but may I use the occasion to ask how one can suggest in print or conversation that there is something wrong with general Christian attitudes if one is forbidden to imply that one's own ideas may be right and others may be wrong. Must one keep quiet for the sake of modesty, or incur the terrible condemnation of being holier-than-thou?

Very fortunately I don't mind at all whether I am regarded as holier-than-thou, sexier-than-thou, chaster-than-thou, or the Scarlet Woman of the Year. What I do mind about is getting Christians to think much harder about people's relationships with one another. Canon Monte-

fiore thinks the Christians do rather well in this respect, healing those in their orbit who need it, and radiating love into our society. I cannot agree, though I am aware of a few Christians who succeed in this.

I cannot agree because nearly all Christian discussion of relationship problems and sexual problems seems to me to be taking place on the wrong level. It is taking place on the level of ideals and of what people ought to do, and almost never on the level of what they can do. That is to say, it is a theological and ethical discussion, and rarely a psychological one. The Church of England report on abortion was almost a classic of this kind of thinking. Most oddly it confirmed most of its discussion to extraordinary situations, in which abortion was thought desirable because of rape, the extreme youth of the mother or the possible deformity of the child.

But this does not happen to be the problem which confronts our society, or at least it is only one tiny fragment of it. Our problem is that thousands of women, many of them married, refuse to go through with having a child, and prefer to endure pain, and to risk infection or worse, in defiance of the law. This is the problem which has to be understood.

It can only be understood, I suggest, by turning away from 'ought' and trying to see what is actually going on. And what is going on, it seems, at least where a woman conceives in a situation where she has no wish to bear a child, is that her unconscious says 'no', and goes on saying it, firmly and insistently, in the face of any well-meant exhortation to the contrary. When a pregnant woman says 'I cannot have a child', she may be speaking the simple truth.

As with abortion so with other problems. Married couples do not live out their lives on the ideal level of text-books, like that of Mr Grimm. His book seems to me to be written on a beautiful abstract level that has little to do with people's real inhibitions and wounds. In all our loving we are in a constant state of conflict between our conscious and our unconscious impulses, but he does not think this is worth mentioning.

The bad thing about Christian thinking, I suggest, is that it cannot heal people on an ideal level, and it scorns to do so on a more mundane level. For to do this often means accepting the validity of another's unconscious processes, and this sometimes means breaking 'the rules'. It may mean accepting that for some women, in some situations (and I don't particularly mean rape, incest, or something extraordinary), abortion may be the right course. It may mean accepting that a marriage has come to an end. It may mean accepting that it is right for a homosexual to live and to sleep with his friend.

So far only the Quakers have had the courage to come off the perch of lofty ethical discussion, and try to build an ethic out of what actually goes on in the real world. It is not surprising that the rest of us are so frightened, since the whole discussion is dangerous, lays us open to making fools of ourselves, and involves a painful self-awareness. But try as I may, I cannot see that anything else is likely to be of much use.

From the Rev. Harry Williams, Dean of Trinity College, Cambridge

Canon Hugh Montefiore writes to Miss Monica Furlong: 'I think you have a genius for words and for many years I have read your writings usually with a chuckle, often with a cheer.'

Other people have had a genius for words. Sophocles, Shakespeare, Racine, Goethe, Ezra Pound, Auden, to take a random selection. For the sake of the church in general and of Canon Montefiore in particular it is to be hoped that these writers have catapulted him from his bed more often than they have made him chuckle and cheer. Chuckling and cheering are considered by many, rightly or wrongly, to be typical of clergymen, indicating their unacknowledged fear of reality and their patently obvious refusal to face it. The clergy, of course, can always reply that this people who knoweth not the law are cursed.

From Mr Robin Denniston, London EC 4

It seems wrong to intrude on the correspondence between Monica Furlong and Hugh Montefiore. But I would very much like to establish whether there is common ground between the two, as if there is and they both acknowledge it, a considerable rapprochement has been achieved.

The common factor of the argument is the person in trouble who consults either Miss Furlong or Canon Montefiore; perhaps a father is hopelessly in love with a friend of his daughter: perhaps she is in love with him and they cannot decide what to do about it. What I would want to ask Hugh Montefiore is, is there any conceivable circumstance in which he would be prepared to accept or even recommend adultery? And Monica Furlong, would you agree that there are quite frequent occasions on which strong advice (compassionately given) to stick to the rules improves the situation all round eventually: that the very sticking to the rules, plus the surprising happiness that abstinence can bring, work their own miracles.

If either party says 'No' or, worse still, 'I don't know what you're talking about', then our hope is in vain. If either or both say 'Yes' – on however rare occasions – here would be progress. On the one hand we would be assured that pastoral counsel is given to help those in need and not to back up the rules: on the other we would feel that rules are not being rejected simply because they are rules.

From Mr Bruce Cooper, Middlesborough

Poor Monica Furlong! She's in for a busy time 'trying to build an ethic out of what actually goes on in the real world', because this seems to change with alarming rapidity, and particularly in the century we're living in at the moment.

How much more comfortable life would be! I could sleep with other women besides my wife, providing, of course, we were all enjoying it. I could fiddle my income tax return without a twinge of conscience. And if I had some perversion (what a pity I haven't!) I need only to consider it on a psychological rather than on a theological and ethical level.

This strikes me not only as sloppy thinking and damned nonsense but nonsense that can damn.

Christian compassion demands that we succour and aid the homosexual, that we do not sit in judgment upon the over-wrought wife who has reached the end of her tether and can tolerate no more pregnancies. It doesn't mean that we toss the crucifixion and all it stands for out of the window, and produce a god (for each generation on Monica Furlong's reckoning) in our own image and likeness, and an ethic that is glitteringly contemporary.

Miss Furlong claims to be old-fashioned. So am I, not about privately addressed letters, though. About a virtue, which I'm surprised Miss Furlong doesn't seem to have encountered, namely heroism. Unlike her, I am amazed at what quite ordinary people can do (a different gloss to her can) and actually do every day of their lives – actions based very much on another old-fashioned word she doesn't seem to like, ought.

I am not sure that Miss Furlong's particular brand of witness is doing the Christian cause a great deal of good, but I don't expect this will deter her from spreading her own brand of confusion.

From Monica Furlong

Mr Cooper, a married man himself we gather, demands that the homosexual should live out his life in total chastity; that the mother who is physically and mentally exhausted should go through with her pregnancy. He then goes on to talk of the cross and of heroism.

I rest my case against contemporary Christian attitudes.

From Miss Valerie Pitt, West Wickham

Monica Furlong suggests that one Mr Cooper, being a married man, has no right to an opinion on sexual ethics and is, what's more, probably cruel and complacent like the rest of us Christians.

Now I deprecate this form of argument for reasons which I have explained many times, but since I suspect Monica Furlong will not listen in an impersonal case, may I put the matter this way. Mr Cooper may be a married man, but I am an unmarried woman and a virgin. I am therefore as aware as Monica

Furlong can be of the physical, psychological and, indeed, social strains of a celibate existence. This does not give me the right, certainly, to talk about 'crosses'. It does allow me to say that the attempt at obedience in the matter of chastity is not the barren observance of law: it is part of a living relationship. I said a living relationship. 'My strength,' our Lord says, 'is made perfect in weakness.'

The difficulty with Monica Furlong's system, or attitude or whatever she would call it, to moral questions is that it is focused, unnaturally, on the person-to-person relationship. Love your neighbour does not mean that one must be perpetually agonizing, or 'engaged in dialogue' with him, over his personal problems. We all have our share of that, and Monica Furlong has no business to suggest that only she and her friends really know what human misery is about. But most of us also have jobs, we handle money, we have votes – and all these activities also engage the conscience.

All this agonizing, however, does lead to a very dangerous conclusion. Nothing, the Utilitarians said, is evil in the fullest sense except pain. This at least is true: pain is an evil and no one should pretend that it is not. But no philosopher suggests, ever, that we ought not to require ourselves, or others, to do things which cause us pain or distress. Even the giving of a cup of cold water is occasionally a matter of personal inconvenience. But Monica Furlong sometimes talks as if any solution to a problem which involves sacrifice is and must be wrong. That is very odd for a Christian. For the one thing we know about love is that it is obedient even to the death of the cross.

I am Sir, yours, no doubt, neurotically,

RELIGION!

The speaker at the meeting on Tuesday, 1 March, will be Mrs Reindorp, the wife of the Bishop of Guildford. Mrs Reindorp is reputed to be a 'Bomb' on the subject of sex, and the Mums look forward to a very helpful afternoon. – *Notice in Aldington Parish Magazine.*

The services of at least five Lady Godivas has been secured at a cost of £10. This was reported at a meeting of the Wisbech (Isle of Ely) Parish Church Restoration Appeal Fund. They are to take part in Wisbech Rose Fair. – *English Churchman.*

Over 200 illegitimate babies are born each day – most illegitimate children being conceived in the month of August, when the church goes on holiday. – *From a leaflet setting out the need for the Project Evangelistic Crusade, Chesterfield.*

Sex has become a grave problem, Cardinal Alfredo Ottaviani, head of the Vatican's Congregation for the Doctrine of the Faith, told the Vatican Sunday paper *Osservatora della Domenica* in an interview today. – *Daily Telegraph.*

The churches should protest at the proposed return of the BBC tv programme 'Till Death Us Do Part'. On 13 February the word 'bloody' was used sixteen times and 'Gordblimey' five. On 27 March there were horrible remarks like 'Take off yer drawers'. – *Letter in Home Words parish magazine inset.*

I – and I am sure many thousands of listeners – are sick of hearing holy men discussing sex so much. Surely it's against their religion for priests to dwell on this subject as this part of their life is taboo to them. All churches should concentrate on getting people to church and leave politics, sex and everything else outside church matters to people concerned. – *Letter in TV Weekly (Wales).*

He (Father Peter de Rosa) is reckoned to be an excellent and very professional communicator, not least after defeating celibacy with Brigid Brophy in an early David Frost show. – *The Guardian.*

TAMAR

Matthew 1.1–16

Exceedingly odd
Is the means by which God
Has provided our path to the heavenly shore:
　　Of the girls from whose line
　　The true light was to shine
There was one an adulteress, one was a whore.

　　There was Tamar who bore –
　　What we all should deplore –
A fine pair of twins of her father-in-law;
　　And Rahab the harlot,
　　Her sins were as scarlet,
As red as the thread which she hung from the
　　　　　　　　　　　　　　　door,
　　Yet alone of her nation
　　She came to salvation
And lived to be mother of Boaz, of yore.
　　And he married Ruth,
　　A Gentile uncouth
In a manner quite counter to biblical lore;
　　And from her there did spring
　　Blessed David the king,
Who walked on his palace one evening, and
　　　　　　　　　　　　　　　saw
　　The wife of Uriah,
　　From whom he did sire
A baby that died – oh and princes a score.
　　And a mother unmarried
　　It was, too, that carried
God's Son, who was laid in a cradle of straw,
　　That the moral might wait
　　At the heavenly gate
While the sinners and publicans go in before,
　　Who have not earned their place,
　　But received it by grace
And have found them a righteousness not of
　　　　　　　　　　　　　　　the Law.

M. D. GOULDER

No Instant Mission: The Billy Graham Crusade

2

A leading article published in April 1966

Faced by an intractable mission situation, the British churches are in the doldrums. This is hardly surprising. For the greater part of Christian history the church has enjoyed a dominant role in Europe. The content of its message, the structure of its organization and the style of its leadership have developed to meet the needs of a static agrarian society in which Christian beliefs were taken for granted and the institutional church stood at the centre of community life. It is, therefore, difficult for the churches to find their bearings in the new situation of the twentieth century.

In this situation the only possibilities open to the church are those of despair, a struggle for survival, or the acceptance of radical reformation. *New Christian* was born out of the conviction that the first two possibllities were incompatible with the Christian gospel, and that the church is being called to new patterns of obedience which must be reflected in new structures of institutional life. This conviction remains, and has indeed been reinforced by the current discussion in our correspondence columns on the function of the ordained ministry.

Two aspects of the church's future strategy seem to us to be of fundamental importance.

First, it is necessary for the new strategy to be considered in the long term. Having reached its present position as the result of forces which have been at work in European society since the beginning of the Industrial Revolution, it is hardly to be expected that the church will light upon immediate solutions to all its problems or that current trends can be reversed quickly. This is not a plea for caution, but rather a demand that the present *ad hoc* decisions made by apparently desperate men should be replaced by policies conceived in terms of a hundred years.

Secondly, it is necessary that society should be taken more seriously and dual is influenced and moulded by social pressures over which he has little, if any, control. Long before the birth of Karl Marx, St Paul had reminded Christians that 'we are members one of another', and in an important chapter in the recently published symposium *The English Church – A New Look*, the Bishop of Middleton has pointed out that while the nation is deeply secularized, it is 'victim of the secular forces surely, rather than an open-eyed, conscious and determined agent of those forces'. A realistic mission strategy must, therefore, incorporate those areas of social life which have a profound effect upon human attitudes and behaviour, and which it is necessary to Christianize before a widespread response to the Christian gospel can be expected. The role of the local church is to be seen primarily in terms of finding points of engagement with the local community.

In the light of these convictions it is impossible to view the forthcoming crusade to be conducted by Dr Billy Graham with anything other than grave foreboding. Like many other misguided Christians, Dr Graham's intentions are good and his sincerity is not in doubt, but the content of his teaching and the techniques employed in his crusades must in the long run be harmful to the spread of the Christian faith.

The techniques employed in the crusades are not, of course, significantly different from those employed in any form of 'soap-box' evangelism where the emphasis is on quick returns in the form of a personal response from individuals whose feelings of guilt have been successfully aroused. The prodigious efforts made to bring large numbers of people within range of this technique speak clearly of an approach to evangelism which cannot think in terms other than those of filling the empty pews of the churches today. That they fail to influence people who are not already committed to church membership is nothing like as serious a matter as the fact that they encourage clergy and laity in their failure to embark upon the hard thinking which must accompany long-term mission planning.

The Graham crusades are also designed to confirm Christians in their current antipathy to constructive social thinking and the consideration of new expressions of the Christian gospel and church life. Dr Graham's sermons, based on a near-literal interpretation of the Bible, reveal a complete failure to grasp any of the insights which come through a Christian estimate of the world, and the sole intention of the preacher seems to be that of saving individual men and women from the perils of life in a world which is degenerating rapidly and which will soon be consumed in the fires of hell. His firm opposition to those who are attempting to proclaim the gospel in twentieth-century terms and who are concerned with a contemporary interpretation of Christian ethics is now well known, and every opportunity is taken to denounce scholars and pastors who are trying to communicate

Christian truth in ways which make sense to those who are at present outside the orbit of traditional belief.

It hardly needs to be said that it is the plain duty of local churches to
welcome and care for the casualties of the crusade, but equally plain is the
duty to discourage participation in its activities and to begin the long-term
mission operation for which there can be no effective substitute.

The Gospel and Mr Graham

A review by James Mitchell of John Pollock, Billy Graham. The Authorized
Biography, *Hodder and Stoughton, published in the same issue.*

This is a story in the classic American tradition of country boy to national
hero. Written by an Englishman, it thus necessarily reflects something of
the uneasiness of a cultural transplantation, and many of the features so
vital in the American genre – agricultural innocence and clean-living long-
limbedness – seem a little out of place over here. It is also, as an account of
its hero's rise to evangelistic stardom, appallingly repetitive and madden-
ingly superficial. Its hagiorgiastic nature palls somewhat too.

If you want a worshipful account of the Billy Graham success saga, read
it. But if you hope for any new insight into Billy the man or Billy the Gospel
you're going to need a lot of native cunning to try and piece together an
honest portrait from the snippets of information and hints which the author
unconsciously leaves lying about. In short, you can read into the story
whatever you are pre-disposed to read into it. As a thoughtful study it gets
us nowhere.

And that is the depressing part, for we need to know a lot more about
Billy Graham, the structure of his personality and his techniques of per-
suasion, before we can assess the probable usefulness or damage of his
summer campaign over here this year.

The book's introduction to this campaign is not encouraging. 'The ear
of the nation,' writes the biographer, authorized by Billy Graham himself
presumably, 'was more attuned to churchmen whose intellectual search, as

it percolated to the ordinary TV viewer and newspaper reader, appeared to
have made the discovery that in this scientific age any authoritative pro-
clamation of faith was childish, that God was not a Person who could be
known, loved and obeyed, that He had never walked on earth, nor had
Christ risen bodily from the dead; that the one absolute was love, and thus
that a true morality must be uninhibited by traditional Christian chastity.
The time cried for another voice.'

This caricature of the new theology (not actually libellous because not
specifically directed) forebodes a sickening season. Here you have it in a
microcosm. The smattering of accuracy covering the propagandist degrada-
tion of truths – some of which truths, nestling up to the blatant distortions
in this passage, are truths which Christians have died for. Christ himself, I
seem to remember, died for the one about the one absolute being love. A
different voice indeed: it is a voice which I don't find hard to recognize.

And yet it is a voice which many find compelling and even attractive. I
did at the age of fourteen and paid a heavy price. While this biography
gives no clue as to why the voice is so attractive (unless that success itself
is such a god in our society that we are all the victims of a snowball idol),
it does give a hint or two as to why it is so necessary for Billy Graham himself to go on uttering it. And from here on I write of personality characteristics which I recognize because I've had to come to terms with them
myself.

The picture we have is of a man on the run from an ever-threatening
sense of depression. One way to avoid this is to keep yourself in a perpetual
state of hyper-excitability. If you can keep the elation steady you can keep
the depression at bay. Psychiatrists call this manic defence. Churchill was
a victim of this – immensely elated in wartime when he was constantly in
demand: desperately depressed in peace when he was not. An evangelist
has the opportunity to contrive a state of steady elation denied to the
politician: fervent prayer, great projects, huge crowds, the ceaseless burden
of maintaining an image, the huge inner expenditure of energy on self-
humiliation – all this activity keeps the enemy at bay. Success is the key:
if you're on the up-grade you're safe: failure threatens the entire edifice.
Failure is thus the devil who must be hounded by the ceaseless brandish-
ment of Christ the American country-boy success.

And so it is that the buses are fixed up months in advance to bring in the
faithful to the stadium from the four corners of the land to ensure the place
is packed – largely with pre-converted Bible-fodder who know the story
backwards already (a feature, incidentally, which accounts for the surprisingly low number of people who 'decide for Christ': the convert figures
are puny compared to the kind of results any political demagogue can

weave out of crowds of similar size under the sway of hysteria).

And with the success syndrome, to maintain this elation, you need the conviction that what you are doing is unique, of exclusive importance, original, vital. Something so precious that it can only be revealed in depth to a devoted group of inner disciples (Graham has twelve associate evangelists) – disciples who themselves become conditioned (through sharing the same manic tendencies) to need the elation in their leader to keep their own elation up to pitch. But you can't guard against life. And the neurotic disorders and intermittent insomnia to which Billy Graham is recorded in this book as being the unhappy victim bear their own witness to the inner ravages which the maintenance of this state renders inevitable.

A sad story is related with apparent approval by the author of a time when Billy Graham was a young man. Two friends at his training college had been found guilty of some 'moral defection'. He had admired and learned from these men and he was shaken. 'He saw that a man may talk piously and help others and then be himself a castaway. Graham determined that nothing should ever be allowed in his life, known or unknown, that could harm the name of Christ.'

It's here that the Graham gospel must be rejected, for it rests on a misunderstanding of Christ's own personality ('no sissie and no weakling . . . no sin and no mar had come near his body') and a rejection of the Christian doctrine of forgiveness. A doctrine which, I believe, involves self-forgiveness – or, if you like, self-acceptance – as well as the forgiveness of others. There is no self-forgiveness here: here is the eternal commitment to self-strangulation.

Christ did not preach this gospel, and there is no evidence that, as Billy Graham believes, he was the most perfectly developed man physically in the history of the world.

My Christ, and I suspect the more likely Christ, was not of this massively controlled unforgiving phallic splendour. He was a defeated, muddled, superb and violent man who some people thought was a little too fond of the bottle. He died in ignominy, believing himself to be a failure.

We do not read much about that in this biography of one man who has committed himself to this castaway's service. We read about a flowing tide of success: success which is something Christianity has never been about.

I wonder what God has in store for Billy Graham this summer? More success? Bigger business? Deeper impersonality? Or the kind of relative failure which is the stuff of the original gospel? I wonder how many things there were in the life of Jesus which would have harmed the name of Graham?

Letters to the Editor

From Dr G. R. Beasley-Murray, Principal of Spurgeon's College, London

It is a long time since I read two such prejudiced statements in a single issue of a paper as the editorial on Billy Graham and James Mitchell's review of his biography. I receive material of this sort quite regularly – from the International Christian Council of Churches – and I listen to the like from non-Christian humanists, but I do not expect to read it in a responsible Christian paper.

Let us grant that Pollock's characterization of modern theologians in the Graham biography was exaggerated: that did not justify Mitchell going berserk with his pen. If Pollock has tended to put Billy Graham in a stained-glass window, Mitchell has done his best to discover him in a psychiatrist's lavatory. But nothing Mitchell said of Graham was as reprehensible as the caricature of Christ at the conclusion of his review; this was the action of a theological mod, heaving a brick through a rocker's plate-glass window – sheer adolescent irresponsibility to enrage the middle-aged and bring the police out.

I can understand Christian people objecting to elements in Graham's biblical interpretation and evangelistic techniques, for there will be differences in these areas till judgment day. But why do we have to lampoon a man's efforts to bring his contemporaries to God? It is unjust to make out that Billy Graham's methods confuse evangelism with filling church pews, and it is foolish to assert that his crusades are designed to confirm Christians in their antipathy to 'constructive social thinking'. And why must it be assumed that there is only one way of spreading the Good News – the *New Christian* way, or any other? Are there not, in fact, a thousand ways? Why cannot we thank God for Symanowski, George Macleod and Billy Graham? Admittedly they have little in common, but they all have something to say – though none of their methods is so important as organizing the laity to fulfil the Great Commission. In one crucially important matter Billy Graham is an example to the church, namely in making the gospel plain to plain people. Who will maintain that the gospel of Christ is being clearly proclaimed in the British churches today in any idiom?

Not mud-slinging, but earnest prayer befits the churches as June approaches. Let us not withhold it.

From the Warden and Chaplains of Lee Abbey, Devon

We write as a group of people from differing theological backgrounds and we represent a fairly wide experience of ministry at home and overseas, in parishes and in the specialized work of Lee Abbey. None of us are conservative evangelicals and none of us are uncritical admirers of Billy Graham, but we have no hesitation in affirming that his past crusades in this country have been of genuine help to many people. We ourselves know of a number of men and women who ten years ago were completely outside any active membership of the church and who are today loyal Christians, expressing their faith fully in the life of society, and well aware of the twentieth-century world. Their conversions were the outcome of Billy Graham's ministry. We know, too, of parishes and churches which have received new vision and understanding of the church's job through the same ministry.

However much we may differ from some of his theology and disagree with some of the methods of mass evangelism, there can be no doubt that Dr Graham's ministry has been blessed by God and is of enormous importance and influence. To suggest, as you do, that all who come forward at the meetings for personal counselling are to be regarded as 'casualties of the crusade' is not only arrogant nonsense: it is perilously near to blasphemy and it ill becomes a paper which would presumably make the claim to be both informed and responsible in its judgments.

From the Rev. Richard Askew, Liverpool

The two articles in your last issue about the coming Billy Graham crusade are interesting in that they highlight the salient feature of the debate between the exponents of the 'new theology' and those who still propagate the traditional Christian gospel. The point on which this debate turns is, in essence, a christological issue.

If, with your book critic, James Mitchell, we hold that Christ 'was a defeated, muddled, superb and violent man who some people thought was a little too fond of the bottle', who 'died in ignominy, believing himself to be a failure', then we shall be bound to search for a purely naturalistic explanation of the phenomenon of conversion – there is no other dimension in which to look. Like Sargant in *The Battle for the Mind*, dismissing St Paul's Damascus road experience in a brief paragraph, or Osborne attributing the Reformation to Luther's constipation, we shall be bound to explain conversion in terms of the evangelist's and the convert's suspected neuroses, and in so doing to explain it away.

If, on the other hand, we accept twenty centuries of Christian experience of the Risen Christ, and hold him to be not only fully human but also supernatural and transcendent, then we shall be at least open to the idea that lives may be radically changed by confrontation with this Christ. Sincere and urgent preaching, recognized by people as relevant to their own life situation, is surely one way in which this confrontation is brought about.

The presentation of the traditional Christian gospel by Billy Graham is both clear and effective; as one of many who find themselves not only within the church but in the church's ordained ministry as a result (in human terms) of this preaching, I personally welcome his June crusade most warmly. The gospel he preaches is 'honest to God'. What gospel can the new theology present?

From Mr R. Lawrence Jones, Crawley, Sussex

As one who greatly appreciated your courageously honest comments on the Billy Graham crusade, I much regret the criticisms you have received from some readers.

What is so disappointing and even alarming is the failure of these critics to face the hard facts (*a*) that Billy Graham's modernized nineteenth-century revival meeting approach is not the one needed for the twentieth century; (*b*) that the growing alienation from the churches has roots too deep and reasons too complex for a 'The Bible says' message even to touch; and (*c*) that so long as we put money, energy and hope into this sort of thing, so long will we avoid the 'New Reformation' needed and increase the condition from which Billy Graham comes to rescue us.

Mr Beasley-Murray anxiously asks on behalf of the crusade's converts: Will the churches be ready for them? I am afraid that all too many churches will be exactly what they will want.

The acceptance of organic unity as the supreme aim of the churches has coincided with a marked swing towards orthodoxy. Even Congregational churches, once noted for their progressive radicalism, have swung to the right.

For each one of the converts of the crusade there are at least a thousand of the *Honest to God* and *The Christian Agnostic* way of thinking for whom few churches are ready. Even the City Temple now offers the Apostles' Creed as its gospel! And the many cannot accept this for three simple reasons: because it omits all the things about which Christ was most concerned; because every phrase in it needs demythologizing; and because if anyone came to the Jesus of the gospels seeking the way to his Father, he would never – absolutely never – offer this creed as the way.

In the light of the real needs, theological and social, it looks to me as though Billy Graham is himself the biggest casualty.

The Case for Dr Graham

BRYAN GREEN

As he preaches him as Lord and Saviour . . . some, I believe, will fall in love with him and—yes, I will use the dirty word—begin to discover what it means to be 'saved'.

The coming of Dr Billy Graham this June for his crusade in the Earls Court Stadium has already aroused interest in the press. It is certain to give rise to a great deal more. Both appreciation and downright criticism will be voiced during his stay in this country. The interest and the comment will not be confined to church circles and the church press. Right outside, in factories and offices, in schools and universities, and within all the mass media there will be articles written about him and his work, and opinions concerning both will be freely expressed.

Judging from what happened during a previous visit, the reactions of ordinary men and women who are not churchgoers are likely to be more tolerant and even more appreciative than the views expressed within church circles, if one can take as an example of this the recent editorial in *New Christian*.

The non-churchgoer's view cannot be dismissed in an airy fashion simply as being naive, without a true understanding of proper Christian strategy or true Christian theology. My experience is that ordinary folk are often very shrewd in their judgment both of a man's sincerity and of the basic value of what he is trying to do. It was, after all, the Pharisees and Sadducees who pretty vigorously opposed Jesus.

It is therefore important, in my opinion, not to worsen the image of the church in the eyes of the outsider by appearing to be unfair in criticism or, because of our frustration, even jealous of seeming spiritual success.

Shared misgivings

Let it be said at once that I myself share some of the misgivings of the critics of a crusade of this kind in England at this time. Also, I do not share much of Dr Graham's theology and outlook. Granted, too, that the large sums of money and tremendous effort needed to promote such a crusade could, as is suggested, have been diverted into more profitable channels for the church's mission – though it must be admitted that it is doubtful if either would have been forthcoming but for an objective to which many diverse Christians could bend their united efforts.

All this and more can be said to give rise to disquiet and misgivings.
Particularly 'grave foreboding' can come to those who believe that 'a realistic mission strategy must incorporate those areas of social life which have a profound effect upon human attitudes and behaviour and which it is necessary to Christianize before a widespread response to the Christian gospel can be expected. The role of the local church is to be seen primarily in terms of finding points of engagement with the local community.'

I see the point of this statement and agree, but my grave foreboding is tempered by the following considerations. How can areas of social life be Christianized without Christians to do it? How can a local church fulfil its role if new and genuine members are not being added to it? In any case, the statement says 'primarily', which suggests there may be secondary and additional ways in which the local church can carry out its role. Is it not possible that Dr Billy Graham has a real contribution to make here?

Part of mission

The winning of individuals to repentance and faith in God through Jesus Christ is, I suggest, firmly based in the New Testament and in the history of the Christian church. It is certainly part of the church's mission to-day. The late Dr Kirk, Bishop of Oxford, made the point that the religion of many Anglicans is 'that of adherence and not of possession'. He pointed out that they needed to know that living personal relationship with God through the Holy Spirit which is implicit in the sacraments both of baptism and of the eucharist.

This is the task to which Dr Billy Graham sets himself with enthusiasm, intelligence and single-mindedness. He believes that man is a sinner, not just maladjusted. He believes that God's free grace and love desire every man to know him and to love him. He believes this offer of God waits for man's response, whether gradual or through a crisis. I believe this, too, and so do a great number of other Christians spread throughout the churches.

It is therefore unfair and untrue to say: 'Dr Graham's sermons reveal a complete failure to grasp any of the insights which come through a Christian estimate of the world.' I do not accept his near-literal interpretation of the Bible, and I regret Dr Graham's failure to grasp many other insights which I believe belong to the Christian viewpoint; but he clearly sees some truth and shares this clear insight with many others.

I have had the privilege of his friendship since 1948, before ever he became famous. We met when I was preaching a mission in the Cathedral of St John the Divine in New York. During the years of our friendship I have been impressed not only by his sincerity but by his humility and charity towards those who disagree with him. He does not denounce scholars and

pastors who try to communicate Christian truth differently from himself;
he does indeed firmly oppose those who, he thinks, are falling into grave
error; but so does your editorial in reverse, though certainly not with the
same charity.

As a convinced Anglican I am glad about the radical thinking of to-day
on all fronts and am willing to learn from it; but I deplore anything which
widens the breach between Christians. With this new re-thinking we need
also the proper Christian belief in the power of God and expectancy of
conversion that many Roman Catholics and Pentecostalists have through
their certain faith in the acts of God in Christ and in his purpose for the
individual.

On balance I come down as a supporter of Dr Billy Graham's Crusade
and agree with Canon Hugh Montefiore's remarks in his letter to Cambridge undergraduates announcing Dr Graham's forthcoming sermon in
Great St Mary's: 'May I say how delighted I am to welcome Billy Graham
back to our pulpit. I do not of course always agree with him theologically
(any more than I do, for example, with my Roman Catholic friends) but
this does not diminish in any way my affection and respect for him as a
great Christian (any more than it does for Roman Catholics too).'

It is the business of the local churches to help forward those who make
some kind of step of faith at the crusade meetings. What a snide and emo-
tive sentence there is at the end of your editorial: 'It is the plain duty of the
local churches to welcome and care for the casualties of the crusade.' Does
this mean that you believe that all those influenced by the crusade must be
classed as casualties? – for you do not suggest that there may be need to
welcome some who may have been helped. Of course there will be some
casualties, but there will also be many converts, and if we think of all converts as casualties we shall certainly fail to be pastors to the sinners who
have repented.

Sympathetic support

I am glad that the Bishops of London and Southwark have sent identical
letters to their clergy calling for prayer for the crusade and asking that,
whatever their views, they will give sympathetic understanding to any
people in their parishes who may have been helped by the crusade. Those
who, like the writer of the editorial, believe Dr Graham's teaching is in the
long run harmful to the Christian faith, will have plenty of time when he
has gone to improve on his teaching and to deepen the spiritual understanding of the converts.

Monica Furlong, in relating how she passed from being a humanist to
being a Christian, describes her experience as being 'as near as anything

like falling in love'. Such an experience can of course be sudden or gradual: what matters is that it is real.

As Dr Billy Graham preaches Christ – with faults of emphasis, like the rest of us, but nevertheless preaches him as Lord and Saviour – some, I believe, will fall in love with him and – yes, I will use the dirty word – begin to discover what it means to be 'saved'.

How Does Graham do it?

GEORGE TARGET

A description of the technique and the degree of careful pre-planning that marks every Billy Graham meeting.

In the overheated acres of mass evangelism, not to be sold and singing about Billy Graham and his methods is accounted by most evangelicals as unrighteousness, and to suggest that he still remembers a few tricks from the sales manual he used as a youngster peddling Fuller brushes in North Carolina, that he's a professional in the chromium-plated craft of manipulating crowds – this is to suffer the vials of instant wrath at the hands of the uncertain, whose certainties have been doubted just that little bit.

Yet this is worth risking, for what happens at a Billy Graham Crusade raises larger problems from the depths than shallow-draught enthusiasm has nets to manage, the implications being such as to put the skids of reasonable doubt under some of the unquestioned theological assumptions from which these campaigns are launched at us.

But first, before considering what happens, who does it happen to? What kind of people make up the bulk of the counted crowds?

Rose-tinted views are ten-a-penny, the evangelical press (especially the sub-division published by the Billy Graham Evangelistic Association Limited) indulges in wistful speculation about revival and the common man, but the facts are unglamorous.

Who goes?

That it is not, for example, a typical football or royal occasion crowd can hardly be doubted. For one thing, most of its members are already

Christians – active, nominal or Laodicean, there by the chartered busload
from all over the country to swell the numbers; enormous choirs, hundreds
and hundreds of ushers and stewards and organizing staff and counsellors
. . . even 25 per cent of all 'decisions' are merely reaffirmations by existing
Christians.

What is open to less doubt is that most are either women or children.
Even on the hesitant assumption that those who respond to the appeal for
'decision' are in any way a fair sample of the whole, 25 per cent are children
below the age of consent, and an average of 65 per cent are women to 35
per cent men – and this ratio often slides into the splits of greater extremes.
For example, during the 1955 crusade in Glasgow 71 per cent were women.
(Unless, of course, the preaching of Billy Graham is that much more
effective with women and children than with men?)

And then many attend time and time again – which means that the
loudly-trumpeted grand totals for attendance are somewhat larger than the
truth has breath for, by no means being the mind-reeling numerical wonders
of publicity.

The crowd attracted, then, is an extremely limited one – not only a
comparatively small number of people when compared with the total
population, but a section severely restricted in age-range and interests,
tending to be drawn from one particular type or class. In other words, a
highly-selective minority of a minority.

What happens to them?

The main effect worked and planned for with some of the most polished
techniques still permissible in a democracy is that worked upon Billy
Graham himself by a Kentucky revivalist, Mordecai Fowler Ham: the
effect reported with such clarity by William Sargant in his already classic
book, *Battle for the Mind* . . . a disturbance of the emotions as a means of
affecting the higher nervous system.

True, there are minor reservations which can be made against some of
the hidden assumptions of this book (and evangelicals have pounced upon
these scraps of comfort with loud cries of relief), but its essential arguments
remain untouched.

A disturbance of the emotions, then, as a means of affecting the higher
nervous system.

Now, as his supporters are swift to claim, Billy Graham is not all that
emotional in the pejorative sense. There are no orgiastic fits, no excessive
ravings and foamings, no Kentuckian 'seeing the devil', very little hill-billy
patter, and he builds up nothing like the head of steam of yesterday's
hell-fire.

But the fires of his anger and emotion are only lightly damped down. His
movements and gestures are violent. He stabs and thrusts and clenches and punches, and there's an apparent need to destroy, flatten, raze to the ground, threaten, crush, throttle, cut off, smash . . . and his images and language betray the same frustrated rage beneath what looks like a merely dynamic approach.

The emotion is there, then – deliberately suppressed to the one end in constant view: decision.

How is it used?

First, nothing just 'happens' – everything is planned, and times are calculated in seconds.

Long before the meeting there is the extended publicity build-up – a very necessary part of the process: people work and wait for weeks and months and years for a crusade to start, because Billy Graham without the ballyhoo would be like Brigitte Bardot in a suit of rusty armour – both need to be seen under the bright lights to be believed, and both need production by experts.

Build-up begins

The potential 'decision-maker' at such a meeting is almost certain to be what is known as a 'seeker after the truth' – else what would he or she be seeking at the microphone of Billy Graham? A person unsure of belief, indecisive, self-questioning, possibly anxious and nervous – wide open to persuasive suggestion.

The audience gets ready for the meeting hours in advance, travels long distances to it, queues and assembles an hour or more early for it, and waits and waits for it to start. There's the sense of occasion, being present with thousands and tens or thousands of other people, and thus subject to all the normal pressures of group excitation so well understood by Hitler and those in charge of state ceremonial – all and everything working for the induction of tension and expectancy.

During all this time their natural and induced tensions are screwed up tighter and tighter by excitement, expectancy, comings and goings on the platform, the entrance of the massed choir, visible signs of preparation for the event they are all waiting for, and even the beginnings of sheer exhaustion. These pressures are then intensified by community singing, which tends to unify the group and lead to self-identification with it and the content of the songs – which are those of full surrender and self-abandonment.

This singing is initiated, led, controlled and conducted by one of the professional song leaders in the team – happy, extroverted, confident, and the feeling is communicated that other people are now in charge, that all

will yet be well, that the inevitable process has started, the rivers of salvation are flowing, the end already in sight . . . the singing continuous, the
dark currents of hope and despair running counter, making for new tensions, new complexities – the words those of confusion, despair, hopeless-
ness and abnegation, the music loud and triumphant, exulting in self-disgust.

The vocal persuaders

Then one of the professional singers in the team will perform a solo – well-
known and well-loved, everybody knowing the words, but not being
allowed to join in, and so mouthing them silently, still part of the experience, but still denied full expression . . . the organ sweet and reverent,
sliding gently across the emotions, the pleasure of memory and recognition
rippling around the multitude, the singer strong, simple, beloved, sincere.

And then the group is made to act as one, standing or sitting or singing
or praying when told to do so – all thus being encouraged to obey instructions, to get used to the idea of obedience, to do what other people are
doing, not to remain out of things, not to be different, not to be awkward,
not to remain one among many, alone, unwanted and unloved, but to
belong, to join in, to imitate, to be part of this great movement: all con-
stituents of the condition which Karen Horney has termed 'neurotic
submissiveness'. This condition tends to the abdication of individual
responsibility for events, to dependence on others, on those in charge, on
those who know, on leaders . . . and the more powerless to influence events
such a person feels, the less of a person and more of a small unit in a big
crowd, the more important appear those who are in charge, who know
what they are doing, who have confidence, who are not at all frightened of
what is happening, who are controlling, giving orders, and having them
obeyed.

This new anxiety to conform and belong is overlaid on all the others, and
interacts with them, and leads to an acute concentration of the normal field
of attention. There grows an inability to respond to the total environment,
to act with normal rationality, but, instead, there is a tendency to react
almost impulsively, to do the first thing suggested or seen to be done by
others.

So, when Billy Graham at last appears, often late by just those few very
significant minutes, the ending of all this unbearable tension is experienced
as profound emotional relief and release, and he becomes the centre of
enormous gratitude and feelings of pleasure and heightened expectancy,
and thus has total and undivided and completely uncritical attention, which
is then concentrated still more upon him by the use of spotlights and other
accessories.

There are no distractions in this carefully conditioned and minutely controlled environment. 'We allow no applause, no outbursts.' Loud-speakers amplify the voice, which seems to come from all directions at once, harsh, metallic, unnatural, larger than life, insistent, echoing out of this world, the voice of no mere man. He is distant and remote, and this sheer distance from the source of all the sound, from the tiny, gesticulating figure on the platform, keeps the audience from testing against their own reality their induced belief that he knows the answers, that he can help them. There can be no deflating personal contact – but there, in charge at the heart and centre of the event, surrounded by his flanking staff, so urgent and passionate and utterly sure and certain, there is the one man in the whole world who can bring peace, answers, safety, security, comfort, love, understanding, forgiveness – even God.

His message is short, simple and repetitive, like a series of advertising slogans calculated for anxiety and the sense of guilt. On the one hand hell, and death and damnation and personal and total unworthiness, and the imminent destruction of our cities by the hydrogen bomb and of our free way of life by the completely overwhelming and merciless forces of atheistic communism . . . and, on the other, the desperate need to make a 'decision for Christ' here and now as the only possible way of escape from the looming and nameless terrors of sudden death and the grave: a simple choice between staying where you are to die, or standing up for your very life – a sudden-death choice between certain death and the hope of life . . . the only hope. . . .

By thus confronting the potential 'decision-maker', already in a very nervous and highly suggestible condition, with such a false and naked antithesis, by denying all other self-expression than to obey the 'call', this call to come forward can be made with certainty of response. All present are told to pray, instructed to close their eyes and bow the head, and the form of words is the auto-suggestive one that hundreds of others are already going forward, finding happiness, peace, love, God . . . the counsellors planted all over the audience make the first few moves, create the sense that the statement is true even when it very often is not . . . they stand close by those their experience and training tell them are being drawn to move . . . the appeal goes on and on, hammering away, ten, twenty times . . . seconds pass, minutes, and still the voice calls on and on . . . there's a break, a pause, the hope of silence, of ending . . . but then it starts once more . . . the choir is singing quietly . . . it might all be true, there might be some nameless peace down there with all the others . . . the tension screws to breaking point and beyond . . .

The wonder is that so few actually obey.

Letters to the Editor

From Mr Philip Nash, St David's College, Lampeter

George Target's article 'How Does Graham Do It?' was a fine expose of the technique of a Billy Graham campaign, one which only such a master demolition expert could have provided. As a vulnerable teenager I attended some of the London meetings of the mid-fifties and can vouch for the psychological pressure to associate myself with what was happening: i.e. to make a 'decision'. I have never regretted resisting.

However, one senses in Mr Target's article a definite aversion to Dr Graham's methods, yet surely theological colleges up and down the country teach their students 'technique' in preaching (we have all heard the 'argument weak, so shout' classic). A mass campaign is only an extension of persuasive sermonizing and, despite the moderate response which Mr Target distinguishes, somewhat more successful.

What is more, the call of the gospel message is to 'salvation', to redeem self by identification with Christ. Undoubtedly the Graham version of the message is over-simplified to the degree of presenting his audience with 'a false and naked antithesis', but at least he does present an antithesis, a choice, which is where so many of our habit-tied conventional preachers, apparently ashamed to take a firm stand beside the Saviour, fall down. We might not like the content of a Graham harangue, but please let us not have these implied sneers at a perfected technique. The Graham gang may treat people like sheep, but it is necessary to separate them from the goats in the first instance. Unfortunately we are far too often inclined to treat man as sacred in his unredeemed highly individualistic state; brainwashing is a useful method, providing your detergent is the blood of the Lamb.

From Mr Dennis Parker, Eastbourne

George Target and James Mitchell have made pretty fierce criticisms of Billy Graham; denigration might be a more appropriate description. May I ask these gentlemen: 'How many have turned to Christ (in the widest sense) as an outcome of your own methods (witness?). You don't like his; fair enough. Tell us better.'

If, as is obvious, they confess, 'less than Graham' (or any at all?), why don't they come clean and tell us that they simply hate his guts? At least we could admire such honesty. So far, they have scarcely been constructive enough to earn much admiration.

From George Target

Dennis Parker calls me a gentleman in such a way as to demonstrate his conviction that no critic of Billy Graham can possibly be one, asks me how many have turned to Christ as an outcome of my methods of witness, then doubts that any have at all, and finally instructs me to come clean and admit that I simply hate Billy Graham's guts.

But I am a novelist, not a professional evangelist, and to tot up an account of my evangelistic activity and good works and whatnot, issue nighly statistics and sound an expensive trumpet before me in the synagogues, would be to do the very thing I question in the Billy Graham Evangelistic Association Incorporated – and Christ has said of such, 'They have their reward'.

And I do not hate anybody's guts. Billy Graham is my brother in Jesus Christ, and merely because I have questioned his use of various honestly-doubted conditioning devices is no reason for Dennis Parker to use such uncharitable language about my motives. Unless, of course, such a panic-reaction betrays him as one of those who prefer their plastic saints to remain untouched by human hand?

RELIGION!

Is God dead? Of course not, preached Evangelist Billy Graham, 47, to the Atlanta Press Club. As a matter of fact, said the reverend, 'I can tell you that God is alive because I talked to Him this morning.' – *Time*.

33 Prayer is evangelism stripped of all carnal attractions. – *Slogan of Billy Graham All-Britain Crusade 1967.*

One lone demonstrator cried out from the crowd 'What about Vietnam?' But he soon quieted as his voice was no competition to eight huge amplifiers that were lifted high in the air by hydraulic equipment. – *Billy Graham Crusade News Release.*

Eastbourne: De-luxe Flat in small block nearing completion, opposite Holy Trinity; 2 bedrooms, large lounge, with balcony, bathroom, separate toilet, kitchen, dinette; £6,750. Evangelical Christians only. – *From an advertisement in the Church of England Newspaper.*

Can any of your readers give me some first-hand authoritative information about the late Dr Martin Luther King's ministry? Did he really preach the Gospel of God's redeeming grace in Christ? Any man receiving such laudatory effusions from leaders of the organized churches at once becomes suspect to Evangelicals. One would like to have one's suspicions allayed, but one can't help regarding these effusions as oblique attempts to boost our government's anti-Scriptural racial integration policy. – *Letter from the Revd Stephen E. Pulford in English Churchman.*

Dr Jones, who would make no compromise with 'modernists' or watered-down Scripture, ran the school, current enrolment 2,000, with an iron hand. Drinking was strictly forbidden; sexually integrated groups were not permitted to use the gymnasium, swimming pool or tennis courts; Hollywood movies were forbidden, and boys and girls going to his school had to keep their bodies at least six inches apart. Evangelist Billy Graham attended the school in 1936, but quit after a brief stay. – *Minneapolis Tribune.*

Asked whether Evangelicals were 'happy Christians', David Pawson said, 'Yes we are. When we are on our own'. – *Methodist Recorder.*

Mr Lynd, sentencing Mr Shaw to six months' imprisonment, said: 'For someone with an evangelical turn of mind it is remarkable that you have 22 previous convictions, including assaulting the police, common assault, malicious damage, disorderly behaviour, larceny, and cruelty to a cat.' – *Daily Telegraph.*

SILLY LITTLE MAN

A silly little man in a pulpit
taught me that God lived in the sky
and that if I were not quite obedient
to the silly little man's book of rules
God would burn me in hell for years,
perhaps for ever.
He also said my badness
hurt God like anything.
And I believed it and so did my mother
and my children almost believed it
but not quite.

But God said, whispering
through my veins and down the wind
year after year till I happened to listen:
Like a fish you swim in me
though sometimes my love is rough.
I go where you go, and your pains are
                                    my pains,
your sins are my sins
and your muddle my muddle,
and I love you, says God,
despite all evidence to the contrary.
And I believe him, though my mother
                                    doesn't quite
and my children are not yet listening.

What I find difficult
is that God says this too
to the silly man in the pulpit
and he means it
although the little man never hears a word.

YVONNE ABBOTT

3 The Coming Non-Church

RAY BILLINGTON

Without the crutches of convention and the millstone of mediocrity, the church will again stand for something real in men's lives.

An article published in June 1966

Any suggestion that the contemporary church is irrelevant, or that it is dying, causes a good deal of resentment amongst those who are involved in the life of the church. It is felt that Christians should not 'rock the boat' and that the church should always be presented to the world in the most favourable terms. My own conclusion that Methodism could not survive until unity grieved some of my Methodist friends, and I am sorry about this, but I believe that we must see the situation that exists, not what we would like to exist.

Methodism is not, of course, alone in this plight. It is in fact one which besets all the major churches of this country, though some more obviously than others. The Free Churches have been losing ground, both numerically and in influence, throughout this century. The Anglican Church, by the consequences of being the established church, maintains the façade of significance on state and other national occasions; but without these special occasions, and by having to do with those buildings and priests that congregations could afford, the Church of England would begin to look decidedly threadbare. The decline in the Roman Catholic Church is less marked; but it is there all right. Work is having to be left undone because there are no priests to direct it; and the downward trend in church attendances is beginning to be recognized.

Those Christians with any genuine contact with non-Christians (genuine, in the sense that there is a real listening to each other on both sides) know how slight is the hope of any revival of religion in its present form. The image of the church in most people's minds is of a well-meaning but ineffectual organization; it may not do much harm, but it is anachronism in contemporary society, rather like an aged grandmother, living on with her children after most of her generation have gone: it is pleasant to have her around, but her outlook is that of a past generation.

Indifference of the young

It is among the young people of today that the most massive indifference to the church is to be seen. In the classes which I instruct in liberal studies (sixth-formers and day-release apprentices) it is rare almost to the point of being unknown to find one with any church affiliation. This is not because of their unawareness of the attempts of various church people to modernize the whole set-up, but springs from a conviction that the fundamental tenets of the church are little more than mumbo-jumbo. The magazine I edit, *Over the Bridge* – organ of the South London Industrial Mission – recently had a correspondence between SLIM's vice-chairman, Kenneth Adams, and Nick Stacey about the need for a new look in the church. A teenage girl wrote in: 'No one can deny that the church is doing a good thing in trying to "reach" the young "outside". May I respectfully point out that it is failing miserably? This attempt to buy the young at the cost of its own dignity is an admirable thing, or, rather, would be if it succeeded. But it does not. Nor would it, even if you had the Stones singing a Lennon-McCartney setting of the Magnificat. Why? Most of my friends do not go to church. This is because they cannot accept the existence of any form of spiritual Being. No amount of beat music or experimental worship could persuade them otherwise. Many older people too would, if honest with themselves, admit that the reason for their failure to attend church was a lack of belief in God. Atheism is not confined to a small circle of highly intelligent doubters. It is for this reason that all teaching that presupposes a belief in God is valueless. It is no good preaching that Christ is the Son of God if people are going to say, "What God?" '

Modernization no answer

I quote this letter in full because it presents the basic dilemma confronting the radical in the church today. What is the use of modernizing an outfit with which the growing generation will have nothing to do? If we believe on the one hand that within the church is contained the 'divine spark' which offers the best hope of a full life to mankind, as even Malcolm Muggeridge admitted in his famous *Weekend Telegraph* article, and on the other hand that this spark is being rendered invisible by the very organization which contains it, do we achieve anything worthwhile by trying to make that organization more efficient?

The answer to this question will depend on whether one feels one's chief responsibility is to the few who do remain loyal church people, or to the growing number – many of them honest, intelligent, enquiring people, desiring to find an ultimate purpose in life – who simply will not identify themselves with the church today at any price. The trouble is that even if you take the first alternative there still remains the problem of those lay-men, admittedly a minority, who are brassed off with the present organization and desperately long to break out of it. Nobody, in fact, can escape from the dilemma except by the process adopted by too many who ought to have more integrity and courage – shutting the eyes and stopping the ears, and whistling to keep the pecker up.

What Christians today need most of all is the determination that the love which was seen in Jesus Christ shall become real among men, whether they recognize the source of it or not. Our task is not to baptize but to make the good news known; not to bring people to church but to take its essential power to them; not to induce guilt complexes but to help people to find the essential depths in themselves; not to talk theology – perhaps not even to talk at all – but to express in ourselves, and by the decisions we arrive at as a result of our thinking together, what good neighbourliness means in social, industrial, commercial, educational and personal life.

In short, our task is to humanize the monsters of our age, so that the full personality of man can begin to flower. In Jesus Christ this is possible, for in him the new humanity has been seen and expressed; but the tragedy and irony is that the church which contains this mystery and therefore ought to be the universal guide into the truth has, through its established position, its top-heavy organization and its crass pettifogging rules, become a monster in its own right. We can tinker with it here and there, but in the end there is only one course of action possible: like a building with dry rot through most of its woodwork, you must tear out the lot and start again.

It is clear that whatever does survive will not be denominational. Nothing in the church today evinces our living in the past so much as the continued divisions. A growing number of people realize this, of course, but there still remain many who assert that their denomination's distinctive understanding of particular truths justifies their remaining in isolation from their brother Christians. These people argue that such matters as apostolic succession, or the inspiration of the scriptures, or the interpretation of the sacraments, are crucial in the life of the church, apparently not realizing that the world amongst whom they are called to minister does not care a penny whistle about the niceties of theological distinction. Can't these apologists for denominationalism appreciate that they are falling into precisely the error of the Pharisees: straining off a midge yet gulping down a camel?

I think the initiative for action here will have to come from Anglicans.

So long as they follow the rule book they help to stifle the faith. What is
needed is for large numbers to act – now – by inviting members of other
denominations to join at their eucharist, and by joining that of others.
Then we might see who's calling whose bluff.

White elephants

The next millstone to go must be the church buildings. A building is like a
pet: so long as you've got it you've got to look after it. And if the pet is
large enough, it takes a lot of time, energy and money to do this. To make
matters worse, most of the buildings are not even useful pets but white
elephants. Is there anything more sickening than to see a group of reasonably intelligent people coming together in a church – many of them with
vital problems to face in their daily lives – and discussing how to raise cash
for their particular shrine? Christian stewardship has been an insidious
element in this situation for, despite all the protestations of its advocates,
it has led to or encouraged two evils: the thought on the part of fringe contacts that the church wants only their money, and the misguided belief
among regular members that maintaining the local church plant is a justi-
fiable use of that proportion of their income which they give away.

Apart from the economics of the problem, there is the fact that a building inevitably becomes a crutch to one's faith, and even an excuse for not
broadening that faith. Would we have half the difficulty in persuading
church members about the necessity and nature of mission if the buildings
were not around, so offering the easy way out for many, that all they need
do is to persuade colleagues to 'come to church'? Would the dualism of
seeing the church set over against the world – which most church members
share to a certain extent, whether they admit it or not – be fallen into so
easily if there were no buildings? Would we be so ignorant of our neighbours if we only had our homes for services? And would we not gain in the
respect of those around us if, like all other organizations, we had to hire a
hall for our public assemblies?

Immediate action on this one could be twofold: those churches with no
building 'problem' could resolve that only the main act of worship should
take place in the building; for the rest of the week it could be hired out for
secular uses – and if its present structure doesn't easily allow for this, let
it be altered so that it does. Better still, let it be sold to the local authority,
to be hired for worship Sunday by Sunday. For those Christians in areas
where a new building is contemplated the matter is simpler: they can resolve
not to build, and in one action throw the local Christians back on their
own resources as few Christians have been in four centuries. With the
crutch removed, people would be forced to stand on their own feet.

The third change needed is an end to the rule of the church by full-time clergy. It may well be that there will continue to be a need for a few full-time people; what is certain is that the great majority must be men and women who have a job to do apart from their leadership in the local Christian community. The clergy can no longer continue to be a group set apart, cotton-woolled from the world by their ecclesiastical duties.

Apart from the good that this would do to the group concerned, the chief value of this development would be similar to that of removing buildings: another crutch would be removed. So long as the full-time minister remains, the rest of the church members are normally going to leave things entirely to him, whether out of deference or from laziness. Why should they spend time visiting this elderly couple, or solving this teenager's problem, or gathering a group of their neighbours together to discuss local issues, when they pay a man to do these jobs? The fact that some non-clerics do this despite the presence of the clergy serves to suggest what infinite possibilities there are for when he is gone. If we can begin to think of all Christians as pastors, and of the clergy as the men or women who emerge as leaders of the Christian community, helping to direct their thoughts on the problems that face them all at work and in their leisure time, and therefore taking the lead in Sunday worship, we shall be approaching, I believe, the pattern of ministry needed in our time. And more clergy can do this now by opting for some form of 'secular' employment.

Mention of the problems men and women face leads to the final and most important aspect of the coming 'non-church': the realization by all that we exist as a body in order that the Christian message can have meaning in the lives of all men. This means that our task is to express love in our own lives, and to make it easier for other people to realize love in theirs. Our aim will be that men may find the 'abundant life' of which our Lord spoke – by discovering the depths which they possess in themselves, and getting beyond the selfishness and materialism which lie on the surface. But it's not a bit of use our imagining that we shall help men to do this by the utterance of pious-sounding phrases or by glib invitations to attend church. It will require careful study of the problems facing men where they are – problems like those of automation, monotony or management-labour relationships in industry, or of race relations, selfish landlords or short-sighted councils locally.

It may well be that we are in for a period when there will be no clearly-defined pattern of the church at all. In some places it may be that *ad hoc* groups, chosen from local personnel (in a factory or a school, for instance), will meet occasionally to discuss how love can be expressed in their situation (though they will probably not speak of it in those terms). *And for these people this will be the church.* Elsewhere groups may gather for informal times of discussion or worship in the homes of those who give the lead. For them this will be the church. Others again will wish to meet occasionally for a celebration of the eucharist – though not in Anglican Cranmerian or Free Church hymn-sandwich style. But these may well be a minority of the whole.

I foresee the breaking down of central structures, and the springing into life of jocular expressions of the Christian community, with different communities varying considerably from one another. The dangers of wrong beliefs and practices creeping into such a situation are offset by the inevitable freedom from the dead hand of conformity which must accrue. It may be that with such a pattern the church will once again begin to stand for something which is real in men's lives, instead of standing as the guardian of a tradition which is generally rejected because its essential worth is hidden behind ecclesiastical jargon, imposing edifices and clerical collars.

The church is dead. Long live the non-church!

Non-Church is Nonsense
ALISON ADCOCK

The picture of the activities of the non-church is an interesting one. In one place a group will meet – 'occasionally' – to discuss how love can best be expressed in their situation. Elsewhere – 'some will wish to meet occasionally for a celebration of the eucharist, though not in Anglican Cranmerian or Free Church hymn-sandwich style'. These groups will meet in a school, a factory, a private house, or rent back an ex-church for an hour from the local authority to whom it has been sold. It will no longer have a churchy look, except for the line of Gothic pillars which had to be left *in situ* to support the roof; otherwise it will have been reconstructed for secular use, and with a bar in the ex-apse, and the ex-nave filled with card tables and ladies' and gents' cloaks in the transepts, it should give quite a human tone. As there is no trained minister, the leader of the group will 'emerge' spontaneously. His qualifications, to judge from current experience of lay-leadership, will be a muggins-like capacity to be bullied into doing work nobody else wants to do; and possibly the possession of a nice big, centrally-situated living room and a docile tea-brewing wife.

'Occasionally' is a fascinating word. What happens? A spontaneous wave of emotion and resolve as one morning all severally suddenly realize that they have an urge to meet each other? Perhaps, like PCC meetings, each meeting-time will be chosen at the end of the previous meeting? The twentieth? No; Bill's sister is getting married on the twenty-first so he'll be busy. Not Sunday, of course. How about the twenty-third? No, Gwen's judo class always on Mondays – and Mary has Red Cross on Tuesday, and Wednesday is Tom's darts night . . .

But anyhow, one only wants these meetings when in the mood, otherwise they get so insincere and forced. So it will have to be done by a whip-round on the phone. 'Gwen? Can you come round to my place at once? Drop everything. Bill and I feel the urge to discuss love with you . . . Would you ring Tom?'

It is, of course, rather tough on the unaligned. He won't know when and where to find the non-church functioning. But no doubt they will draw him in by personal contact, mutterings on the grapevine, little buttonhole pins with 'NC' on them, to give him courage to ask. Maybe we could recapture the old catacomb spirit, with passwords to the pothole, sewer or disused boathouse currently in use for our non-services?

We are abstemious, too. We only meet occasionally. In these bad old days of the church's long-protracted death, there is no restraint, no self-control for Christians; they can get frequent and regular eucharists all over the place, publicly advertised. Some claim to find this helpful. Victims of a compulsive neurosis – eucharist addicts. They will learn to cut down gradually, training themselves to vary the intervals so as to lose the appallingly *routine* behaviour-pattern. And one other perversion we really have to quash. Nobody is to be allowed the stupefying drug of 'Cranmerian' English. Some people like it, obviously, just as some drinkers like meths. But they must be prevented from indulging. Some tastes are too depraved to be tolerated. We will explain to them; atavism, nostalgia, the dreadful second-hand derivativeness of using other people's words.

Talking of other people's words, what about the Bible? After we have jettisoned the course of training in what it meant, in how previous generations interpreted it, are we allowed the thing itself, old as it is? Or would we discard all framework and just sit there evolving loving notions in total fluidity?

I have just remembered that we already have meetings to think about

love and how to express it – Quaker meetings for Sufferings are rather the
same, surely? And Quaker meetings for worship are pretty fluid, and have
no trained leader, and take place in nice plain rooms which are used for
other purposes betweenwhiles. The non-church exists. Its only drawback
that I can see is that while I personally am immensely drawn to Quaker
customs, the Friends are in fact the Christian group with the least membership among the ordinary chaps in the factory and the ordinary housewives
on the estate. They are much admired, but they don't attract actual members from Admass.

This is a problem. The godless teenagers and the man in the street show
no more signs of wanting to sit around in groups evolving ways of showing
love than of wanting to attend old-fashioned eucharists. Otherwise those
Quaker meetings and Toc H meetings would be packing them in. What *will*
Admass and their wives join in? Ten-pin bowling and rave sessions before
marriage: afterwards, possibly, Bingo. Shall we have two-tier non-church
with jukeboxes and coke in the downstairs twilight and legs-eleven upstairs?
We shall have the people, but will they have religion? Or is it perhaps the
unpalatable truth that modern man doesn't want anything to do with any
sort of religion, church or non-church, and if we find a form of togetherness
with popular appeal it won't be religious in anybody's sense of the term?

Meanwhile, in abolishing the trained ministry, you will have destroyed
all knowledge of what religion was about; and you will have destroyed the
buildings that belonged to religious observance. But doesn't this give the
game away? People who seriously advocate adapting York Minster or St
Paul's to secular uses are the same sort of insensitive barbarians as the
people who used the Parthenon as an arsenal, or the people who have
turned the Russian churches into museums. Haven't they read Philip
Larkin's *Church Going?* Church buildings today possibly do their greatest
work between-times.

Think of the average person, sharing his bedroom with a relative in the
matchboarded compartment of a block of flats, with the thuds from above,
the squalls from below, the transistors right and left all impinging on him;
he gets up to the radio, eats amid family squabbles and jokes; dashes for a
crammed bus; works all day in a roaring, blaring, bellowing workshop;
lunches in a canteen that resounds with male voices echoing off breeze-
blocks . . . This man is never, never alone and still in silence. But he can be,
in a church. And, in strange fact, you do find people in church, on weekdays, alone, on tiptoe, drinking up stillness and timelessness while their
nerves cool and untwist and the perspectives of living swing back into focus.
The otherness, the dimness, the chill, the tremendous 'unignorable' quiet
are the very stuff of religious experience, along with the venerable peace of

Stonehenge, the colossal majesty of Angkor, the shimmering splendour of
the Shwe Dagon pagoda.

To destroy the last oases of truth and silence in our cities so as to belong more completely to our own age (more secular in the literal sense of less eternal) may merely mean that we destroy our last bridge to sanity and give ourselves over entirely to bedlam, because not many people have the sense to come up for air. Suppose our way of living really is bad for us, corrupting and degrading us. Suppose it is because we are so far gone in our opiates that we have lost the appetite for better things. Then to destroy the last outposts of the other kind of life will be disaster, not the dawn of a brave new world. It will mean blocking up the door of the cave in which we live among the shadows, so that it ceases to be possible for anyone to leave it and find the real sunshine outside. This, incidentally, will apply to our liturgy – to the ancient poetry, music and drama. After all, we don't abolish Shakespeare as antique. We even revive Aeschylus on our stages. Bach and Mozart are available to those for whom they speak, those who can savour them. We don't tell lovers of poetry to put Shakespeare into the modern idiom or jazz up Palestrina for electric guitars. It could be that, to its shame, our modern world is barren of vehicles for worship, just as computers cannot see visions or typewriters make symphonies.

God is an almost lost secret, worship an almost dead art; but the worship of God is something which for the health of our souls and bodies we must somehow keep alive and rediscover. There were black days in Israel when there was no open vision, the Lord seemed to have withdrawn himself, no prophets spoke and shrines were little used. But the river still flowed beneath the soil and in good time burst forth again. Nobody then considered it a sacred duty to seal up the springs with cement and make an unreclaimable desert. Will it be our privilege in this modern age, at the same time as we are poisoning our songbirds, choking our seabirds, eliminating our buttercups and daisies, bombarding our moon with hardware and showering our soil with strontium 90 – to slam the door irrevocably on the God of our salvation in whose will is our peace and without whom our souls must wander restlessly in dry places? *Absit omen.*

Letters to the Editor

From Moira Megaw, London SW

It is unfortunate for Alison Adcock's argument that she should have chosen an illustration that simply reinforces Mr Billington's point. Has she read Philip Larkin's poem *Church Going*? She seems to have missed the irony of the poem completely. As the double meaning of the title indicates, 'Church Going' is the 'Going Church', i.e. the disappearing church, and the same irony underlies the poem from the first line, 'Once I am sure there's nothing going on', to the last, 'If only that so many dead lie round.'

As the ironic undercurrent of the poem demonstrates, the church is disappearing because it has only one thing it can talk effectively about – death – and the reason it speaks so well about death is that the dead are the only people who still seriously use the church. Larkin concedes ceremony to religion but does not suggest it really affects life. The church chiefly serves as a meditating point on extinction, an extinction to which the church's own irrelevance bears witness. All this underlines Mr Billington's point that the church is no longer in touch with life and its buildings are therefore *memento mori*.

Mrs Adcock is right that love can't operate in a vacuum – certainly not in the vacuum of an empty church building or Stonehenge. The necessary context was pointed out by Christ in sending his disciples out into the world.

From Mr Douglas J. Derbyshire, Cheadle

I agree with Alison Adcock, Ray Billington *is* hopelessly in error in suggesting we disturb the even tremor of our ways. It is sacrilegious to speak against the ordained ministry and the parish system. For wasn't the Christ, before his baptism, duly examined by John the Baptist to see he had suitable sponsors, an adequate degree – at the best university – and had passed the GOE? After his baptism, wasn't the Christ inducted and instituted into the spiritualities and temporalities of a quiet Galilean parish church? Didn't his parishioners spend many a quiet hour there in seclusion from the bustling world and the noisy crowd? I myself cannot remember the chapter and the verse where it is written, but I am sure it must be so! Don't you agree?

It was that horrible man St Paul, the perverter of the simple gospel, that caused all the trouble. I *do* know this, he wasn't qualified; he was never instituted and inducted by the 'proper' authorities to a quiet little parish church; because he tells us brazenly in his letters that he held communion services in people's homes; he tells us that *he went out* and *met* people; that he was all things to all men in order to win them for Christ! How ridiculous can you get? Win men for Christ!

No, I agree with Alison, none of this Pauline non-church nonsense for me, it's not Christian, Christ wouldn't approve it! Or would he, that's a thought!

Niponese Non-Church

HOWARD WILLIAMS

Some years ago Emil Brunner described a Christian movement in Japan called *Mukyokai*, non-church. It is the result of the work of a great Japanese evangelist Kaizo Utschimura. Following his death, the work prospered through his writings and by the zeal of his disciples. Brunner described this movement as standing 'unique in all Christianity'. If Brunner had lived a little longer and become a reader of *New Christian*, he would have seen the desire for non-church manifesting itself in Britain. Ray Billington would have astonished him with news of an emerging church in February which had developed into the coming non-church by June of the same year. This swift merging of being into non-being would have been too much even for Brunner.

The Japanese movement is of considerable interest. It is lay, Bible-centred with an attraction to the Greek text, and has a deep suspicion of any subtle theological questions. There are no paid theologically-trained ministers – the sort who are cushioned from the world by their work – and the Bible study seems to be done in summer vacation by intellectuals (of non-theological faculties) who have time to spare, or by others who earn a little by their writings and who receive occasional gifts from charitable friends. *Mukyokai* has no love for institutions, and no outward or visible structure is allowed to interfere with the action of the Word of God and the Holy Spirit. With Luther they believe that the Word alone will do. There is no wilful opposition to the church, and it may be that, again with Luther, they believe the peasants and uneducated need churches in order to maintain their relationship with God.

Top response

Mukyokai grew among the intellectuals, and this statistical success has some attraction for those who dwell in wilting denominations. The Japanese non-church found much support among the highly educated, even a lively interest from the Imperial family, but gained little response from humbler ranks of society. The Japanese, with their tradition of Confucianism and Shintoism and the consequent feudal structures, have found it especially difficult to encourage any movement coming from the people. Non-church seems to have had no success in this. They withstood any appeal that the churches might have had, not because they were socially superior, but because they regarded them as a foreign infiltration. Western forms of church life were resisted.

There are, I suppose, good reasons in the history of Japan for the *Mukyokai* movement. The president of the Christian University in Tokyo has explained recently that the Japanese have not reached the stage where the individual has attained self-identification apart from the group. Group movements find fertile soil because they are needed, becoming a kind of intimate family. The houses seem to have been designed by delinquent Methodists who are attracted to non-church. In the country, at least, the Japanese house is one big room divided from time to time by thin sliding partitions made of paper. This is an admirable alternative for those who want to get rid of our church buildings. Since silence seems to play a significant part in non-church worship it should be possible to practise it under the protection of a decently partitioned non-building.

The extreme of this non-church view is the belief that people have no need of churches or services of worship. Indeed Luther and others have asserted this, usually making some provision for those not as enlightened as themselves. Presumably this is what the common use of non-church implies. Being weary of church buildings, denominations and paid clergy, the sponsors suggest possible ways of ignoring history altogether. The buildings in some paradoxical way become both a burden and a crutch, and ordinary life, whatever that may be, is distinguished, sharply, from the work of a minister day by day. There seems to be no attempt, however, to dispense with academic disciplines – providing they are non-theological.

Worthwhile burden

Now I approve of a great deal in this protest. I recognize that buildings are frequently a burden, although it is a mistake to think that they exist to keep people from the world. Many buildings are simply the places from which people are sent into the 'secular world' – and this, so I understand, is a good thing to do. My fellowship at Bloomsbury seems to have no privileges at all. The members give their money to provide a place of worship and fellowship primarily for other people and for any kind of people. During the week most of them are content to be Christian where they are, without making a lot of fuss. They could, of course, meet in homes, but since the family is rather a big one they need a big house – like a chapel. Instead of hiring buildings they seem to prefer both to accept the labours of their fathers and to let other people, from time to time, use the building which they provide. Since the membership and table are open to all, the whole fellowship is as universal as anything I can yet imagine.

The church, clearly, is facing problems. It is, if you like, at the cross roads. Evangelicals use terms to describe the divine life in the church and others speak of the servant church, but none of us is very clear about what we are supposed to be and to do in the world. When I think of the swift movement of events in the world, I sometimes marvel that the church has any word to offer or any life to nourish. I think that there are good human and psychological reasons for rejecting the talk I have heard about non-church. There is much in the modern church which annoys, much which disappoints. I can see the dilemma and I feel the burden, but I do not believe that there is any solution by trying to escape either from the church or the world. There are three things I should like now to mention which the church needs to bear in her heart and mind if we are to move into any real future.

Three thoughts

The first is the claims of history. *Mukyokai* (non-church) in Japan rejected the churches as foreign infiltration. There are some obvious reasons why this suspicion should be felt. Yet the churches and clergy we now have in Britain were also a foreign infiltration – but that was a long time ago. Reform and renewal we need, but I should not welcome any attempt to have Christ without taking history with him. Few groups in this country were treated so shabbily by church and state as the groups known as Congregationalists and Baptists. I can still feel pride in their resistance, their love of freedom and even in their separation. The needs now are different from the needs then, but nothing will be gained by uprooting a growth for which we have no right to feel shame. The fundamental point here is that you cannot ignore the roots, just as the Christian faith will grow thin if it tries to forsake Israel.

Secondly, there is incarnation. This is not a New Testament word, but it witnesses to a truth at the heart of the Christian faith. It speaks of the risk God took in becoming man. It reveals a hidden meaning in a stable, an insignificant country, a dirty river, a cross and a tomb. Now it may well be that the church in the continuing ministry has been wrong all the time. I prefer to believe that the failures in terms of pride and pomp, persecution and heresy are a part of the risk. You simply cannot keep the church clean, pure and undefiled except in the vision. You may think that you achieve this by pietism or by being 'spiritual' but you end up by denying incarnation or withdrawing into a sect. I recall Jocelin's words in *The Spire* – 'I had a vision, you see, a clear and explicit vision. It was so simple! . . . But then the complications began. A single green shoot at first, then clinging tendrils, then branches, then at last a riotous confusion . . .' My own denomination began in this simple way. It is not like that now, but I think the risk had to be taken. We shall go on with these attempts to transform the vision into matter – until the church becomes superfluous. But that will not be until the world becomes the church, where the life of the kingdom is enshrined in a universal community. The New Jerusalem needs no temple – but London, New York and Moscow need the church.

Thirdly, the place of theology. It may sound liberating to discount theology, but it is not. The fashion of theology changes, but it is man's attempt to deal with the fundamental meaning of life and especially the 'mystery' made known in the Christian story. There will be no renewal or reformation without it. I read somewhere that the theologian is responsible for saying what it means to be a Christian and how that meaning affects men's other attitudes towards the world. You will get emotional spasms without theology, but no abiding word for the world.

The Tedious Church Reformers
RAY BILLINGTON

An appeal to modern Christians to stop trying to bolster up dead causes and instead turn to some new expression of human awareness.

Published in May 1968

If the art of conversation is all that anthropologists claim it to be, it constitutes one of the main distinctions between man and other animals. It is also, according to sociologists, a dying art. So I shall no doubt appear to be both inhuman and anti-social when I say that most of the conversation, whether in speech or in writing, of most of my Christian friends makes me long for the silent companionship of the animal species and the lazy loneliness of a desert island.

Not so long ago I was having a pre-lunch drink at a friend's house with two of the best known 'reformers' in the Church of England. Both are men with powerful minds who could have made a success of many jobs in spheres other than the ecclesiastical. Yet from the moment they arrived until I left they spoke of absolutely nothing else but church affairs, appointments, bishoprics, who's in, who's out – completely crowding out any attempt to change the subject. I'm told by another guest who remained that they did not change the subject throughout the meal or after it. Is it any wonder that some of us are beginning to view these people like drug-addicts who, however much they may long to be free from their addiction in their saner moments, find it impossible to shake it off? And is it any wonder that we no longer find it possible to respect them?

In his book *Include Me Out!*, Colin Morris has criticized the church for its frittering away of time and energy on church matters when weightier matters like world poverty, racialism and injustice are demanding human concern. What he seems incapable of realizing is that as long as an ecclesiastical organization remains, its main concern – however much the 'secondary' issues may be considered – must be with the preservation of its own way of life. The laws which governed the evolution of the species apply just as much here. If the church were not to concern itself primarily with its own preservation, it would soon die. Seen in this light, the attempt hitherto of most of the 'reformers' must be seen as little more than sewing new skins on old garments.

I am bored by all this for the simple reason that it no longer matters two hoots whether the church survives or not. I doubt very much whether Jesus ever wanted, or even expected, a church to evolve; and its record through the centuries does not, with the exception of occasional individuals or groups, fill me with pride. What does seem to matter today is the question of *how man is to live*. What meaning can he find in his life, what values, what purpose? It may be answered that the church can provide the clue through the doctrines it proclaims. But two things militate against this. First is the almost total disinterest, on the part of most people, in anything associated with the church. I know that parsons were voted top of the list of 'useful' people in ATV's Gallup poll two years ago; but this must be seen as a survival from earlier generations of a reverence for the religious element in life. The important point is that, in this form, this reverence makes no demands on the individual. Anyone can say that he respects parsons, without feeling that he must therefore *do* something about it. One wonders, in any case, how many of those questioned were under the age of twenty-five; my own experience of this age-group is that, with rare exceptions, parsons are viewed as little more than parasites.

Much more important than this, however, is the second factor, and the amazing thing is that, though lip-service may be paid to it in the conversations and writings of the reformers, it has seldom been allowed to be more than a disquieting thought at the back of their minds. I am referring to the

rejecting of belief in what, in short-hand terms, we can call the supernatural. In effect, this means the rejection of those tenets of the Christian
faith which are summed up in the creeds. The reason why this development
is the most important of all is obvious: the church depends on their
acceptance for its own *raison d'être*. Given a belief in a personal God, and
the acknowledgment of Jesus as a unique manifestation of him, the con-
tinuance of the church as the focal point for worship of him is natural. The
real malaise today is that with the massive rejection of her basic beliefs she
has, in the eyes of many people, lost 'the ground of her being'.

So we reach the nub of the matter. Granted that the 'renewers' are wasting time because they are only painting over a façade, is it possible to find
a new way of expressing the church's beliefs which will give them validity
and so give substance to the ecclesiastical organization? This is the main
concern of the Bishop of Woolwich and a few others. Are they likely to
succeed? Two years ago I could have replied affirmatively, but I can no
longer do so. I accept the fact that 'God' is dead, and it therefore seems
pointless to try and revive 'him' in a new guise. If God is not the God of the
classical theologians – eternal creator, omnipresent, omnipotent, loving
personally all his creatures, the source and goal of their lives – what is the
use of declaring in effect that he is someone else with the same name? It
may be argued that we must give some name to 'the ground of our being',
and that 'God' is far better than such clumsy constructions as 'I-Thou'.
I can't for the life of me see why any name at all is needed, and most of
the population share this perplexity.

The fact is that the old myths, forms, symbols, images, are finished; and
it is no use trying to reshape them in a contemporary outline. We need to
put out of our minds what we have received and begin here, where man now
is. If we are to express ideas and ideals about human life which give that
life meaning and purpose, we must discover some expression of human
values which does not depend for its validity on any more than the experience of being human. We must work and think from the ground up, not
from heaven down.

This may well sound like an argument for 'humanism' and an attempt to
drag man up by his own bootlaces; and on both counts, it will be argued,
it has been tried before, and has failed. On both counts, I disagree. Inas-
much as official humanism has its own system of beliefs, even if these are
mostly negative, it is akin to Christianity in offering a list of tenets for the
consumer. No 'received' tenets, of whatever kind, are going to make any
impact on the coming generation. It is only too manifest that all the 'isms'
so far produced have completely failed to solve the world's most basic
problems: poverty, racialism, war, population and (a product of all these)

depersonalization. Anyone who thinks he has the answers in a set of beliefs
is a fool. So I feel as little sympathy for Brigid Brophy as for Billy Graham,
for a Marxist as for a bishop.

What is needed is for all those people – and they will be primarily young
people – whose attitude to received systems is a simple 'plague on all your
houses' – including the disenchanted members of these different houses –
to come together in order to think and work creatively, to construct out of
our present impasse an expression of human values which will tackle the
major problems of our time, and will enable more men everywhere to discover the infinite depths and ecstatic heights of human nature. We may
well begin by stating the unity of all men, refusing to think of ourselves in
terms of nation, race, colour or class – in other words by refusing to be
pigeon-holed. We may go on to say that we are looking for qualitative
rather than quantitative life: that man is a creator, and finds fulfilment in
creativity – a rare commodity in our mass-produced society. But whatever
we shall say and do, the essential need now is for us to stop trying to bolster
up dead causes, whether religious, political, philosophical or moral, and
instead turn to some new expression of human awareness.

One of my correspondents on the subject of non-church a year ago said
something like this when, after a marvellous diatribe against those who
still invoke great names from the past in their discussions, he exclaimed,
'Damn your blasted dead!' Within non-church there has emerged a sharp
division between those who, however sympathetic, feel that their chief concern must be with the renewal of faith within the church, and those who
share the above sentiments and desire to venture out into hitherto untried
paths. Some have argued that by taking this direction in my thinking I
have broken faith with those who responded to my earlier call for a re-
discovery of life in terms of Christ but untrammelled by ecclesiasticism.
To these I say:

First, I feel that Jesus, although naturally restricted by concepts relevant
to his own age, was essentially working in this direction. His words about
abundant life were geared to the present, and, 'demythologized', amount
to an affirmation of human values. But, secondly, it would be a paradoxical
denial of this if at every turn we were committed to the invocation of his
name. So long as we do this, we shall be restricted by the myths and
images which have been attached to it through the centuries. If we are to
discover what were his basic concerns, we shall do so only by refusing to
make him into a God.

Letters to the Editor

From Mrs Pauline A. Mills, Leicester

At 10.30 p.m. precisely a very tired mother of three has just thrown the latest *New Christian* across the room. With 'nightcap' and biscuits to revive me I have enough energy to take up my pen to say that if Ray Billington is bored, I am not only bored by his latest exercise in your pages, I am beginning to be very angry, too. So it does not matter two hoots whether the church survives or not? Those of us in our early thirties, members of that sometimes sad and floating section of the populace, the meritocracy, who are now faced with bringing up our children, need not look to Mr Billington and non-church for help. Can you gather figs from thistles? If Mr Billington cannot see why God needs any name at all, let him try answering the penetrating questions of a five-year-old. If we are 'new' Christians, these children of ours are even newer. If there is going to be a future, they are it, and I'm not putting my money on Mr Billington's wild and woolly thinking. Thinly disguised humanism is not and never was Christianity. One page of the work of Mr C. S. Lewis, 'out' as he may be, is worth more than a thousand articles such as that produced by Mr Billington. The fact that from its beginnings the church has been consistently engaged in working for the whole man (hungry, uneducated, unloved, unwanted, etc., etc.), seems to have escaped the notice of many *New Christian* contributors. So I am sticking to the New Testament, supernatural and all. I shall tell these children of mine that I believe Jesus to have been God in a human life. What other explanation can account for this extraordinary man? Sitting on the fence just will not do. I shall still subscribe to *New Christian*, however. Perhaps other parents in the same position will understand and agree. 'I trust I make myself obscure.'

From the Rev. Anthony J. Wesson

Is the non-church a non-starter? This is the question prompted by Ray Billington's article. The attraction of the non-church concept arises, for many people, as a result of deep dissatisfaction with the church and the ministry as it is now organized. As Billington expounds the conception, however, it becomes less and less credible. Before the non-church idea can have any real effect it must be more carefully expounded. His article is full of half-baked themes and hidden assumptions. A critique of his contribution may help to crystallize the issues.

On the superficial level one could wish that Billington exercised his critical faculty on contemporary attitudes as much as he does in regard to. the church. The people who write parsons off as 'parasites', in my experience, usually hold similar views of lecturers in liberal studies at Colleges of Further Education, and often with more justification since they are not usually involved financially in the payment of the parson! Evidence from the recent history of the church would also contradict some of his affirmations. For example, the missionary movement from Europe makes nonsense of his claim, 'If the church were not to concern itself primarily with its own preservation, it would soon die'.

The central issue, as Billington rightly indicates, is the theological one. But his discussion of this is confused, and somewhat tendentious. I can only indicate the issues at stake here. His wholesale rejection of the 'supernatural' without any attempt to define what he means is positively misleading. Does he include in this the classical distinction between the divine, supernatural and the preternatural? He appears simply to equate 'supernatural' with 'other-worldly', and this only makes confusion worse confounded. His bland acceptance of the 'death of God' phrase also suggests that Billington has not grappled with the issues. It is a sort of non-theological issue. Is God the kind of reality of which death can be predicated? The perplexity of the population at large needs to be carefully analysed. Does it arise over the idea of God they have been taught to associate with the name? Or is it a genuine refusal to believe that life is anything other than surface and immediate?

Billington's hidden assumptions are also theological. He wants us to start the search for the non-kingdom of heaven on the basis of the unity of all mankind. But on what grounds is this call made? The unity of all mankind is certainly not 'given' in the facts of contemporary life. If that is to be the basis upon which the future of mankind is to be built, then it must be justified on non-empirical grounds. I fail to see how that can be done without raising the theological issue. Billington has made the simple mistake of ignoring, or perhaps confusing, the primary and secondary causes of any action. The fact is that none of the really fundamental questions that concern man can be faced without, in the end, raising the theological issue. To attempt to 'ground values in the experience of being human' is notoriously difficult, since it assumes an understanding of what being human is. And this is an issue that is open for debate.

Billington's attitude to structures is also highly questionable. I suspect that at heart Billington is really a manichee. Any expression of spiritual realities (in the broadest sense) must have a material manifestation. To reduce the Christian concern for love to individual acts, and nothing more, is to trivialize it. To make it anything more demands a community.

The question which is basic to mankind today is not merely how man is to live, as he suggests, but also where is man to find the resources to enable him to love? In this the non-church is apparently as perplexed as the church.

RELIGION!

Major W. F. Batt (Norwich) said that the State Prayers gave most people the only opportunities they had to obey the command of the Holy Spirit. – Church Assembly report in the *Church Times*.

As a Christian, I am entirely opposed to the use of the swings on God's Sabbath, and I regret the eventual decision. I may say that practising

Christians with whom I have discussed the matter are in agreement. We are in danger of adopting the Continental Sunday, and the results of this are evident to anyone who looks at the European situation.

There is, however, one further point upon which I am not clear. I have a pet budgerigar which has a swing in its cage. I have made a practice of disconnecting this swing each Sunday and not putting it back into use until Monday morning. Is this in accord with strict Christian principle? – *Belfast News Letter*.

Feb 5   Controversy arises over removal of Victorian windows in chapter house of Salisbury Cathedral.

Sept 7   Manchester win *Church Times* Cricket Cup.

From Principal Church Events of 1967. – *Church Times*.

HOUSE CHURCH

Suppose the church had been wrecked last
  night
By a 'plane flying into the steeple,
Why now the parish would have to be run
With nothing left but the people.
The services wouldn't be held any more,
And no going to church next Sunday;
But though we should miss our accustomed
  rite,
Would anyone know on Monday?
Would anyone mind if we met no more
In our long-loved Gothic aura,
With our monuments, pews and altar-rail:
Would anyone else be the poorer?

The sacrament bringing our work to God
Might less seem idle fables
If the body and blood God gave for us
Were offered at laymen's tables,
The heavenly bread more down to earth
If blessed from a housewife's baking;
More might partake of the wine of life
If less archaic the taking.

The wreck of a church in rubble and dust –
Would less not have moved you, my
   daughter?
Yourself strike the stone and flow among men
As rivers of life-giving water!

ILSLEY INGRAM

CHURCH GOING

Once I am sure there's nothing going on
I step inside, letting the door thud shut.
Another church: matting, seats, and stone,
And little books; sprawlings of flowers, cut
For Sunday, brownish now; some brass and stuff
Up at the holy end; the small neat organ;
And a tense, musty, unignorable silence,
Brewed God knows how long. Hatless, I take off
My cycle-clips in awkward reverence,

Move forward, run my hand around the font.
From where I stand, the roof looks almost new –
Cleaned, or restored? Someone would know:
  I don't.
Mounting the lectern, I peruse a few
Hectoring large-scale verses, and pronounce
'Here endeth' much more loudly than I'd meant.
The echoes snigger briefly. Back at the door
I sign the book, donate an Irish sixpence,
Reflect the place was not worth stopping for.

Yet stop I did: in fact I often do,
And always end much at a loss like this,
Wondering what to look for; wondering, too,
When churches fall completely out of use
What we shall turn them into, if we shall keep
A few cathedrals chronically on show,
Their parchment, plate and pyx in locked cases,
And let the rest rent-free to rain and sheep.
Shall we avoid them as unlucky places?

Or, after dark, will dubious women come
To make their children touch a particular stone;
Pick simples for a cancer; or on some
Advised night see walking a dead one?
Power of some sort or other will go on
In games, in riddles, seemingly at random;
But superstition, like belief, must die,
And what remains when disbelief has gone?
Grass, weedy pavement, brambles, buttress, sky,

A shape less recognizable each week,
A purpose more obscure. I wonder who
Will be the last, the very last, to seek
This place for what it was; one of the crew
That tap and jot and know what rood-lofts were?
Some ruin-bibber, randy for antique,
Or Christmas-addict, counting on a whiff
Of gown-and-bands and organ-pipes and myrrh?
Or will he be my representative,

Bored, uninformed, knowing the ghostly silt
Dispersed, yet tending to this cross of ground
Through suburb scrub because it held unspilt
So long and equably what since is found
Only in separation – marriage, and birth,
And death, and thoughts of these – for which was built
This special shell? For, though I've no idea
What this accoutred frowsty barn is worth,
It pleases me to stand in silence here;

A serious house on serious earth it is,
In whose blent air all our compulsions meet,
Are recognized, and robed as destinies.
And that much never can be obsolete,
Since someone will forever be surprising
A hunger in himself to be more serious,
And gravitating with it to this ground,
Which, he once heard, was proper to grow wise in,
If only that so many dead lie round.

PHILIP LARKIN

Philip Larkin, 'ChurchGoing', from *The Less Deceived*, Marvel Press, 1966.

4 The Parson's Role Today

MONICA FURLONG

The clergyman must live much more in a state of being than in a state of doing.

The substance of a paper given at the Wakefield Diocesan Clergy Conference in April 1966

Throughout this century the clergyman has suffered a decline in status. This is indicated, as well as accentuated, by the fact that his income is frequently less than that of the majority of his parishioners. In some cases he earns about the same as an unskilled worker, and this is perhaps how an unchurched society is coming to think of him – as someone who is not qualified as the twentieth century understands qualification. In an age which is not particularly interested in faith, it is difficult for people to understand what the clergyman is up to, and so they are apt to suggest that he isn't up to anything in particular. He is thrust on one side where serious issues are being discussed – he isn't a social worker, he isn't a psychiatrist, he isn't a doctor, he isn't a probation officer, or a teacher or a welfare officer. He is granted a little elbow room in hospitals or prisons – after all, it is well known that when people are unhappy, ill or dying they like a bit of religion, and the clergyman can at least talk about God without getting uncomfortable. But I believe there is a growing feeling in the community as a whole that the church is played out and the clergy with it, and this is perhaps as obvious in the exaggerated respect – an almost superstitious awe – which is sometimes shown to the clergy and which indicates how little religion is a part of people's ordinary, everyday lives – as in the directly unkind or obtuse remarks on the subject among intellectuals.

The clergyman who, historically, has played such a vigorous part in the life of this country in the movements towards general education and in framing social attitudes is, I think, entering a new phase, a phase in which he finds that if not actually despised and rejected, he is set on one side, ignored, the victim of others' indifference. He isn't a success as the twentieth century understands success, and his income will not allow him to enter the status race.

Growing loneliness

My first, rather depressing conclusion, therefore, is that clergymen are in for a period of growing loneliness, of being misunderstood. I would suggest that this will only be endurable if they expect this, understand the reasons for it, and do not cast too many envious glances over their shoulders at the easier circumstances enjoyed by their predecessors.

I also want to suggest that out of the suffering which this will impose upon them, out of the growing and deeply disturbing sense of loneliness which has already affected some of the clergy in terms of breakdowns or despair or a throwing over of the job, something new and exceedingly valuable is going to grow, has already started to grow.

In order to see what form this can possibly take, we must look outwards at the society which has to be served. In England in 1966 we see a great emphasis on security – the security, that is, that is offered by affluence and a Welfare State. There is great emphasis on success and on status – it is important to be in the right job – a job which carries prestige. It is important to be insulated against suffering of any kind – an attitude that is easy to sympathize with and to some extent to share, but it also begins, I suspect, to be important to be insulated against having to have close contact with other human beings, and if I am right in my diagnosis, then this may be an indication of a schizoid tendency within our whole society.

From self-service shops to our grossly over-crowded schools, from mass-communications to the glib jargon with which some, though not all, sociologists attempt to talk about the human condition on these islands, one can sense, and I don't think I am being fanciful in this, a tendency for people to shrink from one another, to lose their identity in the crowd, to lose the precious sense of themselves as persons of value to others, able to enjoy fruitful and satisfying exchange.

A substitute

We cannot yet see where this is taking our society. We can sometimes get a terrifying glimpse of what it is doing to individuals when we listen to the depressed, those who have had breakdowns, those who are trying to cope with a bereavement or some other great blow, those who feel isolated and unable to communicate, let alone give or receive affection, with other people. People's desperation also expresses itself in the growing amount of violence, and the growing preoccupation with sadistic fantasies (in the form of films, books, etc.), a preoccupation which is known to be a substitute for close, warm, openly affectionate relationships.

Into this scene let us set the clergyman, though not so that he may
thunder shocked abuse as he might once have done. Let us just see him
standing there, and see what a contrast he makes to his surroundings.

In a society which sets great store by financial security he makes himself
obvious by being hard up. In a society which values status and success he
again sticks out as someone who will not enter the race. His job carried
status once, but everyone knows that those days have gone. In a society
which sets scientific observation and verification in an exalted place, he
talks of, and lives by, faith – a commodity which cannot be observed or
verified except in ways which would fill the scientist with suspicion.

If this were all, he would be a highly subversive and non-conforming
member of society, but this is not all. At the centre of the clergyman's way
of life is the word 'love' – a word which fills our contemporaries with a
mixture of wistfulness and fear.

I wonder sometimes if it is not because we are afraid of the word love
that we have developed such highly specialized techniques for dealing with
people. I don't wish to decry the value of training for social workers, for
psychiatrists, for doctors, for nurses, but if one has much to do with any of
them it is possible to see that they can, if the demands become too great,
escape from having to offer love to or receive love from people they are
caring for, and take refuge in acting the part which their training has led
them to play.

The clergy, of course, also often act a role, and indeed it is difficult for
them to help it, since their parishioners and others often thrust it upon them.
But since the clergy stand so uncompromisingly for a belief in love, and
since the Christian faith is intangible, and since it is difficult to imagine
what the job is if it is not about love, then it is harder for the priest to
escape successfully into an act than it is for the social worker.

At this particular time there is perhaps a strong temptation among some
members of the clergy to adopt a social worker act, to take refuge behind
one of the comforting and reassuring masks which others in the helping
professions are lucky enough to be able to wear. At least these roles are
something which the world can understand.

Refuse to compete

I cannot speak for other laymen, but this is something I deeply regret. I am
clear what I want of the clergy. I want them to be people who can by their
own happiness and contentment challenge my ideas about status, about
success, about money, and so teach me how to live more independently of
such drugs. I want them to be people who can dare, as I do not dare, and
as few of my contemporaries dare, to refuse to work flat out (since work is

an even more subtle drug than status), to refuse to compete with me in strenuousness. I want them to be people who are secure enough in the value of what they are doing to have time to read, to sit and think, and who can face the emptiness and possible depression which often attack people when they do not keep the surface of their mind occupied. I want them to be people who have faced this kind of loneliness and discovered how fruitful it is, as I want them to be people who have faced the problems of prayer. I want them to be people who can sit still without feeling guilty, and from whom I can learn some kind of tranquillity in a society which has almost lost the art.

I want other things too, which you can probably imagine for yourselves, but what I want most to stress now is that what I think is very dangerous is when the clergyman becomes so desperate that he is driven to trying to beat the layman at his own game.

Whereas the layman longs so much to be shown how to break out of the iron grip of a society which cuts people off from one another, makes love difficult to practise, and which tries to tell him that his spiritual life is something unimportant.

Breaking through

I believe that Christianity may be one of the most significant movements at work in our society in breaking through the growing isolation imposed by a mass-society. But if this is to happen, then both priest and layman must learn something more about offering love to others, plainly and unashamedly.

This is all rather grandly idealistic, and clergymen will say, I expect, that I have no idea of the problems involved in keeping the fabric of a church building in decent repair and in keeping the whole organization ticking over, and of how much time and effort it all takes.

And I think this is fair criticism. But it may also be true that it is only in so far as the clergy start by exploring their inner loneliness and its relation to Christian belief that all their hard work is going to reach others who, for one reason or another, are alone, and so begin to heal our society. If they do not begin from a vast clearing of quietness around the offering up of worship, a quietness in which they can discover who they are and so enter into genuine relationship with others, then they are indeed second-rate social workers, and it were better that they were swept away. But I have great hope that the clergy will rise to this challenge as, historically, they have risen so admirably to others.

From here on, I want to suggest, the clergyman's great strength will lie in the fact that he has no strength except the strength of love. He is closer to Christ than he has been for centuries because, like Christ, he has so few defences against the world. Where once he kept a stable, hunted twice a week, and had a whole army of servants, he now runs an old car and helps with the washing-up.

Where once he was the most educated man in his community, along with the doctor and the squire, he is now no better educated than a large number of the population. Where religion was the most important thing in people's lives, it now takes second place to other, more shallow influences.

Now much of this is stripped away, but with it much that encouraged self-deception. Like Christ, if he is brave enough, the priest is now free to offer the best gift of all – himself. Without any certainty that it is going to be understood and appreciated, he goes out to other people, able only to offer his relationship with God, his longing to help, to love and to heal. He is prepared to be vulnerable, to make a fool of himself, in a way which only the Christians still attempt.

This, then, is my second conclusion. That the clergyman's role must be to decrease his activity, to live much more in a state of being than in a state of doing. I don't underestimate just how difficult this is in practice; I only want to say that to this one layman the clergy who help and impress most are those who live in a state that is neither laziness nor hyper-activity.

I don't suppose that I have to elaborate the point that in order to succeed in this, the priest has to be very open with himself about his own problems, his own inhibitions in dealing with others, his own need for others to be dependent on him, and any problems which may exist within his own family circle. It is within his family that he can learn most about himself and his difficulties in loving other people. Should the difficulties prove intractable, then I would think that out of loyalty to his job, he would seek expert psychiatric help.

So that my third conclusion, a fairly obvious one, but none the worse for that, is that the clergyman must face his own private and personal problems and not use his job as an escape from them. Heartbreaking letters from clergy wives which sometimes appear in religious papers, and comments made in conversation, sometimes indicate that some clergy can love everyone but those closest to them – a situation which needs much insight and probably some outside help.

And so I come to my final conclusion, and it is one which I hardly know how to put into words at all. Clergymen find themselves in their present job because they have had, like other Christians, some apprehension of God. This can take a variety of forms, from mystical experience to a simple discovery of inexplicable joy and goodness in another human being. But whatever the initial experience, we have all come to stake a good deal on the fact that there is a reality behind and beneath and through our everyday world.

As our lives continue, and the pressures of the everyday world become heavy and insistent, we wonder if we are not making 'charlies' of ourselves in trying to hold on to this original vision. And we wonder this particularly when others are indifferent to our vision, stay away from our churches, or when they come to church but make it clear by their words and actions that they have no intention of letting the love of Christ penetrate their attitudes to other people. When this happens the clergyman must wonder whether there is any point at all in struggling on, whether he was not somehow duped or deluded to start with.

And if this is the case, then I should like to offer my own conviction that love is one of the great healing forces in our society, a force which works towards health and hope, even when the results are not instantly obvious.

The Loneliness of Doubt
ALISON STUART

Last Saturday night my husband cried in my arms in despair because he had two sermons to preach the next day and he had nothing at all to say. His mind was blank – no thoughts, no words. What could he do? What could he say? The scriptures appointed for Sunday seemed meaningless to him; he did not know what he could preach and yet maintain his integrity. That was bad enough. But far worse than this was his acute awareness of his own emptiness and hollowness – the feeling that he himself had no real being, that there was nothing there – only the ache of appalling emptiness. It was a frightening experience. He has known it before and it is quite likely that he will know it again.

At other times, he suffers from an utter lack of direction. It is as though he wanders alone in some unsignposted wilderness where there is no indication of what he should do, where he should go, what he should become. This is inner loneliness and bewilderment which results in outward enervation and ineffectualness in daily living.

He endures periods of radical doubt about the very ground of his faith, the actual existence of God himself. This means that he sometimes questions his vocation as a priest. Ought he to abandon it? What would he do if he did? His years in the ministry have left him unqualified for any work he might otherwise have done, and he has a family to support. But does he really want to quit? Perhaps the doubts he now experiences are but the projection on to his outward circumstances of his deep internal conflict? He cannot be sure. But, if this is so, he wonders if he will ever be able to face the naked conflict itself. (As Monica Furlong knows well enough, the expert psychiatric help which she recommends does not, if it is to be more than a palliative, quickly remove all difficulties. It rather enables the sufferer to enter more deeply into his pain and so learn from it.)

If I understand something of my husband's suffering beyond what I see and hear in our life together, it is because my own experience is in many respects similar to his. I, too, know the lack of direction and the sense of terror which follow the abandonment of some of the old hysterical and schizoid defences against life. I, too, blunder at times in the darkness of unfaith and know the intense longing for a God who seems always absent. And I can be extremely irritable, explosive and uncomfortable to live with because years of suppressed rage against life are at last able to find expression.

Why do I write all this? Because this is something of what is involved for the parson or anyone else who takes seriously Monica Furlong's advice to 'face his own private and personal problems and not use his job as an escape from them'. This is the result of facing 'the emptiness and possible depression which often attack people when they do not keep the surface of their mind occupied'. This is what Miss Furlong asks the clergy to do. I do not quarrel with it.

I do, however, quarrel with her request that they shall also 'by their own happiness and contentment' challenge her ideas about life, that they shall be people from whom she 'can learn some kind of tranquillity in a society which has almost lost the art' and that they shall 'begin from a vast clearing of quietness around the offering up of worship'.

Just what does Miss Furlong want? She must make up her mind, for I say most emphatically, speaking from within the situation, that she cannot have it both ways – not yet. The man who dares to attempt the desperate spiritual and emotional adventuring which she asks for will be neither happy nor contented; he will certainly not radiate tranquillity, and the offering up of worship may be one of his major problems.

I agree that 'the clergyman's rôle must be to decrease his activity, to live much more in a state of being than in a state of doing'. This is surely true for all busy, over-active Christians. But, as Miss Furlong realizes, ceaseless activity is part of our defence against our inner selves, and it is not possible to move from a state of doing to a state of being in a day, or in a month, or in a year. A course of lectures at theological college, a few days' annual retreat, will not resolve this one! There will be a period of transition – a time of 'becoming' – which will be protracted, bewildering and extremely painful. Despite moments of insight and growth, even of joy, distress is often acute. This is the agony of rebirth, the cost of being 'transformed by the renewing of your mind', which part of us resists every step of the way.

Any parson who submits himself to this discipline is going to suffer, and whilst he does so, others will suffer with him. Thus it is inevitable that my husband and I should sometimes hurt each other deeply in the process of our own 'becoming'. Somehow we have to learn to accept these hurts, without raising our defences against them, in order that we may both grow.

The parish also suffers. The parson cannot opt out of its life whilst he wrestles with his problems and confronts his frightening loneliness. Indeed, would it really help if he could? We have learnt that it is in the happenings and relationships of ordinary life that we find our deepest insights and that these provide the material with which we must work towards maturity.

So the life of the parish goes on regardless of the parson's private dilemmas. There are still sermons to be preached somehow or other. If the church roof is falling down, the initiative for its repair will still rest with him, even though he feels that his whole world is falling around his ears and the roof can go to hell. And what if the Church Council is bloody-minded? It will not be less so because he seems more incompetent, less on the mark, than ever. People still come for advice and expect him to know the answers. He has abandoned the old paternalistic attitude (if ever he had it) and can no longer give the simple authoritarian reply they seek. Others look to him for deeper help than this. He has to try and mediate the love of God to them however little he may be aware of it for himself. He has let go of his former assurances; he no longer speaks the old language and has not yet learnt a new language which can reach the level of their need.

People begin to ask what good he is anyway. He also asks himself this and knows his answer to be the same as theirs.

And this is where I ask my question. Are Miss Furlong, and other laymen, prepared to accept what is involved in their demands of the parson? Will they accept and carry his helplessness, and bear with his ineffectualness and unpredictability, as he makes his inner explorations and risks all the uncertainties of 'becoming' in the desperate hope that one day he may possibly 'be'? If they are logical they can hardly do less.

Letters to the Editor

From Mr R. Brown, Leeds

Monica Furlong's article was excellent. I believe she has restated the classical ideal of the contemplative life not so much in terms of spirituality as in terms of self-knowledge through loneliness and humility.

There is also a deeply humane strata in the picture of the parson standing for humanity, as a symbol, in a dehumanized world. This is where the misgiving starts. This ideal view of the clergy is in danger of becoming a variation on the 'leave it to the parson theme'.

The really crucial issue for me is how the layman can maintain his vision if he is drawn powerfully to the contemplative idea, i.e. being rather than knowing or doing, rejecting the dehumanized values of the power money complex, believing in the necessity of love (*eros* and *agape*) and the value of personal relationships for their own sake, instead of using people?

The classical/Furlong solution will not do for a man placed in the economic, personal, psychological milieu of a family and community.

The solution is to become a double person, to have a facade of minimal conformity to the world; how otherwise would you get through the day? But inside is the secret, subversive inner monk, but not in my case particularly poor, chaste, or obedient.

It is like being a spy, equally subversive to the values of the admass etc., equally dextrous in avoiding being caught and brainwashed, or if the world retaliates it is probably like being an alienated, exiled Jew.

As for the 'apprehension of God', what is this?

To me God is more like waiting, groping in the 'cloud of unknowing', 'the stranger in the night'.

From Mrs Anne Lobstein, Jordans, Bucks

In his letter Mr Brown says 'The really crucial issue for me is how the layman can maintain his vision if he is drawn powerfully to the contemplative idea . . . The classical/Furlong solution will not do for a man placed in the economic, personal, psychological milieu of a family and community. The solution is to become a double person, to have a facade of minimal conformity to the world: how otherwise would you get through the day?'

I am a woman placed in this situation, with a family to bring up alone and see through school and university, etc. Until quite recently, six years ago to be exact, I was an atheist and proud of being so. Then a series of strange (perhaps mystical) experiences occurred to me and left me in no doubt whatever of the existence of God as the real basis of my being.

But these remarkable times of grace could not stand up to everyday life. I longed for them, I needed them, I prayed for them and, if I had no dependents, would, I am sure, have attempted the life of a contemplative. For several years I see-sawed heavily between the memories and occasional experiences of these states and the emptiness and tawdriness of everyday life without them. Gradually, but only gradually, I became stronger within myself, see-sawing more gently, more able to practise faith without evidence; to know the absoluteness, the God-ness of all things without needing another dimension of consciousness for it. I began to realize that faith – that unique leap over the abyss in which one leaves all known things behind – is a major part of the answer.

But even so daily life troubled me very much. For one thing, I felt I was so bad at it; for another it seemed wrong that there should be a dichotomy between my outer and inner life. This year brought the whole thing to agony point and gave me the answer, which is why I am writing this letter.

This is my first year of teaching and I teach in a secondary modern school. I have found it frantically tiring – exhausting in the worst possible way, so that at the end of each day I have felt as though my whole personality had been dragged out and torn to pieces. I had no spirit with which to meditate and every day was spent in trying to salvage and preserve a little inner stillness and peace – unsuccessfully. Two terms passed this way and then, in the middle of this term, it suddenly came to me with the force of given knowledge that I was hopelessly wrong in the way I was looking at the situation. What was I trying to preserve? God? Me?

In the moments of grace I had always understood that I had been able to respond and receive them because I had given myself up, initially through despair and then gradually through love. Now I saw that for me this was the only way of living properly and that it didn't just apply to those moments. I must give myself totally up in love to whatever the next situation was and whoever the person in front of me happened to be. No matter what the demands were and no matter how I was received (and this ceased to matter, anyway), this particular moment in time, and the shape that it took, should fill me to the exclusion of myself.

It worked immediately and has gone on working. I feel now an integration between my inner and outer selves. There is now no need to preserve an inner life because there need be none there – it is given up daily and very happily to the outer. I am immensely grateful for this because it is such a workable grace. It gives meaning to the prayer 'Thy will be done on earth as it is in heaven'. The act of giving oneself up in love to anything, even if it is a picture on the wall or the washing up, is a means of creating heaven on earth, at least in terms of personal happiness.

In November 1913 I relinquished my charge of a Baptist church in Northamptonshire, and a week after, in December, I entered upon the pastorate of a Unitarian church in Lancashire. None of the people immediately concerned in these matters knew that in the following August, the Foreign Minister of Britain, Sir Edward Grey, would say 'The lamps are going out all over Europe: we shall not see them lit again in our lifetime'. – *Faith and Freedom, Spring, 1966.*

Unlike Canon John Collins, Precentor of St Paul's Cathedral, who is disappointed that none of his four sons wants to follow him into the Church, I find that the Queen's Succentor at Windsor takes an opposite view.

'It is very difficult for a man who does not have a considerable private income to exist on present clergy incomes,' said Mr Nourse, who lives at Windsor Castle and teaches divinity at St George's choir school. – *Daily Express.*

Close down the churches for a month and let the ministers go on strike. Advocating this course of action, the Revd John McNicol, Baptist minister and founder of the National Association on Drug Addiction, said that this would bring the country to its knees. – *Methodist Recorder.*

The Pope told an assembly of Roman clergy that the desire to become part of society was basically good but could prove a most seriously mistaken suggestion which could ruin a priest's vocation. – *The Guardian.*

RELIGION!

A wrestling match between two women will be held in the Territorial Army drill hall, Portsmouth, on March 25 in spite of many protests. Women's organizations have described the match as 'disgusting and degrading'.

The referee of the bout, between Jenny Peel and Sugar Pie Harlem, will be the Revd Reginald Thompson, aged 62, Vicar of Moulton Chapel, Lincolnshire. – *The Times.*

RETREAT 1967

Where shall we go to
Out from here
Two dozen clergymen
Black and alone?
Where shall we go to
Out in the cold?

Nobody loves us
And we love nobody
Not very much at
  least
(Wives excepted)
Out from here
And out in the cold.

We've been with the
  Lord
Or, have we
  (*rallentando*),
I wonder?
Where shall we go to
Out from here?

Tomorrow we're
  back again
Out from here.
Back where we
  started from
Out from here.
And now we begin
  again
Out from here.
Where shall we go to
And what shall
  we do?

The answer to that
  one
Is
Out from here
Out in the dark
And out in the cold
Where He who is
  (*rall.*)
Will/ there/ meet
  me/ again/
Out in the dark
And out in the cold.

D.G.H.

Angel Time 5

A leading article published at Michaelmas 1966

Those who observe the developed Christian Year of the Roman and Anglican traditions will soon be called upon to take account of the angels. Michaelmas Day and the week following will find many Christians in church thanking God for the angels and praying that the said angels will succour and defend them during the time of their earthly life. Most preachers will by now have abandoned the 'our feathered friends' approach, but it will be surprising if the majority of congregations are not given some information from the pulpit about the supernatural beings who are believed to inhabit the heavenly places and to act in the capacity of messengers.

It is, therefore, relevant to enquire what preachers and congregations really make of all this. Bearing in mind that only a few people have ever claimed to encounter an angel, and remembering that the Bible was written when belief in angels was an important part of contemporary mythology, it is surely not too outrageous to suggest that the angels ought to be subjected to rather closer scrutiny than has previously been their lot, and that their disappearance from the Christian scene might be one of the more profitable fruits of demythologizing. Twentieth-century thinkers could hardly be expected to mourn their demise.

Now it seems more than likely that a large number of clergymen, and even more laymen, have already written off the angels and will be somewhat relieved when the embarrassing season of Michaelmas is over. But embarrassment, like patriotism, is not enough. If Christians are to face the world as honest men, they must sooner or later sort out their basic convictions from those aspects of Christian belief which belong to the past or to the realm of pious opinion. It is obviously unnecessary to believe that a man named Jonah was swallowed by a big fish or that Adam and Eve were the inhabitants of a pleasant garden in the East, and it would be foolish to propound these stories as basic elements in the Christian faith. The angels could just as easily be allocated a similar place in biblical mythology, and their removal from the pulpits, the Sunday School lessons and the liturgies would surely be a real gain.

Letters to the Editor

From May Blew, London SE

Your leading article highlights the blind alley into which the present confusion between faith and fantasy seems sometimes to be leading us. Unfortunately, however, in this short article confusion is worse confounded.

There appears to be an underlying assumption – based on what? – that where there is fantasy there cannot also be fact. Co-existence is deemed impossible. While it is suggested 'that the angels ought to be subjected to rather closer scrutiny', it is a little depressing to find that no attempt at such scrutiny is made before leaping to the conclusion that 'their removal from the pulpits, the Sunday School lessons and the liturgies would surely be a real gain'. Without the attestation of any real evidence here the passion for demythologization is clearly running past itself.

I am reminded of the remarks of Fr Bernard Basset SJ, made not without humour, in his book *The Noonday Devil* (p. 15), where he writes of 'doubts about childish concepts which we should have discarded years ago. An intelligent woman, troubled with doubts, at length had to admit that she had lost her faith in angels and this because she could no longer swallow the feathers in their wings. This may sound ridiculous but it happens to be true.'

There is no logical connection between the 'childish concept' and the doctrine of angels, that is, of the existence of spiritual beings. Here again Fr Basset is apposite (p. 63). He refers to the pictures of Fra Angelico and Botticelli as 'ravishing but often spiritually absurd', and continues: 'The fault lies not in the masters themselves but in our own untrained imaginations which have usurped the place of thought. Fra Angelico offers us through his skill an interpretation of reverence, sanctity, divinity in three dimensions and in flesh and blood. The effect is uplifting and leads to a fuller realization unless we spoil it by taking it all too literally.'

It is this 'fuller realization' which is so often missed when its image is discarded. Is not one

great weakness of the demythologizers simply this – that they are too literal? Granted that we reject the old-time imaginary picture of angels, there are surely no grounds for assuming that beings (e.g. angels) other than ourselves cannot exist simply because they are not visible within space and time. A naive assumption!

It is questionable, to say the least, whether imagery in Christian belief can or should be lightly discarded. Imagery is after all bound up with our life and experience. Some people are endowed with highly pictorial mental processes, and, as Bruce Cooper says on p. 8 of the same issue of *NC*, 'abstractions do not have the same hold on our imaginations as attempts to visualize and depict'. Can there not be a true as well as a false imagery? At any rate, it might be illuminating to hear what other readers consider the place of such imagery to be in Christian faith, particularly in relation to the teaching of children. To be practical: If we believe in angels (though not in 'feathered friends'), can – or should – this be taught without the use of imagery to the very young? If so, how?

From the Rev. Mark Potts, Carisbrooke, Isle of Wight

Very well, the twentieth-century church repudiates its doctrine of angels.

Throw out the Preface from the Liturgy: and the Sanctus – Isaiah clearly must have taken Mescalin. We must put the Nicene Fathers right over that word 'invisible'. Honest silence should reign over the awkward opening quotations in the Gloria culled from the angel mouths.

NT references to so many angels should never be mentioned except with a knowing smile. Next year we must find something else to read for the Epistle on St Peter's day.

It stands to reason that the Lord's own reference to angels shows just how mistaken he was about that other world in the light of what we now know. And Dionysius, Aquinas, the Schoolmen, are plainly barking up the wrong tree.

Apart from the hypothesis that your opinion might be mistaken, may you not also, on your own showing, be determined to limit the unlimited creativity of God to what your own thought considers desirable?

From Mrs Gladys Keable, Bognor Regis, Sussex
About angels: Like you, I shall never see one. I have come across one double-headed lamb; two marginal cases of speaking with tongues; two recognizable saints (one with the stigmata, one healthily normal and British) and several runners-up; no magicians of any competence; one completely 'impossible' miracle; two doubtful ghosts; no flying saucers; several authentic spiritual healers; one 'devil-possession'; and alas no outstanding man of genius. Reliable friends vouch for a hermaphrodite, and for a fire-walker.

All these phenomena are rare, and every meeting with the rich and strange has been of incalculable value to me, and puts me constantly on the watch to clarify my estimate of the literal, the psychological and the spiritual levels of experience, and their influence on one another. Angels, too, are rare, yet I know three reliable people who 'see' them; one of them is highly intellectual and a man of prayer, the other two are artists. Psychologists tell me that the experience springs from a function of the mind called 'active imagination', and that without this faculty we should lose most of the world's great (as well as not so great) art.

By all means let us push back or abolish the category of 'supernatural', but not at the expense of throwing away as rubbish experience on the frontiers of human understanding simply because it is rare or cannot be proved in a test-tube, though we must 'try the spirits' to discern from what source they come.

Surely the positive Christian attitude today is a zestful, though critical, openness to other people's experience, though we must avoid gullible credulity. I grant that it is impossible for the parson to teach what he does not believe; for my (easier) part, I shall continue to present to my grandchildren and the Sunday school the fine music of the trisagion and the great angelic pictures and stories which have genuinely nourished me; but when I am questioned I must frankly admit that I do not *know* about angels because I am not among the chosen ones who have this rare vision.

From Mr John Smyth, Billesdon, Leicester
You ask us what we think of angels and suggest they are myths. As I have seen one you might care to have a description. He was travelling along a fairly good track at a rapid pace. I should say he was hurrying, and as the terrain was arid semi-desert he was hot and dishevelled. The main outgarment of his clothing was brown, as was his hair, and his clothes were worn and torn in parts. There was a general air of authority in his manner. He was covering the ground at an impressive pace without actually running. When he came on the track to speak to me where I sat, he surprised me by kneeling by my feet to give me the message he had brought. He spoke briefly and to the point and then continued on his way.

Place of the Angels

JOHN A. T. ROBINSON

A sermon preached in Canterbury Cathedral

The church has just celebrated the festival of St Michael and All Angels, and to coincide with it *New Christian*, that *enfant terrible* of Christian journalism in this country, celebrated its first anniversary with an editorial saying that the time has surely come when angels may go: 'Their removal from the pulpits, the Sunday School lessons and the liturgies would surely be a real gain.'

If we are honest, I am sure there is a large part of each one of us which would echo that sentiment. For most ordinary people angels simply add to the cocoon of fantasy and unreality in which the Christian gospel is wrapped. So far from making the faith more real, they undoubtedly make it more unreal, remote and airborne. I simply do not see how this can be denied. In so far, therefore, as one is trying to start from where people are and make the Christian faith meaningful in terms of what is real to them, I agree with *New Christian*.

Having said that, let us have a look at what has happened and see whether, starting from the church's end (which is not the same thing at all), it is possible to interpret what belief in angels is really about. For it is a belief that is *meant* to add to, rather than detract from, the reality and richness of life. If it doesn't, has something important been lost? And, if so, how can we restore it?

Loss of reality

The story of our modern world is a story of the steady loss of reality suffered over the centuries by these ethereal beings. In the Middle Ages everyone believed in angels, and took them desperately literally. In their odd moments, theologians, when they were not arguing whether an archdeacon could be saved, spent their time disputing the number of angels that could dance on the point of a pin. Angelology was already on the way to being little more than an intellectual puzzle, a sort of medieval substitute for *The Times* crossword.

Later, with the Renaissance, angels became domesticated, and we find
them appearing as cherubs – sweet little boys with wings, whose blissful smiles certainly bear little enough resemblance to their counterparts on earth.

Then, with the Romantic Movement, they got sentimentalized as those sexless creatures who float through pre-Raphaelite paintings and stained-glass windows.

By this time they had become so thoroughly vapid and meaningless that it is not surprising that most people have now dismissed them altogether. They have become part of the fantasy world, with fairies and Father Christmas. A survey would doubtless reveal more people prepared to believe in flying saucers than in angels. We have reached the end of the road.

What do we do now? The one thing I am sure we can't do is just to go on as if nothing had happened. I remember years ago when I was on the staff of a theological college listening to a Compline address on angels from a leading Anglo-Catholic vicar, with whom I have joked about it since. But at the time I was angry. Just because we were in chapel we were exposed to a devotional fundamentalism that could only conceivably survive unquestioned there, and which I felt was an assault on the young men's critical faculties. It simply took for granted these invisible denizens of space as medieval men had believed them.

Expressing a conviction

Far be it from me to be dogmatic on the other side. In this age of constant fresh discoveries by radio-astronomy no one is going to be so foolish as to *deny* what may be around the universe. But I cannot say too strongly that it is no part of the Christian faith to put one's belief in hitherto undetected cosmic agencies. For believing in angels is not committing oneself to statements in the field of astrophysics any more than believing in Adam and Eve is committing oneself to statements in the field of anthropology. In neither case are we required to believe in the existence of actual beings who are or were around the world as we are. For angels are not literal entities that could be picked up on radar if we got their wavelength. Rather, like Adam and Eve, they are ways of representing, of picturing, certain convictions – theological convictions, not scientific convictions – about the meaning of life. They stand for the belief, if we may so put it, that there is always an inside to events, a personal as well as an impersonal aspect, a spiritual as well as a material, that the entire universe is shot through with God and his living activity. Whether angels are any longer the best or most helpful way of expressing this conviction is another matter. But let us try to understand it.

First, however, let us clear up one misunderstanding. For the men of the Bible angels were the communications system between God (who was in heaven) and men (who were on earth). Obviously for getting about they must be imagined as having wings – and in the visions of heaven in Isaiah or Ezekiel or the Book of Revelation they are represented, in highly poetic imagery, as winged creatures. But when angels appear to men and women on earth, there is nothing whatever to suggest that they are feathered or look different from ordinary people. In fact they *are* ordinary people, either real or in dreams, who are seen at the time or subsequently as having something to say from God. The classic case of this is Abraham, who, according to the Epistle to the Hebrews, 'entertained angels unawares'. The three men for whom Abraham and Sarah cooked lunch were three men – and there is no suggestion in the story that they looked or were anything else. They were afterwards (though not, interestingly enough, in the Genesis story) called 'angels' because they were recognized as bringing a message from the Lord. If God was in an event, then the human agents or interpreters of it were seen as angels. For an angel is what an angel does.

We have the same usage in the phrase 'be an angel', which does not mean 'go and get yourself feathers' but 'do something angelic'. The Greek word *angelos* simply means a messenger. It is that used of John the Baptist, who was indeed a man sent from God; but certainly he did not have feathers or wings. And St Paul applies it to the Christian ministry. Sometimes indeed there is doubt whether a person should be described in terms of his physical aspect or of his 'angelic' function and significance. Thus, in the earliest account of the Empty Tomb in Mark, we read that there was 'a young man' sitting there in 'a white robe'. In Luke it has become 'two men' in 'dazzling apparel', and in Matthew an 'angel' whose 'appearance was like lightning and his raiment white as snow'. I suggest that what the women actually saw was, as we should say today, a man in a white shirt. But what he had to say was seen as a message from God. So the event becomes written up in language that any first-century reader would instantly recognize as symbolic.

As I said, angels for the Bible stand for the conviction that within or behind all that happens there is a personal, a spiritual reality to be reckoned with. It is the biblical way (or, rather *a* biblical way) of denying a final materialism, that everything can be explained by the outside of events, merely in terms of the physical and the impersonal. Expressions of this spiritual dimension to all reality are the angels of the nations in Daniel, the angels of the churches in Revelation, and the angels of children in Jesus' own words (Matt. 13.10).

Let me try to interpret this spiritual dimension, what the Seer of Revelation so vividly calls a 'door opened into heaven', from three areas of experience.

1. There is, first of all, the meaning of the whole process of creation. Consider this breath-taking scene from the Apocalypse (Rev. 5. 11–14):

> Then as I looked I heard the voice of countless angels. These were all around the throne and the living creatures and the elders. Myriads upon myriads there were, thousands upon thousands, and they cried aloud: 'Worthy is the Lamb, the Lamb that was slain, to receive all power and wealth, wisdom and might, honour and glory and praise!' Then I heard every created thing in heaven and on earth and under the earth and in the sea, all that is in them, crying: 'Praise and honour, glory and might, to him who sits on the throne and to the Lamb for ever and ever!' And the four living creatures said, 'Amen', and the elders fell down and worshipped.

What a stupendous vision of the entire created universe as one gigantic act of worship, as spiritual in its ultimate, inner significance. We shall indeed be impoverished if we cannot catch its thrill. It is this interpretation that the dimension of 'angels and archangels and the whole company of heaven' is intended to supply. Let us not write it off. It is what is conveyed in modern terms by the sweep of Teilhard de Chardin's *Phenomenon of Man* or more soberly and scientifically by Sir Alister Hardy's recent Gifford lectures *The Living Stream* and *The Divine Flame*, though it is significant that neither of these think of mentioning angels.

2. There is the field that today is occupied by the powers lying beyond the threshold of conscious control, the ideologies and -isms that grip men in groups, the forces of the collective unconscious, the Archetypes of Jung, the Shadow, the Censor, not to mention the highly mythological figures of Oedipus and Eros and Thanatos, or the ghoulish monsters of science fiction. No one doubts their psychological reality, and it doesn't take much imagination to translate the biblical language of the world-rulers of this darkness, or the spiritual wickedness in high places, or the vision of Michael and his angels warring with Devil and his angels, into analyses of race riots or the individual psyche. 'The heights' and 'the depths' of which St Paul speaks in Romans 8 as powerless against the love of Christ, are essential to the scope of the Christian understanding of man and the cosmos.

3. And then, at the more homely level, there is the conviction of God's constant presence in ordinary life. For the men of the Bible, angels came in and out of everyday events entirely naturally. 'An angel appeared to Joseph in a dream' means simply, as we should put it, that Joseph had a dream in which he was told to get out quickly, and that in this he saw 'the hand of God'. Such incidents need not be miraculous interventions: simply

ordinary events on their 'inside'. The way the men of the Bible registered that these were not just accident or coincidence was to talk of angels as we still talk of providence. *God* was at work wonderfully, graciously.

I am not suggesting that we try to make this dimension real for people by pressing upon them the language of angels. In that I agree with *New Christian*. For it will probably have precisely the opposite effect. But I do not want to throw out the reality or cut the life-line of its connection with the biblical imagery and myth. For this has great evocative power, which one day we may be able to accept as the poetry it is. Above all let us stop being so desperately prosaic and pedestrian about it all. Angels are a *jeu d'esprit*, part of the dance of life. And maybe if we cannot take them from the theologians we can still glimpse them through the words of the poets. So here, to end, is Francis Thompson:

> The angels keep their ancient places;
> Turn but a stone, and start a wing!
> 'Tis ye, 'tis your estranged faces,
> That miss the many-splendoured thing.

Letters to the Editor

From Mr Neville Boundy, Bristol

Can someone tell me why we need angels? Regardless of their Zoroastrian origins, I would have thought that a fully incarnate Christ and a fully operative Holy Spirit rendered them and their intermediary functions entirely obsolete.

From Mr Philip Walker, Newthorpe, Notts

Your correspondent, May Blew, has hit upon the crux of the argument when she writes that the trouble with the demythologizers is that they take everything so literally. They are actually opposed to the doctrine of the incarnation, dismissing God's creation as an inadequate vehicle for his self-revelation: or else, naively, they have confused the true meaning of the word 'myth' with its popular corruption as something which is not true. And if we discard the traditional symbols and imagery which contain these myths in favour of some cold abstractions – the inward and spiritual grace without the efficacious outward and visible sign – then, we shall find that all kinds of magical myths will be created in order to replace the loss of the true myth.

The real question is not between symbol and abstraction, but whether the traditional symbols still have the power to reverberate in man's subconscious mind: how far the archetypal symbols are still archetypal: how far a symbol should be simple and self-explanatory, or whether there is a greater value in retaining the traditional symbols even if they require some explanation.

Dorothy Sayers recounts in *The Mind of the Maker* how she was once taken up for using the word 'dynamite' instead of 'TNT' as a word indicating great explosive power. She chose 'dynamite' because of the associations which that word has and which 'TNT' lacks.

If we think bread and wine are not significant symbols today try substituting coffee and biscuits and see what an impoverishment there is then.

Dismiss poetry, the imagination, the creative

spirit which can fuse together in a symbol the dust of the earth and the insubstantial light of heaven, in favour of a philosophical concept, if you like, but don't be surprised if men go chasing after other symbols of more dubious worth in order to establish meaning for themselves.

From Mr Reginald Payne, Dover
You may have had enough of the angels, but I venture to submit a largely borrowed reply:

I do wish *New Christian* would leave us
Alone in our innocent state –
They are saying there's no Father Christmas,
And he doesn't descend to the grate!

It's all a made-up fairy story,
The adults were having us on;
There aren't any heavenly reindeer,
Rudolf the Red-nosed has gone.

(Triumphant music)
And yet all my life I shall see them,
Up there on the nursery wall,
Santa's boots and his robe and his whiskers,
And his sack of good things for us all.

All right, they weren't real, I admit it,
But still, thirty odd years ago,
They were vividly real to my brother,
And he was aged seven or so.

My faith may be somewhat retarded,
I *prefer* the things I can't see:
Three cheers for the old superstitions,
For incredible mythology.

Most people find it ridiculous,
Irrational, escapist and such,
But there's several like me in the parish,
So that doesn't worry me much.

I suppose the *New Christian* would tell us
It still is in favour of God,
That science and faith go together,
And that seems decidedly odd.

WITH HOMAGE TO MARTIN LUTHER KING

What if an angel is a messenger sent by a god
  from a kingdom beyond our ken? Maybe
    not seen at all
  or hardly heard, sometimes gold wings that
    fall
around a sunset in pattern of a cloud
as once I have seen. Or a tremor on the shroud
  of one we loved. Or from some shrine a low
    call
  'kneel here and pray . . .' Or after battle a
    shawl
of misted light over a field of blood.

But more than all, one burning flame still
  moves
  my spirit to adoration. In human form
  its radiance lurks and leaps from thousands
    of faces
bearing the modest signature of a Hand that
  roves
  all Time, signing *Love*, *his mark* on faces of
    all the tribes and races
    the Face that suffers, and subdues the storm.

EDITH ANNE ROBERTSON

The Romantic Mr Eliot

The romantic pursuit of love is a far better way of overcoming lunacy, violence, stupidity and greed than classical discipline can ever be.

On the first anniversary of T. S. Eliot's death, ABC Television broadcast a controversial memorial programme by John Wren-Lewis which attracted considerable attention. Mr Wren-Lewis was asked to write this article based on his programme.

In his much maligned last play, *The Elder Statesman*, Mr T. S. Eliot makes his heroine say to her lover:

I've loved you from the beginning of the world.
Before you and I were born, the love was always there
That brought us together.

Such an extremely romantic sentiment is not at all what common opinion would lead us to expect from Mr Eliot. All his life he represented himself to us as firmly anti-romantic, the arch-exponent for our day of the great classical traditions in both art and religion. In his reflection on his own practice of the poet's art in *East Coker* he deplored 'undisciplined squads of emotion'; in his critical writing he insisted that art which deviated from the order and discipline of tradition into any form of individual self-expression must necessarily be inferior art; and in a broadcast talk he once asserted explicitly that the next best thing to Catholic Christianity – probably an essential precondition for the Catholic faith – was the Stoic belief in Fate overriding all merely personal emotions, the Great Universal Law to which all must be obedient.

Beneath the surface

But a close examination of Mr Eliot's work will show that his position was not quite so straightforward as he was wont to profess. I believe we can find under the severe classicism a high romanticism trying to get out, and in this I think he exposes a general truth of the utmost importance for our whole understanding of religion, namely, that the classical approach to religious belief (the idea of a Grand Design in the universe to which we

have to learn to submit if we are to lead the good life) is in fact always a
rationalization arising from disappointed romantic feelings.

To put the same point in another way, I believe Mr Eliot's powers of poetic expression were so great that they were able to give the lie to a very common notion about religion which he himself in his prosaic moments tended to support, the notion that the 'mainstream religion' of mankind is the classical belief in Grand Design and that romantic (or 'Protestant') appeals to individual feelings are at best a minor tributary of this mainstream, with the danger of becoming a dangerous diversion from it. This notion has an astonishing power of persistence amongst theologians and religious thinkers generally, although it actually flies in the face not only of all the best anthropological evidence about religious origins, but also of simple logic where the Jewish/Christian religious tradition is concerned.

If it were true that belief in God originated from a conviction of a Grand Order in the universe, as erudite theologians and Sunday-school books alike commonly suppose, then the various dualistic heresies which proclaimed that the physical universe was not God's creation at all, but the work of an evil opponent of God, could simply never have arisen. The real origin of the idea of the divine must have been something quite different – and, on the other side of the same coin, it is surely very hard to believe that anyone contemplating the strife and chaos of the natural world would ever conceive the idea that it was a Grand Design *unless he already had some other motive for doing so*. We gravely underrate even primitive man, and certainly the Old Testament Hebrews, if we think they were unaware of this aspect of nature: maybe we today have a little more evidence of it from science, but the basic facts have always been staringly obvious for all to see.

What then could be the origin of religious belief? The general weight of psychological and anthropological evidence points towards the idea embodied in the lines from *The Elder Statesman* with which I began, the idea that the sense of the divine originates in the romantic feeling that love is 'bigger than both of us', the feeling which lies at the root of individual self-consciousness – and there is good evidence for this in the Hebrew/Christian tradition too, once we have eyes to see it, not only in the obvious case of St John's assertion that God is love but also in the Rabbinic statement that 'God dwells in our togetherness', or in the assertion of the Koran that 'where two are met, Allah is the third'. *This* is the real mainstream, and if this is once recognized, it is perfectly possible to see how the 'classical' view of religion, with its deep suspicion of romantic feelings, might arise out of it: it could happen because of the sense that the romantic feeling of the infinite value of love seems to run completely counter to the whole direction of the natural world. Hence another world is posited to account for it, and then people are confronted with the alternative of denying this world altogether, as the puritanical, dualistic cults did, or else pretending that the natural order is in some way a necessary part of the divine will.

Disillusionment

Now one of the great virtues of Mr Eliot the poet is that he actually shows us this process of disillusionment and subsequent rationalization at work. The idea that there must be another world because we have feelings of infinite value that make this world seem hopelessly sordid comes out in Sir Claude Mulhammer's description of what he gets from contemplating pottery in *The Confidential Clerk*:

> To be among such things,
> If it is an escape, is escape into living.
> Escape from a sordid world to a pure one.

But the fullest articulation of the subject comes in *The Cocktail Party*, where the whole theme is explored in detail with immense psychological insight.

Of the four characters in this play who approach the priest-like psychologist, only one has any sense of religious belief, and that is the girl Celia, who gets it from her experience of love for Edward, the husband of Lavinia:

> I have thought at moments that the ecstasy is real
> Although those who experience it may have no reality.
> For what happened is remembered like a dream
> In which one is exalted by intensity of loving
> In the spirit, a vibration of delight
> Without desire, for desire is fulfilled
> In the delight of loving. A state one does not know
> When awake. But what, or whom I loved,
> Or what in me was loving, I do not know.

And because this vision comes to grief, Celia confesses to the sense of sin, very strange to one brought up in a typically modern atmosphere as she was. She makes it plain that this sense of sin has nothing to do with having 'been immoral' in the conventional sense, since Lavinia did not want her husband: it comes from the betrayal of the infinite vision of good which her love for Edward had given her:

> And then I found we were only strangers
> And that there had been neither giving nor taking
> But that we had merely made use of each other

Each of his purpose. That's horrible. Can we only love
Something created by our own imagination?
Are we all in fact unloving and unlovable?

But now comes the crucial point. The psychiatrist tells Celia that this
betrayal is no merely personal fault, but something inevitable in this world.
Those for whom love leads on to marriage, he says, betray the vision as
surely as she has done. They

Maintain themselves by the common routine,
Learn to avoid excessive expectation,
Become tolerant of themselves and others,
Giving and taking, in the usual actions
What there is to give and take. They do not repine;
Are contented with the morning that separates
And with the evening that brings together
For casual talk before the fire
Two people who know they do not understand each other,
Breeding children whom they do not understand
And who will never understand them.

The description is reminiscent of the couple playing a game of chess in
The Waste Land:

I never know what you are thinking. Think.
I think we are in rats' alley
Where the dead men lost their bones.

This, insists the psychiatrist of *The Cocktail Party*, is the human condition, not anything that a married couple could possibly remedy. Nature is
like that, so if Celia wants to pursue the infinite vision of love, it can only
be by contracting out of natural life altogether in favour of the supernatural
– first, becoming a nun, and then being martyred. And although Mr Eliot,
the exponent of the classical tradition and of Catholic Christianity, tries to
argue that acceptance of the human condition is an equally good way, he is
forced to say 'you will not know how good till you come to the end', and
he justifies it merely by the fact that it avoids the worst horrors of the
natural world: 'In a world of lunacy, violence, stupidity, greed . . . it is a
good life.'

For the truth is that Mr Eliot the romantic knew perfectly well that anyone who had ever really glimpsed the vision of infinite love would never
want to settle for that. A few pages later the psychiatrist expresses his real
feelings about Edward and Lavinia's marriage in terms which give the lie
to the protest about it being a good life, and show that in fact it is seen as

hopelessly sordid:

> What have they to go back to?
> To the stale food mouldering in the larder.
> The stale thoughts mouldering in their minds.
> Each unable to disguise his own meanness
> From himself, because it is known to the other.
> It's not the knowledge of the mutual treachery
> But the knowledge that the other understands the motive –
> Mirror to mirror, reflecting vanity.

And since this is what the natural world is like, it follows that acceptance of the world is not really a happy acceptance of sanity and balance at all, but a way of crucifixion quite as certain as the literal crucifixion which Celia meets at the hands of the savages. The so-called 'world-affirmation' of the classical outlook is not really opposed to the overt world-denial of romantic dualism of the Gnostic, Manichaean or 'puritan' type at all: it is merely the opposite side of the same coin, for both deny that the infinite vision of love, which alone makes life really human, can ever be found in this rats' alley of a world. World-acceptance on these terms means conscious acceptance of death in the belief that it is somehow a preparation for another world: in the unforgettable lines of *East Coker*:

> Our only health is the disease
> If we obey the dying nurse
> Whose constant care is not to please
> But to remind of our, and Adam's curse,
> And that, to be restored, our sickness must grow worse.
> The whole earth is our hospital
> Endowed by the ruined millionaire,
> Wherein, if we do well, we shall
> Die of the absolute paternal care
> That will not leave us, but prevents us everywhere.

When the matter is fully displayed in this way, I believe it becomes evident that the 'world-affirmation' of the classical outlook and the world-denial of the romantic agony *both* represent failure of faith, inability to believe that the infinite good glimpsed in the experience of love can ever really have the power to *change* the patterns of nature. Insofar as either of these views calls itself Christian, it is Christianity stopping short at the Crucifixion:

> Who then devised the torment? Love.
> Love is the unfamiliar Name
> Behind the hands that wove

The intolerable shirt of flame
Which human power cannot remove.

But surely genuine Christianity begins with the faith that human power is not unaided, that the infinite good glimpsed in love is in reality the Power before whom all nature is merely plastic. Real Christianity goes beyond crucifixion to resurrection, not merely as an ultimate hope but as a present reality in the world, and in *that* faith it is surely possible to believe both that ordinary commonplace marriage *can* be made to embody the infinite vision of love and that technology is not merely wasting its time when it searches for ways to prevent the corruption of food in the larder. I believe it was because he came through to this faith at the end of his life that Mr Eliot was prepared to be so unashamedly romantic in his last play. I see it, not as the work of an old man whose powers were failing, as most critics have held, but as in some ways his greatest affirmation, the discovery, amongst other things, that the romantic pursuit of love is a far better way of over-coming lunacy, violence, stupidity and greed than classical discipline can ever be.

Quotations from T. S. Eliot's *The Elder Statesman*, *The Confidential Clerk*, *The Cocktail Party*, and *Collected Poems* (The Waste Land and East Coker) are by permission of the publishers Faber & Faber.

6 Doubt among the Doubles

and still the cat is blessed

BRUCE COOPER

I was recently invited to talk to a youth club on 'Why I am a Catholic'. Although I lecture frequently to various voluntary and professional organizations, I have to go back twenty-three years, when I was still in my late 'teens, to remember the last time I spoke on such a topic. It was to a Presbyterian Youth Club in Edinburgh.

That was in a Calvinist citadel, and in those pre-ecumenical days there was an organization called, I think, the Protestant Action Committee, who were not above heaving the odd brick at the stained-glass windows of the Catholic cathedral.

How times have changed. So have I. And religion. I was in my first year at university, fresh from six years of indoctrination at a Catholic public school. I trotted out the familiar arguments, the church was one, holy, catholic, indivisible, etc., and the Catholic Church was the repository of all truth and the mother of us all, that papal infallibility was necessary to safeguard us against truth and error. Probably I went on to talk about the Immaculate Conception and Our Lady's bodily assumption (or hadn't that doctrine been declared then?). I seem to remember saying something on purgatory. Though I hope I never approached anything near Swift's poem:

> We only shall be saved,
> All others will be damned,
> There is no room in heaven for you,
> We can't have heaven crammed.

I was strongly aware of demarcation lines. I was at any rate talking to an audience avowedly Christian, to whom such terms as grace, sin, the resurrection of the body, supernatural life had some meaning.

Enter the knight

How different the scene was the other night. The setting a pub. Tables groaning under beer and snacks. A raven hair-dyed teenager coolly accepting a double whisky from the club leader. The lads nattily dressed pulling away at their fags. 'None of them believe very much at all,' the youth club leader has assured me over the phone the previous evening. I felt a bit like a medieval knight in shining armour, a relic of the past, something one looks at with curiosity in the foyer of a stately home.

This was not Immaculate Conception country in any sense of the word, theological or physiological, for half the boys freely admitted they were sleeping with their girls, anxious to tell me about it in fact (lending substance to the Schofield Report). A different approach was called for. What approach, though?

Some of the familiar landmarks, the bedrock certainties, seem to be crumbling. The Catholic world used to be solid and unchanging, marked by purple vestments, the liturgy in Latin, indulgences, chocolate-coloured statues of St Antony of Padua with ever-burning candles, relics, pious objects, benediction, holy water stoups. There was an aura of mystery and awe, some might say superstition. For the broad mass of Catholics there was nothing very theological about this world. It was a world bound in by devotion, pious practice, unquestioning belief. It was a world of modest frugal material wealth, of close parochial community life.

But modern communications and technology have shattered it. Parish boundaries are meaningless. Education has helped to erode these. Catholics, too, are living in a world of bikinis, transistor radios, central heating, the family car, bingo. Life has become so much better that we do not need to solace ourselves by the promise of another life. I would say that Catholicism is becoming more middle-class. Life no longer revolves round the parish church in the way it did. People seek elsewhere for their entertainment and community life. Religion is becoming a more individual matter – personal commitment. The expression of this may be dutiful attention to one's religious practices or a greater concern in social matters, but less mass popular devotion.

Place for persecution

Look at any congregation, slumped in their pews on a Sunday morning; little ardour in the preacher's eye. The vernacular seems to have made absolutely no difference at all in involvement or commitment. To the outside world it looks like another gimmick. What is that verse?

> We've given them milk, we've given them buns,
> We've taught them in Greek and in Latin,
> We've put them in first and given them runs,
> But the public, alas, isn't batting.

To the Catholic the removal of Latin makes them less exclusive. The great battle hymn 'Faith of Our Fathers', sung with such lustiness, recalling the days of bitter persecution, rings rather hollow in ecumenical days. And yet was it not for the mass in Latin that some of those Jesuit priests went to the gallows at Tyburn? Perhaps Muggeridge is right, a little persecution, slightly fewer worldly goods, be they purple hearts or fitted carpets, is a more fruitful soil for ardent religion.

Add to this that the Catholic Church to the outsider seems to have nothing to say about the issues which press in on all sides – birth control, nuclear warfare, racial integration – that it doesn't really speak to the mum with seven kids in a Liverpool slum who is at the end of her tether, in terms that are meaningful for her, and I felt in a rather different position than I did twenty-three years previously.

What were the certainties that remained? Even these sounded anachronistic to my audience. I believed in God, that the Word was made Flesh, that God spoke to us through Christ, that he died for us, that there was an after life, a sacramental system, that prayer, devotion and worship were human instincts – plus the usual arguments that the existence of God made life intelligent and purposeful.

But the real difficulties centred on such subjects as heaven and hell. It helped when people could visualize God as looking about a hundred years old, sage and revered with a long white beard, sitting on top of a golden throne way up on a heap of cumulus cloud, that angels looked like saintly fairies with golden wings, that hell was a bit like Guy Fawkes night and heaven like Kew Gardens in mid-June. We have jettisoned all that bric-a-brac. But abstractions do not have the same hold on our imaginations as attempts to visualize and depict. If you can't hold to the concrete because it looks ludicrous by modern standards, dismiss it entirely.

'You don't believe all that jazz about women being turned into pillars of salt and men walking on water. It isn't scientifically possible.' I told them I believed in miracles, that I had been on a pilgrimage to Lourdes and learnt of many miraculous cures, but my credulity was stretched by some of the claims of Scripture, but here again the prosaic, ordinary mind has been trapped by the figurative. Adam eating a Cox's Orange Pippin watched by a slimy snake; God, like Merlin with Excalibur, waving some magic wand and the earth appearing in seven days. People have been educated to scientifically dispose of myth but not sufficiently educated to think in concepts and abstractions about religion. A good man, yes. Goodness, no.

Square one

Education and technology have helped to make us more self-sufficient. 'I don't need a God. I do as I like. What do you mean "sin"?' The Christian

today is back in square one. He can't make any assumptions of common
culture. He has to think out rationally and emotionally his basis of belief, declare his faith and convictions, embody them to the best of his ability in his daily life, and leave it at that. The Sermon on the Mount, the beatitudes, do not speak easily to a self-sufficient generation.

'I liked your talk,' said the double-whisky girl a couple of days later when I chanced to meet her. 'I'm not really religious; my sister is. I forgot to tell you we had the cat blessed with holy water when it was poorly. The priest came round.'

See what I mean?

Make Love and War

MICHAEL DE-LA-NOY

In his article 'Doubt Among the Doubles' Bruce Cooper related how he had turned up to give a talk on religion to a youth club; it appears that at least he got a hearing. In the East End club I have been trying to run, Mr Cooper wouldn't have got a word in edgeways whether his subject had been the Virgin Birth or the Beatles.

Over the past few months I have constantly had to remind myself of the Chinese proverb about the man without boots. I realize that if the club I have been involved with is more chaotic than the one Mr Cooper was asked to talk to, there are clubs far more difficult to organize than mine; chaos, like practically everything else, is relative. But I was certainly not prepared for my first evening.

Two days before I took over, the club enjoyed a full-scale riot. Thinking to restore morale, I imported an American folk singer, who arrived complete with smashing girl friend and guitar. How he stuck it I do not know. He sang against a deafening barrage of talk and tomfoolery, against a built-in refusal to believe that anyone could be there to entertain or educate. I doubt if Houdini would have held their attention. When the singer left, he simply remarked that I had got my work cut out all right, but even so, it was paradise compared to New York.

After this shaky start it still took me several months to accept that the sixty teenagers in my club were little savages. Before I joined, a youth officer on the committee that interviewed me asked how I planned to cope.

'Love is the only way' I told him. He beamed. But the one professional
sociologist on the committee resigned. He may have had a point. How *do*
you love kids who steal money from your wallet, pinch your keys, raid the
store cupboard and chuck the contents to their friends in the street, break
into the club at night to smash up your office and the coffee bar (which they
built themselves), send your assistant leader and one of their own number
to hospital for stitches over their eyes, and then paint swastikas all over the
doors and windows?

I know the 'Christian' answer as well as anyone else. You continue to
open the club night after night, remain behind to sweep up the glass, and
finally have a nervous breakdown – unless, of course, you happen by birth
to be so Christ-like that they mistake you for the real thing, as has happened
to a few saints in history, and then you are protected by a sort of mystical
armour. I know one youth worker who pioneered holidays in the Lake
District for boys from industry, and welcomed each batch by personally
washing their feet. He never had any trouble.

But those of us seeking the 'Christian' approach to youth work on the
children's own home ground, our city slums, always assuming there is a
specifically Christian approach, have to love in a youth service that says,
among other things, that you only get financial assistance so long as you
cater for x-number of children never mind whether the area you are working in is Pinkneys Green, Palmers Green or Bethnal Green, or whether you
have a dozen voluntary helpers or just your wife. In other words, we have
to find practical methods of loving in a sociological situation that frequently says, 'Here are sixty disturbed kids who all need a lot of individual
attention; and here is one paid helper, now get on with the job.'

The youth service, like the church, is not of course the really important
factor, it is only a framework in which people move and have their being.
It is what the people do that matters. The other day some of the boys in my
club kicked down the door of the games room instead of asking for the key,
and then threw the billiard balls through the windows. When I related this
incident to a friend, he asked with a sigh, 'What *are* things coming to?'
And tempted as I often am to share his rather fay pessimism, I am bound
to say, after reading a book like *The Roots of Evil*, that things are in fact
becoming better and better.

The children some of us struggle to serve *are* little savages, and some of
the things they do *are* rather horrid, but they are humane savages; they are
no longer actually brutalized, and neither are the school teachers, police-
men, swimming-bath attendants and youth leaders on whom, from time to
time, they take out their boredom. In the year of the 1832 Reform Bill a
boy of nine was hanged, and children were flocking to watch executions.

Nothing that happens today, in our clubs or outside them, is as bad as this. When a fourteen-year-old boy murders a policeman now, the publicity given to his action only reflects the infrequency of such acts.

Although I suppose it is violent to kick down doors and smash windows, it is a suppressed sort of violence, something the children themselves know is not natural to them. In a club like mine, where a quarter of the members are convicted and a quarter are smoking drugs, it's not their delinquency that shocks one but their restlessness. There is a constant movement from room to room, an almost pathological inability to concentrate on any activity or conversation for more than a minute or two. They shout instead of talking, and run instead of walking. You get grabbed hold of for attention, and spat on by the girls, who lean over the landing, waiting to treat visitors with the contempt, or perhaps suspicion, normally reserved for something the wind's blown in.

There is, too, a sad loss of innocence, a loss of faith in the natural good-will of the adult running the club. This can be a severe test of love, and an alarming exercise in introspection. You too come to doubt your motives. There are very few things my club members want to know about me. They are totally unworried by my posh voice, they do not much mind that I do not live in the same district, and they aren't interested how old I am. But they are obsessed with finding out how I react to them sexually. At fifteen, I find them so hard-bitten that the other day I took five of the boys off for a drink at lunch time, quite forgetting that I was breaking the law. The publican gave me a funny look, but not before he had overcome his own scruples and taken the money.

And then, suddenly, you remember once again that they are only kids, prematurely aged by the ad man, unimpressed by Mack the Knife, Wilson the Wizkid or Paul the Pope. At half past one I suggested they ought to be back at school. 'No, we've got another five minutes,' one of them told me, slowly downing his pint. 'There's no point being on time. In fact, we *have* to be late. See you back at the club.'

RELIGION!

No visitor to the Churches, Schools and Youth Clubs exhibition which has been staged in the Horticultural Halls, Westminster, from Tuesday to today, could complain that youth work was being divorced from religion. The visitor could not get far round the stands without seeing a chasuble or some other church manifestation. – *Church Times.*

A Methodist spokesman said yesterday: 'Previously, in the North of England, the Mayor or the Lord Mayor, as often as not was a Methodist, and in Sunday schools there were Methodist cricket teams. All this helped to serve the Methodist way of life, but it is not having the same attraction for youth.' – *The Guardian.*

7   Time for Consent
NORMAN PITTENGER

The time has come for the church to alter its attitudes to homosexuals.

An article published in March 1967. A book was subsequently published under the same title by SCM Press and reprinted in an enlarged edition in 1970.

This article is an attempt to look at homosexuality from a Christian stance, taking into account what we have learned in recent years from psychology, anthropology, sociology, and biology. It makes no pretence to be anything like a 'full-length' study; my purpose is to be programmatic, as they say on the continent, rather than definitive or exhaustive. My concern with this particular matter arises from a considerable experience of 'counselling' with homosexual people of the male sex, and men whose anguish over their feeling of rejection and dismissal by the Christian church in its various denominations has led me to think afresh about the whole question. Furthermore, I am well aware of the dangers one runs if one takes, as I shall take, a permissive position in respect to homosexuality: but I am prepared to run this risk, if what I say can help the people for whom I feel such a deep, and I believe Christian, concern.

Numbers involved

Are there more homosexuals today than in the past? It is difficult to say; but certainly it can be said that the fact of homosexuality is more apparent, and there is a more honest recognition of the presence in our midst of large numbers of men and women who must be classified as either latently or overtly homosexual. Statistics are not very reliable, but it has been estimated, conservatively, that perhaps 5 per cent of the total population, both in Britain and in North America, fall into this group – which would mean that in the United Kingdom there are some two to three million, in Canada somewhere between 750,000 and a million, and in the United States a total of approximately eight to ten million persons. On any reckoning, this is a large segment of the population; equally certainly, it is impossible to dismiss *all* these men and women, out-of-hand, as just 'disgusting perverts'.

Man is a psychosomatic organism, whose self-expression inevitably
includes sexual activity. Made in God's image to be a lover, in the deepest
sense, like his 'creator' who is the cosmic 'Lover of souls' – and bodies, too
– man finds through sexual activity a chief way in which fulfilment is
achieved in 'one of his own kind'; and this, for a Christian, is an instrumentality in which the Love who is God is also known and served. That is
why in many Christian circles marriage is seen as a sacrament and in all
Christian circles human sexuality is a holy thing, constituting a kind of
'holy communion' which is a genuine created good. But if man is made to
be a lover, he is in actual fact a frustrated lover whose ordering of his loving
is in need of divine grace and correction: so St Augustine could pray,
'Order my love'. *Distorted loving* is in fact man's basic sin, for it is nothing
other than pride in action.

But what constitutes the sinfulness in distorted loving? Here I should
differ, I suppose, from much that has been said and written. It seems to me
that the sinfulness is found, not so much in the *person* loved, as in the *way
in which* the person is loved. The sinfulness of our distorted loving, then, is
its failure in mutuality, fidelity, genuine tenderness, respect for the other –
in a word, in the attempt to possess and use the partner, rather than to give
fully and wholly to another self who also gives fully and wholly. Our
various traditional moral codes and regulations are best seen as guide-lines
to that kind of totality in giving-and-receiving, rather than as arbitrarily
imposed divine law with little relation to the basic desires and drives of
human beings as persons who must give love and receive love if their true
nature is to develop according to the divine intention for them.

In *this* context homosexuality, like heterosexuality, must be seen and
understood. The homosexual is different from the heterosexual in that for
various reasons (the experts disagree here, some stressing sociological,
others psychological, and many physiological factors) his or her sexual
attrait is for a member of the sex to which they belong.

Most Christians, I believe, are prepared to grant that the person who has
this kind of *attrait* is not for that reason in sin, as we put it. That is his
condition; in all likelihood he cannot 'help it' since he did not himself
choose it, or at any rate as a given fact he has become such a person. Where
the sinfulness lies, it is said, is in *acting upon that attrait* in an overt manner
– in other words, concretely loving a person of his own sex and expressing
that love in physical contacts of one sort or another.

Constructive relationships

The Quaker Report disagrees here; so do other advocates of 'contextual'
or 'situational' morality. In varying ways, these writers have said that it is

both absurd and unrealistic to expect from the homosexual a total abnegation of his sexuality in its concrete expressions – and this, not from specifically vocational conviction, as with the monk or nun, but because the
the *action itself* is essentially sinful in nature and hence must be rejected
under any and all circumstances. But for the homosexual himself the real
problem with which he comes (when he does come) to a priest or counsellor,
is not whether there shall be any overt expression of his love for the person
of his own sex with whom he wishes to share his life, but how he can make
of their relationship something constructive and up-building for both of
them; indeed, how he and his partner can build a truly loving union of
lives. If the homosexual is in any sense a Christian, as I have learned from
those with whom I have had to do, he feels also, often with much more
strength than is commonly recognized, that the union can only be a good
one when in some fashion or other God is consciously known to be present
between them, with them, and in them.

Will he be told, then, that there is no hope for him and no chance of a
good relationship with the one whom he loves? Or is the *only* way in which
that relationship can be good to be found by the complete abjuring of all
physical contacts between the persons who believe themselves to be deeply
and truly 'in love'? Generally speaking, he will be told exactly that. And it
is at this point that I cannot agree with the usual advice.

Nobody, I hope, would wish to defend promiscuity between men, any
more than he would wish to defend it heterosexually. Nobody believes that
seduction of one man or woman by another, whatever the sex, is desirable:
that, surely, is of the nature of sin. I am not speaking here, then, of male
prostitution, female prostitution, promiscuity, the 'one-night-stand', the
coercion of others into relationships that they would not themselves choose.
I am speaking of the person who may be called, if I dare use the phrase, a
conscientious homosexual whose only hope of finding *any* sexual life is
with another man or another woman. Such persons cannot be expected to
'give up sex' altogether. And if it happens that one is dealing with a couple
who, so far as one can see, deeply and truly love one another, it is pretty
close to spiritual homicide to separate them, or to try to do so, just as it is
death-dealing tactics to demand that they shall never, in any way, give
physical expression to their love.

Meaning of 'sin'

Most men and women are, of course, sexually attracted to the opposite sex:
there is every reason to assume that this will continue to be true, so long as
man lives on this planet. But there are a considerable number who *do* fall
into the homosexual category: what about them? Supposing the law in

this land, and eventually in other countries too, is altered, as seems very likely. Church dignitaries and moral theologians tell us that this would mean that homosexual physical activity, under proper safeguards as to age and privacy, would no longer be accounted as 'crimes', subject to legal penalty; but such would still be 'sins'. My question is: would they? – or better, are they?

It all depends on what we mean by sins. If my argument is correct, what constitutes sin, from the deeply Christian understanding of man, is that which introduces coercion, fails in mutuality, lacks fidelity, has no concern for the other person, manifests no abiding tenderness. I know that to many all this sounds rather 'sloppy' and 'sentimental'. But here we are concerned with the deepest nature of man: made to love, frustrated and twisted in loving, needing to be made free to love – that is man, in the Christian view. I cannot see that the fact that one loves a person of the same sex, and wishes to act upon that love, is in and of itself sinful; nor can I see that acting upon that desire, when there is the true intention of love with the mutuality, fidelity, respect, and tenderness I have urged, is in and of itself sinful.

I do not pretend that this is a conclusive argument. I know that it is rejected by most of my fellow-Christian theologians. But I have yet to be convinced that it is wrong. And I know of a number of cases where pastoral help along these lines has had eminently constructive results in aiding towards enriched and fulfilling relationships for committed Christian persons – results which, however 'sloppy' and 'sentimental' some may think it to say so, seem to me to be of the sort that our Lord himself, as Love enmanned in our human existence, has been ready to bless.

On the Fringe of Society

'I used to wonder whether the neighbours were shocked by two men living openly together...'

A personal account of a homosexual's background and attitudes. For obvious reasons the authors must remain anonymous.

It grieves me that I have to write this article pseudonymously. I am not in the least ashamed of being homosexual, the law which makes me a criminal is absurd and about to be changed, and with a very few exceptions I don't care whether people know I am queer or not. The exceptions are, inevitably, my own immediate family. My parents are highly conventional middle-class people, and though they must at least subconsciously realize by now that I am not interested in girls, either 'suitable' or 'unsuitable', it would hurt them more than I or they could bear to have to face the fact of my queerness. Nothing now would be gained by forcing them to a knowledge they don't want. It might, ten years ago, have helped me to tell them; we might have avoided a lot of secrecy and lying and evasion which I regret. It would make me much happier if, when I take my lover to stay with them, they could accept him for what he is and try to love him as they love my brother's wife. It is sad that I can never be absolutely honest with them. But, since they are what they are and I am what I am, the friendship we have for each other is perhaps the most we could hope for anyway.

I am a writer by profession, which means that apart from writing my own things I have to do a lot of journalism to make a living. No one, as far as I know, has ever given me a bad review or not asked me to write an article because I am queer. They *have* not asked me because they have dis-liked me or my writing, but that's perfectly all right by me. I do not flaunt my queerness, but I make no effort to conceal it, either.

I am quite sane, really, and live in a quiet London street with a lorry-driver on one side and a garage mechanic on the other, both of them mar-ried with grown-up children. I used to wonder what they thought of us, whether they were shocked by two men living openly together, whether there would be hostility. But there has never been a sign of it. Our houses all have small front gardens, and in the summer we envy each other's flowers; we discuss the threat to pull the street down and band together against it; we complain about the aircraft noise. Either the neighbours don't know we are lovers, or they know and don't mind so long as we don't make a fuss about it. Or perhaps they do mind, but feel sorry for us and are too polite to say anything. Whatever the truth may be, neighbourly rela-tions could not be better.

Understanding

We lead a very normal life. It is difficult to convince people just how normal it is. Because we are both men and indulge regularly and with great delight in sexual acts which are alleged to shock a large part of the nation, people think we must feel different. We are different, of course, but we hardly ever feel it. Our sexual behaviour isn't self-consciously 'abnormal'; on the con-trary, to us it is the natural and obvious way to have sex for our mutual pleasure. We think we feel for other men what most men feel for women; there may be subtle differences between homosexual and heterosexual love, but we are not aware of them. Ours is the only kind of love we understand or want. We love each other, we kiss and caress and copulate the same as any other couple – only we are both men, so it isn't exactly the same, of course. But the differences seem far less important than the similarities. Sex can be the expression of love in any number of postures; ours do not strike *us* as unnatural or abnormal or anything but satisfactory. I think there are far more homosexual couples like us than people realize. The emphasis in books and articles is on the 'gay' life and promiscuity. Well, that exists, and if you are not 'married' it's convenient and sometimes even genuinely gay. But for most queers, normal life is domestic, quiet, loving, serious, dull.

The beginning

Of course it is not always like that, and I am lucky to be in a profession where liberal attitudes predominate. Nor have I always been as happy as I am now. It was not till I was twenty-eight that I settled into 'married' life. I first became aware of sex at boarding school. There, from the age of fourteen onwards, I began to have sex with other boys, always of my own age-group. We began with mutual masturbation, and as we advanced academically so did we sexually till in our last year we were practising sodomy and fellatio. It was all very exciting, with midnight meetings, bicycle rides to distant woods, changing-room assignations and all the rest of the schoolboy apparatus of romance; only romance absolutely never entered into it, our emotions were never for a moment stirred, our sole object was the achievement of orgasm. We achieved it often. For a whole year, when I was fifteen, I thought of nothing else. Every object, every idea, had a sexual charge. It was highly enjoyable, but very bad for my work.

In the holidays I was romantically in love with a series of local girls. We used to meet at dances. We wrote passionate and suggestive letters to each other during term-time, and were embarrassed when we met again. I once had two girls writing to me at once, much to the admiration of the boys I was having sex with at the time. It never for a moment crossed my mind that I might be homosexual. I found a copy of Havelock Ellis and read about the homosexual stage of adolescence and was pleased with myself for going through it in such an admirably ordinary way. As far as I know all my sexual partners from school are now married. Perhaps they sometimes have nostalgic thoughts about their schoolboy sex. I don't myself.

It was only at the end of my schooldays that I trumped up a love affair for myself in the conventional manner. It was very much the done thing for older boys to have crushes on younger ones, and I fell self-consciously for a choirboy in another house. It was a most unsatisfactory business and

quite unreal and it did not last. But I was deeply shocked when I discovered
on the last day of my last term that my most regular lover had been having
quite a serious affair with a younger boy in our own house. I do not know
whether I was shocked because I wanted the boy myself, or because I felt
my friend had let me down – not as a lover, but as a prefect. I was head of
my house, and by that time I strongly disapproved of such romantic relationships becoming physical. I brooded on the treachery for months, yet
knew perfectly well that my friend had done little more than I had myself.
I became very depressed. I did not understand why I should feel it so badly.
I do not think I really do now. But perhaps the violence of my feeling was
caused by a subconscious revulsion from my own unacknowledged homosexuality. There seemed something in the relationship between the two
boys beyond the merely physical, and I was frightened of what it might be.
This trivial incident obsessed me for a long time.

Seeking normality

Doing national service, I began to fret for proof of my normality. One
leave I went with a friend to Paris where we egged each other on to pick up
tarts. I managed all right, and came away immensely pleased with myself,
quite certain that I was a normal, heterosexual womanizer, and pretty
accomplished at it, too. Some weeks later, boasting of our minimal heterosexual exploits, another friend and I found ourselves sufficiently excited for
mutual masturbation. This happened once more. I had no more sex for
four years.

There is nothing I now regret more in my life than that prolonged sexual
abstinence. It nearly drove me mad. I went to a university after national
service, still imagining myself heterosexual, but there I fell in love with a
male undergraduate, and then with another, till I could no longer disguise
from myself that I was hopelessly and exclusively queer. Girls no longer
attracted me at all. All the young men I fell in love with were normal;
though they were sympathetic about my plight, they refused adamantly to
solace me. I painfully came to understand how much normal men like
being admired by other males; I am sure there must be a Greek play about
it somewhere, but if there is, I had not read it, and I had to learn for myself
that the unrequited admirer in those circumstances gets no satisfaction
whatever. I lived in a permanent state of anxiety, worked furiously hard,
drank too much, even contemplated suicide. I desperately needed advice,
but there was no one to go to. I needed, I think, to be gently and kindly
seduced, to be shown that the physical side of love can be enjoyable by
itself. But no one obliged, and I continued in a dreadful torment of spiritual
love, hating myself as I carved my heart to new and more grotesque and

tortured shapes. From eighteen to twenty-three – the best five years of my sexual life from the homosexual point of view and, I dare say, from the heterosexual too – I was virtually chaste. Youth matters in men as it does in women, and I wasted my youth in abstinence, struggling not with my conscience (I was all too eager for sexual life) but with a self-defeating heart. I am sure it was not accidental that I loved only those who were not available. I was, obviously, scared of my own nature. I wish to God that someone had taken pity on me in those bleak years and taught me to accept it.

Finally I took the task into my own hands, went to a place where I had heard homosexuals gathered, and allowed myself to be picked up by a middle-aged South African business man. I thought he was personally loathesome, quite apart from being South African (I was earnestly not buying South African grapefruit at the time), but I have never felt more relieved in my life than when I was walking home that night. After that I allowed myself to drift slowly through the homosexual sub-world, learning to accept myself and to enjoy sex, to say 'No' as well as 'Yes', to discover what it was that I wanted. I had a disastrous affair with a psychopath, many 'one-night stands'. I travelled a lot and worked hard, I sowed my belated, not very wild, oats. Then I decided it was time I stopped wandering and settled down. I found somewhere to live and furnished it. But my evenings were lonely, and a terrible restlessness would drive me out night after night, not so much for sex as for company. Like anyone else, I wanted to marry. I met my lover in a 'queer' club, an unpromising place – but that is what the clubs are for, really. I fell in love with him, terrified that he would not fall in love with me. But he did. We never go to the club now, though he enjoys the excitement of promiscuity which I am delighted to have given up. He is less faithful than I, and we quarrel about it. We quarrel about the washing-up sometimes, too. But our mutual love and dependence grow all the time. We're awfully normal.

We live opposite a church. It would not occur to either of us to enter it. I don't really see what business it is of Christians, old or new, to fuss about us. But I recognize that I am much more fortunately placed than most homosexuals, and perhaps better able than some to cope with the difficulties. The real problem it seems to me, is not social or legal but psychological. Unless you can love yourself, you can never love anyone else. Many homosexuals find this very hard; they feel guilty, anxious and afraid. They are, after all, psychologically 'different'. All Christians can do is what everyone else can do – treat the homosexual's need to love and be loved as a natural one, nature being so comprehensive, and encourage each individual to accept himself enough to love someone else.

Letters to the Editor

From a priest

The understanding of Dr Pittenger may gladden the heart of those within the church (for those outside ignore it) who have to live with the problem of being a homosexual, but it heavily underlines the difference between what might or even ought to be, and what actually is.

I am paid by an organization which condemns me. When the relationship in which I had discovered real love (and in which words like 'the love of Christ' had become a life-giving reality) came to an end, I told my superiors I was sorry that I had lied by saying nothing about the relationship, but I am not sorry, indeed I rejoice that I had, at last, discovered real love the only natural way that a homosexual can discover it. I was told not to be sentimental, and that I must regard the whole relationship as a cancer, which, by the mercy of God, had been removed. I did not, and I cannot.

But now I have to do one of three things. 1. Pretend that I have no feelings of love towards anyone, and so suppress the power that ought to make the whole church move. (I am not asking that I might corrupt all the choir; I merely say that I must stifle at source any feelings of affection.) 2. I can hope that I might fall in love again (and know again the freedom that the marriage service speaks of – 'a remedy against sin'), and yet know that such an event would necessitate lying by default. 3. Leave the church before 1. drives me crazy, or 2. gets a chance to occur.

And please do not come the old guff about the problem for the homosexual being no different from that of the heterosexual who wants to get married. The heterosexual does not have to hide his feelings (preferably even from himself) for safety's sake – he can show that he is going steady, and he also has the hope and possibility of a marriage which his friends can know about.

From the Rev. Raymond J. Foster, Nottingham

Dr Norman Pittenger's article 'Time For Consent' with its balanced, compassionate appraisal, is a breath of fresh air among Christian discussions on homosexuality. The 'conscientious homosexual', to use Dr Pittenger's phrase, has for too long been forced to bear the tension between what his or her whole being cries out for and the harsh unyielding attitude of the church and society. The homosexual is conditioned to see himself as an enemy of society, and yet his homosexuality is so integral a part of his nature that he cannot – nor should he be expected to – accept the role of a monster whom society has the right to put in chains. Sooner or later, every homosexual must choose between accepting or rejecting a relationship with another man or woman. All too often, this is a painful decision, taken alone, resulting either in the torments of conscience, or in the awful knowledge that the possibility of establishing a love-relationship has been lost. Those who succeed in accepting themselves fully and in establishing a love-relationship are a fortunate minority.

The pressure of society's prejudice against the homosexual is very real, leading to a sense of rejection so that he either retreats into solitude and frustration, or seeks the society of others like himself. One of the most distressing characteristics of those who are overtly homosexual is the veneer of cynicism, adopted to compensate for the disrepute in which they are held by society. This atmosphere of cynicism, and the precariousness of the homosexual's status in the eyes of the law, can hardly create a situation in which real love-relationships are possible.

The church should accept homosexuals, not as it would like them to be, loving each other according to the principles of Platonic idealism, but as they really are, persons whose need of sexual fulfilment is as great as any other man or woman's. This is not a plea for special privilege, but simply a plea for the acceptance by the church and by society of the homosexual's freedom to live in a mature relationship with another man or woman, through which each may attain fulfilment. There is every reason to hope that a more liberal attitude would lead not to an increase, but to a decrease, in promiscuity, since a more stable and compassionate attitude in society as a whole would surely create a more stable atmosphere in the homosexual society, an atmosphere in which more satisfactory relationships might flourish.

From the Ven. T. Dilworth-Harrison, Newark, Notts

You will know that *New Christian* is read in theological colleges (and not impossibly in the upper forms of public schools). I submit that the article 'On the Fringe of Society' with its strongly emotional content does grievous disservice to young men, and the assumption that it is quite normal for public schools to be honeycombed with vice is gratuitous. This article can but disparage those who strive after personal purity, and would shrink from the very idea of corporate sex orgies, to say nothing of sodomy.

After describing a year of complete abandonment to such activities as 'highly enjoyable', the author turns to 'romantic love with a series of local girls'. This suggests that his proclivities derive from adoption, not birth. If a homosexual were exclusively loyal to his 'partner' for life, it would be conceivable to see in such a relationship a true example of love, but (speaking as a priest who has had a fairly long experience) one has never known this to be the case.

One may ask with all courtesy, what high purpose is achieved by printing an article which can easily be an incentive to sin? The strict standards of the Gospels and Epistles may be old hat – they are certainly not New Christian – but when St Paul says 'It is a shame even to speak of those things that are done in secret,' his remedy is not to sweep them under the carpet, but to assert with conviction born of experience 'in all these things we are more than conquerors through him who loved us.' Yes, but how to bring that love home!

From Mr John E. Roberts, Wesley College, Leeds

The Venerable T. Dilworth-Harrison reproaches you for publishing the article 'On the Fringe of Society' on the grounds that we, the innocents in theological colleges, may be incited to bouts of homosexual activity. Let me, sir, report on the situation in Leeds!

Because of the Easter holidays we found two issues awaiting us. Within minutes of our reading the copy of 23 March latent passions were aroused, and a mad, glorious frenzy of corporate sex orgies and sodomy was enacted. Satisfied at last, we then turned to the current *New Christian*, and read 'Cheaper Than Alcohol'. O the bliss! Within minutes we had dragged out our pipes and were having a marijuana session in the common room.

The next issue is awaited with eager excited anticipation, what further thrills lie ahead!

Searching for Truth

A leading article published in August 1967

As is well known, though all too frequently forgotten, the context in which a statement is made is normally as important as the statement itself. Christians have every reason to know how much distortion is caused when words

are considered in isolation from their setting and without reference to the   96
circumstances in which they were uttered. The Bible has suffered more from
this than any other piece of literature.

Canon Hugh Montefiore's paper* at the recent Modern Churchmen's
Conference is the latest casualty of this particular form of human per-
versity. In the course of a learned and devout lecture entitled 'Jesus'
Significance Today: the Revelation of God', Canon Montefiore spent some
time discussing 'those characteristics of Jesus that seem to differentiate
him, as a man, from the other men of his time, and which give a special
flavour and quality to his human personality'. Amongst these characteristics he noted the fact that Jesus was unmarried and went on to suggest
reasons for this. Men, he said, usually remain unmarried for three reasons:
(i) because they cannot afford to marry or there are no girls to marry;
(ii) because it is inexpedient for them to marry in the light of their vocation;
(iii) because they are homosexual in nature. The third reason, he thought,
could not be ruled out in the case of Jesus and if, in fact, Jesus was homosexual, this would be one more example of his identification with the 'outsider' – the lonely and the outcast.

All this was, as Canon Montefiore recognized, entirely speculative, as
indeed is almost every attempt to discover the significance of particular
aspects of the life of Jesus. But it was a serious speculation and, in the context of a paper which included an affirmation of the lecturer's belief in the
complete obedience of Jesus to his Father's will, was not by any means
unedifying.

Much more disturbing is the almost hysterical reaction to the newspaper
reports of Canon Montefiore's paper. Without waiting to read the lecture
in full, churchmen denounced its author in most violent terms and suggested that he was unfitted for office in the church. Apart from the lack of
integrity which lies behind statements made on the basis of inadequate
information, the attack on Canon Montefiore must be deplored on two
other important grounds.

First, the search for the significance of the life of Jesus should not be
inhibited by the presuppositions of those who mistakenly believe that they
have already discovered all the answers. Scholars and others must be
encouraged to pursue the search and their discoveries and speculations
considered strictly on their merits. In no other way can the Holy Spirit be
left free to guide men into the truth about Jesus and themselves.

Second, it is quite mistaken to assume that homosexuality is sinful and

*The lecture by Canon Montefiore was published, along with the other papers from the
Modern Churchmen's Conference, by SCM Press under the title Christ for Us Today,
edited by Norman Pittenger, pp. 101–16.

that it is therefore impossible for Jesus to have been homosexual in nature. There may be good theological grounds for suggesting that the perfect human nature of Jesus required him to be as the majority of other men are, but there is nothing in present knowledge of the homosexual condition to give the slightest assistance to those who would like to assert that *all* homosexuals are depraved. If, as Canon Montefiore suggests, there is some evidence that Jesus may have been homosexual, this calls for serious consideration and an assessment of the significance, if any, of such a possibility.

The difficulty is that Canon Montefiore has challenged the views of many Christians in some very sensitive areas of their belief, so he must not be surprised if he becomes unpopular in certain quarters. It is to be hoped that he will regard the unpleasant side of the present outcry simply as an occupational hazard, and continue the task of helping the present generation of Christians to discover the significance of Jesus for today. This is, after all, what theologians are for.

Letters to the Editor

From the Rev. Dr Erik Routley, Edinburgh

I am worried by your report of Canon Montefiore's suggestion that Jesus may have been a homosexual. Not having seen the full text of Canon Montefiore's paper (and, by the way, agreeing wholly with what you say about the irrational expressions of horror which the out-of-context quotation provoked here and there), I am yet unsure whether I am quarrelling with you or with him.

I venture no judgment at the moment on homosexuality (except perhaps to say that I don't see how a perfect being can be homosexual), and I would not be so impertinent as to question even Mr Montefiore's wisdom in including such a conjecture in a paper written for a Christian audience. The one point that worries me stiff is the argument that if in fact Jesus was homosexual, this would be one more example of his identification with the 'outsider – the lonely and the outcast'.

In what sense did Jesus 'identify himself with' the outcast? I understand from the gospels that he healed the sick and made the mad creatures sane; I understand that he went to dine with Zacchaeus and changed Zacchaeus's life for him; I understand that he spoke quietly and rationally to the woman taken in adultery and told her to go and 'sin no more'; I understand that he said to a certain lame man both 'rise up and walk' and also 'sin no more'. In fact, I understand that whenever he met somebody who for one reason or another was 'outcast' he changed their lives; when he had done with them they were in a position to diagnose and, if they really wished, to get rid of their 'outcast-ness'. And I interpret this as Scripture's testimony that Jesus did this every time by bringing people face to face with God the Father, and removing their central conviction that he was their enemy. 'Sin' I take to be basically the conviction that the author of all being dislikes you and therefore does not care for you. Every miracle of our Lord's, in my view, was a miracle because it removed that from somebody's life and therefore set him free. Sometimes we know many details: at other times (as in the case of Mary of Magdala) we know nothing but the result.

Very well. Then, if a homosexual is an outcast – as he still is in our society, and as I agree he should not be – what would an encounter between him and Jesus achieve? It would achieve the conviction in the homosexual that he was not disqualified by his homosexuality from enjoying the privileges and meeting the demands of life 'in the kingdom', any more than a sick person is disqualified by his sickness or a tax-gatherer by his tax-gathering.

But, you will say, sickness was removed, according to the gospels. I would answer – were there no occasions when Jesus admitted a person to the freedom of the kingdom without removing his sickness? I would answer – it was never only the sickness that needed to be removed (otherwise why, so often, the demand for, or recognition of, faith?). I would answer, how does anybody know that Zacchaeus stopped gathering taxes? Matthew did, but did he?

If we believe that Jesus, encountering a homosexual, would work the work of grace in him, our belief must have one of two corollaries: either (if we say homosexuality is as much a bar to the 'kingdom' as the unregenerate selfishness of Zacchaeus) the homosexual became heterosexual: or (if we believe that homosexuality is a condition without moral associations, like being red-haired or having a squint) the homosexual remained homosexual but was 'set free' in his Father's house by grace.

So far as I can see, it makes not the least difference if we claim that Christ may have been homosexual. On balance it is better to withdraw the claim until we can be sure that a perfect being could be so. It is as misleading to try to claim positive advantages for Christ in being homosexual as to claim (and this claim is too often advanced nowadays by implication) that there are advantages in the church's being shabby because shabbiness is the traditional aspect of a servant (test that by asking whether the image suggested by 'servant' is that of a head waiter). Therefore I think that either Mr Montefiore or your interpretation of him is being too humanistic and unnecessarily confusing in its exposition of the divine compassion.

From Mr L. J. Leppard, Rudgwick, Sussex, President, Stock Exchange Christian Association

You say that 'it is mistaken to assume that homosexuality is sinful'. If that is so, how can the following facts be explained?

1. It was because of this practice that Sodom and Gomorrah were destroyed.
2. In Leviticus 20.13 it is stated to be an abomination for which the penalty is death.
3. In the first epistle of St John we are told that 'sin is transgression of the law'.

Jesus, himself, taught that the whole law would remain in force for all time and condemned anyone who taught otherwise (Matt. 5.18–19). Surely it is clear from this that whatever we may think about it God regards it as sin. Are we not in danger of forgetting that the law was given for our good and unless these standards are upheld our society will suffer corruption?

From Timothy Beaumont

Your leader on Canon Montefiore's suggestion leads me to suggest that it may have even more foundation than he seems to have given it, although I have only read the newspaper reports of his paper.

In *One in Twenty* by Bryan Magee – a study of homosexuality in men and women – the author suggests that human beings cover the whole range between the small proportion of men who are exclusively heterosexual, through the large majority who are to some degree bisexual, through to a small minority of completely heterosexual women. He goes on to say 'quite a large proportion of the human race does regard bisexuality as the norm. It may be deeply taboo in the Christian countries, but these account for only a minority of people – in the Muslim countries, for instance, it seems to be accepted as commonplace. Perhaps bisexuality is the norm, and always has been. If this is so it means that heterosexuals are virtually all inhibiting some homosexual responses. This is perfectly credible, and would be accounted for by the conditioning to which we are so heavily subjected.'

This does seem to be very credible, and if it is true it would be no surprise to find that representative or perfect man representing the whole human race was bisexual.

So much on the theoretical plane. On the practical plane it is a matter of common observation that many of the best pastors, schoolmasters or youth leaders have strong feminine characteristics. It would not, therefore, be surprising to find that the Great Pastor was the same.

I think that if only we could get away from the idea that when we are talking about homosexuality we are talking about sexual expression instead of psychological make-up, and if we could, as you suggest in your leader, stop inhibiting our thoughts by accepting certain presuppositions which may not stand up to examination, we would find this suggestion attractive.

From Mr D. F. A. Ray, Chester

Mr L. J. Leppard, who emphasizes the sinfulness of homosexuality by biblical quotation, would do well to go further and notice another sin for which death is the penalty. In Ezekiel 18. 10f. we read: 'If he . . . lends at interest, and takes increase, shall he then live? . . . he shall surely die.'

The members of the Stock Exchange Christian Association should be in a good position to see whether these standards too are upheld, to avoid 'corrupting our society'. Matt. 5.20 makes it clear that high standards are demanded of the Christian.

From Mr Edward Quinn, Clifford, Yorks

There is no need to bring in dogmatic considerations or the implications of being 'perfect man' to refute Canon Montefiore's suggestion. Even in its very negative form and as a mere hypothesis there is not a shred of evidence to suggest that Jesus might have been homosexual. If a reason is required for his not marrying, there is ample evidence in the gospels (even allowing for a late awakening of the 'messianic consciousness') of the second given by the Canon: it was inexpedient in the light of his vocation.

A public speaker must expect a learned paper to be selectively treated even by the most responsible newspapers: he must therefore consider the impact of certain expressions on a wider public and, as a Christian theologian, avoid giving scandal to the weaker brethren by statements that cannot really be taken seriously by the more enlightened.

From Mr John W. Cotton, London, N

Timothy Beaumont's letter in response to the controversy over Canon Montefiore's recent suggestion that Jesus may have been 'a homosexual' has raised the argument from the ideological, dogmatic level to the empirical. The argument might never have arisen had Canon Montefiore shown himself better acquainted with current scientific literature on the question of homosexuality. The term 'a homosexual' is normally used in our society to refer to a person (generally male – corresponding females tend to be called 'Lesbians') who engages in physical intimacy, or is strongly tempted to do so, with a fellow member of his gender, such intimacy involving stimulation of his reproductive organs.

Kinsey's statistical surveys in the USA, however, have shown that such people are not of a different kind altogether from the rest of the adult population; rather, they are to be found at one end of a scale representing a wide range of experience and behaviour, with the entirely heterosexual at the other end. It is, as Mr Beaumont points out, powerful social conventions or taboos in so-called Christian countries, which give 'homosexuals' the feeling that they are different, socially outcast, 'queer'. According to Kinsey, however, 'homosexual' is an adjective that can be applied to most people.

It would clarify our thinking and, I believe, lead to greater acceptance and understanding of people with different characteristics from ourselves, if we stopped this loose talk about 'homosexuals'. Instead, we need to recognize two polarities in the field of human sexuality: the biological male/female polarity and the masculine/feminine, which is cultural and psychological. The polarities are no doubt hard to separate, but it remains true nonetheless that 'male' and 'masculine' are by no means synonymous terms.

Those who are worried about preserving for Jesus the status of a 'perfect being', need to ask themselves what they mean by 'perfect'. Are they perhaps wanting their image of Jesus to conform to some ideal man of their own, someone who represents the qualities most admired by their social group? If so, they are clearly not very interested in the question of what Jesus was really like – a question you cannot begin to ask seriously unless you abandon all dogmatic standpoints. They may, however, be acquainted with ancient Greek and know that the original idea behind the word 'perfect' is that of *completeness*. In speaking of Jesus as perfect man, early Christian writers were in the main asserting that he was completely human, whatever they might say about him also being divine. In other words, not half-man, half-God.

If so, Jesus must necessarily have been limited, unless biologically speaking he was a very rare freak, to being male. I doubt, personally, in view of certain sayings attributed to him, if he was exclusively attracted by fellow males. But I find it hard to account for his tremendous influence on the history of our species if his personality was not 'well-rounded' with what, in *our* contemporary culture, we would call feminine as well as masculine traits.

From Mr Francis Absalom, Ongar, Essex
Surely two points stand out in the continuing debate about Canon Montefiore's remarks. The first, as noted by Mr Quinn, is the sheer impossibility of knowing the truth of the matter one way or the other. This goes for other opinions about what Christ was really like: primitive communist, lonely, muddled, violent, to list only a few. It follows, therefore, that notions of this sort are just speculation, and related more to their authors' personal concerns and interests than to any real evidence of

Christ's character. In this connection one might adapt an aphorism deriving from Karl Popper and suggest that sufficient conflicting material can be found in the gospels to support almost any hypothesis one cares to put forward.

My own theory is that Christ was an early flower child and LSD experimenter – after all, he led an unsettled life; he took frequent 'trips' (where the gospel says 'journey' this is a subtle ambiguity intended for initiates, who appreciated that the plane was psychological; only Pharisees and Old Christians were fooled into thinking that it was geographical); he enjoyed spiritual experiences subsequent to group activities which might have been primitive love-ins (in this connection the idea of *agapé* is highly significant); and he was always making remarks about lilies of the field and so on. Finally, much religious art makes him look like Maharishi Mahesh Yogi. What more evidence is necessary?

RELIGION!

I find the Revd E. J. Edmundson's protest about footballers kissing each other very amusing, particularly in view of the fact that the Archbishop of Canterbury recently kissed in public both His Holiness the Pope and His Beatitude the Patriarch of the Rumanian Orthodox Church.

I wonder if Mr Edmundson lodged a similar protest on those occasions? – *Letter in 'Ipswich Evening Star'*.

Corridors of Compromise 8

A front-page article published in March 1968

There is no point in recounting the horror story of the new Immigrants Act. The facts are well known, the government's actions have been deplored by almost every responsible organ of opinion in the country, and the passing of the Bill must inevitably go down as one of the most shameful actions in British history. The only course now open is to work ceaselessly for the repealing of the Act.

This raises immediately the question of political allegiance, and brings an acute problem to the many people who once believed that the Labour Party stood for social justice and was, in a special way, on the side of the underprivileged. Is the Labour Party any longer credible as a political expression of the ideal of brotherhood, or is it just the instrument of a certain section of society whose sole concern is to improve their own economic status?

If the 1968 Immigrants Act were an isolated, albeit disastrous, lapse on the part of a government which had a fine record of concern for social righteousness, it might be possible to light upon a few crumbs of comfort and discover somewhere grounds for reassurance. But this is not the case. Recent events provide emphatic confirmation of a long-standing fear that Mr Wilson and his colleagues are motivated less by moral principle than by fear of losing power. At least this truth is hidden no longer.

Since the government came into office in 1964 it has been faced with three major issues in which a clear moral principle was involved. First came the seizure of power by a rebel regime in Rhodesia and with it the distinct possibility that the four million Africans of a British colony would find themselves permanently enslaved. Had the boot been on the other foot and an African minority had threatened to subjugate a European minority, there is little doubt that an appropriate military operation would have been mounted and the virtues of equality and democracy extolled. In the event there was nothing more than diplomatic verbiage, half-hearted sanctions and an assurance to Smith that under no circumstances would force be used to remove him from power.

Equally disturbing has been the government's support for American policy in Vietnam. Described by the Secretary General of the UN as 'the dirtiest war in history', millions of innocent peasants have been sacrificed on an ideological altar and the US operations have become a source of acute distress to many intelligent, sensitive and patriotic Americans. But such a distress has not driven Downing Street to dissociate Britain from American policy. On the contrary, President Johnson has been assured of British support and the Foreign Secretary evidently believes napalm to be one of the sacraments of brotherhood.

As if this were not enough to reduce any reasonably humane person to despair, there follows the deplorable tale of an immigration policy which has been frankly racialist in concept and of which the latest Act is but a logical development. Although it used brave words to denounce the immigration proposals of the last Conservative government, the present government has done nothing to redeem its promise to repeal the 1962 Commonwealth Immigration Act; on the contrary it has produced even more restrictive regulations. There seems to be neither the resolve nor the skill to deal with one of today's crucial problems, and the victims of the old British colonial policies can hardly be blamed for believing that the leopard does not change his spots.

Underlying the government's failure on these three issues has been the difficult economic situation which it inherited from its predecessor and which it has never come near to mastering. A showdown in Rhodesia must be avoided at all costs lest South Africa be implicated and Britain's trading interest irreparably damaged. President Johnson must always be humoured lest US support for sterling be withdrawn. There must not be too much accommodation of coloured immigrants lest the threadbare nature of housing and other social policies be too clearly exposed. Avoid at all costs any course of action which might have sharp repercussions on the economic position of those whose votes are needed to keep a Labour government in office. So important moral issues have been burked in the hope that political power might be retained.

It is not that the government is composed of wicked men who are contented with the situation in Rhodesia and Vietnam and who detest coloured people. Had the right solutions to these problems been easier and not involved the risk of electoral unpopularity they would doubtless have seized them gladly. The real charge against Mr Wilson and his team is that they have failed to recognize that it is not the primary function of any government to cling to power at all costs. There are occasions when moral principle must be given absolute priority and it is the task of wise leaders in a democracy to discern when these occasions arise and to accept the risks involved. Having failed over three crucial issues in the space of four years, it is apparent that the present government lacks both wisdom and courage and the time has come when it should be turned out of office, even at the extortionate price of a Conservative succession.

Wilson's Wobblers
HUGH MACPHERSON

On the night before the second reading of the Commonwealth Immigrants Bill a group of interested Labour MPS met with Mr David Ennals, the Under-Secretary at the Home Office, in a room at the House of Commons. Mr Ennals was closely identified with the anti-apartheid movement. Now he is ranked among the many poachers who have become gamekeepers in the present government. One of the MPS present asked what would happen if there were a sudden solution to the Rhodesian problem which gave power to the African majority and the white population wanted to come to Britain in hundreds of thousands. This would be very difficult for them, explained Mr Ennals. His response was greeted with what is most delicately expressed as some cynical ribaldry. And that cynicism has permeated every influential section of the country.

Two facts which seem to have been under-reported are worth putting on record. The first is that, far from Britain being an island bursting at the seams, there is a steady net loss of people from the country. In 1964 this amounted to 60,000 people; in 1965, 74,800; in 1966, 82,500. These figures would even be greater were it not for the large number of aliens who are admitted. And that is the second fact worthy of notice.

During 1967 more than 18,000 aliens were accepted for residence after four years in the UK. More than 22,500 came in during the same period for visits of twelve months or less, whilst those entering for periods in excess of twelve months with Ministry of Labour permits exceeded 23,000. In 1966 just about the same number of aliens were admitted as Commonwealth immigrants, and not much fewer in 1967. These figures do not include those who have been accepted for permanent residence after a four-year stay.

The above statistics have not yet been published in even a provisional form – and it is not hard to see why. Mr Callaghan who, having so successfully emulated Philip Snowden at the Treasury, seems intent on surpassing Henry Brooke at the Home Office, may speak all he likes about the nature of the choice of immigrant being geographical. It is in effect racial – and we are all responsible for the natural consequences of our actions. (At any rate, has he realized that if the absurd rule about having a British-born grandfather had applied to all aliens we would have been denied both the business abilities of Mr Robert Maxwell, né Jan Ludwich Hoch, and the equestrian talents of the Duke of Edinburgh?)

But the reason for the steady retreat from any semblance of principle into the soft pragmatic centre of politics mainly lies in the strength of the former Gaitskellite group in the Government. Characteristically enough there have been a few cries (though not from the inner members of the group) that Gaitskell would have taken a stand on principle. He probably would. For did he not say in a previous debate on limiting immigration, that it was 'a plain anti-Commonwealth measure in theory and a plain anti-colour measure in practice'?

But the stand which Hugh Gaitskell took does not seem to have rubbed off on the disciples who gathered round his feet on Mount Frognal in Hampstead. Indeed it may be adjudged that the Mahirishi Maresh Yogi has had as much effect on Mr Ringo Starr as Hugh Gaitskell had on his followers in this vital area of human relations.

Even the one who leant most closely on his breast, Mr Roy Jenkins, after making an excellent reputation for himself at the Home Office, was singularly lacking in fight during the Cabinet struggles. He seemed to adopt the extraordinary pose favoured by strip-tease artistes: when fully exposed, don't move. But, of course, the Sunday 'heavies' received a leak which explained that no draft bill was left at the Home Office on his departure.

Resistance in the Cabinet was carried on by George Brown and George Thomson. As for the Left wing, Mrs Castle didn't seem interested, and Anthony Greenwood continued his normal function of providing the most handsome profile in the Cabinet.

The main trouble with the soft-centre policies of the old Gaitskellite group is that they are the very stuff on which the most reactionary forces in any mixed society feed. Their great cry against the Left in the days of opposition was that politics was about power. Well, they have had it effectively since the 1966 election and the results are with us now. They have been eaten alive by the people they imagined they could persuade. It is true that politics is about power. It is also about principle. This was a resigning issue. And the shame of the present government is that not a single member of it – junior or senior – found himself at the breaking point.

Mr Harold Davies, the genial Sancho Panza of Harold Wilson, has been going the rounds of the House of Commons informing the men of the Left that poor Harold does his best to resist the pressures of the Gaitskellite group who see the present troubles as a way of finishing off the Left and finding a true centre party. The Left have responded by sending a letter through Harold Davies to the PM suggesting that he clarifies the issue by sacking Messrs Gunter, Healey and Gordon Walker for a start (although in the last case only a decent interment in the Lords is required). Then Barbara Castle, possibly Labour's greatest electoral asset after Edward Heath, should take over George Brown's function as Deputy Prime Minister, leaving Brother George to continue on his merry way at the FO.

There is, of course, not the slightest chance of Mr Wilson doing any of these things, but it would be a rather interesting situation if he did. What most radicals now gloomily await is a disastrous defeat at the polls in the next election, and a re-alignment of radical forces (with the Liberals?).

If the foregoing seems cynical it reflects the state of the political world and the view of almost everyone I have met of a radical disposition. I may even seem to have destroyed everything but the government's backbone. There, alas, God forestalled me.

Letters to the Editor

From Mr M. W. Smart, London SE

I was sorry to see *New Christian* departing from its usual standards of responsibility in political comment in your leading article of 7 March. I should be extremely surprised to find any evidence for the statement that 'the Foreign Secretary believes napalm to be one of the sacraments of brotherhood'. Nor am I at all impressed by a protest at the restrictions on the immigration of the Kenya Asians which takes no serious account of the problems faced by inner city areas in providing housing, jobs and social services for immigrants. Such protests do not deserve to be taken seriously unless they are accompanied by concrete proposals for adjusting housing lists or school places – including an indication of who is to pay or go back in the queue.

It seems infinitely hard for Christians to shake off the bad legacy of 'other-worldliness' in dealing with political problems. Either they contract out altogether or else – which is really the same – they find it easier to strike moral attitudes at no serious cost to themselves than to face the hard and prosaic work of producing solutions which take account of *all* the people involved in the situation. Not forgetting harassed working class families in Wolverhampton or Bradford (both white and coloured) who find it difficult to make any connection between the protesters' high principles and their own urgent needs.

From Lord Beaumont of Whitley, Chairman of the Liberal Party

In your admirable leader on the Immigration Act you start by saying that the only course now open is to work ceaselessly for the repealing of the Act. You finish rather illogically by saying that the time has come when the present government should be turned out of office even at the extortionate price of a Conservative succession.

I must confess that I myself thought that the actions of the Conservatives over the Immigration Bill were even more shameful than those of the government. It was their own pledges that they were being asked to go back on. Of course there were honourable exceptions – particularly in the House of Lords, the Marquesses of Hertford and Lansdowne – but the Conservative front bench did not act in such a way that we can regard it as preferable to the present government.

To resign from the Labour Party at the moment and to join no other party would be to set a very dangerous example in the present reaction against politics. May I suggest that the logical conclusion to your leader, which your connection with myself may have somewhat inhibited, would have been to suggest that people join (and work for) the Liberal Party which throughout this government has stood for so many of the humane and social standards which the Labour Government was elected to champion.

From Mr R. A. C. McClure, Oxted, Surrey

If Christianity is to be political, all the relevant facts must be faced. The chief points about immigration are as follows:

1. To pay our debts and maintain our standard of living, we must be a first-class trading nation. At present our industries and services are greatly overmanned as compared with our international competitors. Therefore we must face up to much redeployment of labour with accompanying problems of redundancy during the next decade. This is the only practical way to the growth which will make full employment sustainable.

2. It is inevitable that there will tend to be discrimination against coloured immigrants or resentment against those in employment while natives are unemployed. To take a moralizing line that this ought not to be so, is either abdicating responsibility or taking responsibility for much human misery.

3. Non-European immigrants, of different races, customs, beliefs, traditions and personality, are particularly difficult to integrate into our society.

I think that it is wrong on moral grounds to encourage the creation of abnormal conditions which will overstrain the ordinary human capacity for love, to the harm of both the subjects and objects of the failure.

Surely we have a colossal task already on our hands, and all immigration from whatever source should be stopped until we have become a properly integrated community. We can then see what fresh responsibilities we can conscientiously undertake.

From Mr A. H. Bennett, Bletchley

Mr Tatham has a point in protesting at discrimination against coloured British citizens in favour of white Europeans; not so in respect of the Irish, whether or not from the Republic. Whatever politicians may say or do, these islands are a unity, and the homeland of the Anglo-Saxon and Celtic races. Accordingly, any restrictions on the entry of the Irish would be as unjustifiable as are those imposed on Australians, New Zealanders, and Canadians. If this is 'racialism', so be it.

From Mr Michael Tatham, Bedford

Mr Bennett and Mr McClure raise a number of issues which I believe deserve a reply. I believe it is now generally accepted that there is no such entity as 'the Anglo-Saxon and Celtic races', and that in this context the word 'race' meaning a distinct human type is, at best, extremely imprecise. Equally, it is surely obvious that the British Isles are not 'the homeland of the Anglo-Saxon and Celtic races' – but merely one region among many inhabited in fairly recent times by caucasoid Indo-Europeans.

In asking for preferential treatment for white aliens from the Irish Republic and Australians and New Zealanders and Canadians – but not presumably for the aborigines, Maoris or American Indians – Mr Bennett is in fact expressing a racialist point of view. It is at least something that he appears to recognize as such himself.

Mr McClure's suggestion that all immigration from whatever source should be stopped until we have a properly integrated community is certainly quite just; the trouble is that all immigration will *not* be stopped and in this realistic context one has to become aware that the attitude of mind which uses the problems of immigration as a reason for limiting coloured immigration *only*, is the very attitude which retards integration within the community.

I am sure that racism is to some extent grounded in those deeply-seated impulses to conformity and group solidarity which produce so much coverage and self-sacrifice in national wars. The measure of its power for good or evil is exemplified by the heroism of the Vietnamese people and the racial murders of America. To suggest that at some future date all will be well – the community nicely integrated – is to evade the present and our moral responsibility for here and now. Time, as Martin Luther King wrote, is neutral; we have only the present to build on.

A few specific points:
1. Over-manning and redevelopment – issues far too complex to be dealt with briefly – but there is every reason to suppose that a purposefully used immigrant labour force could assist rather than impede development and redeployment. And if we are really so grossly over-manned we should obviously begin by refusing work permits to white and coloured *aliens*.
2. To suggest that those of us who resist racism are responsible for 'much human misery' is simply absurd. By the same fallacious reasoning Martin Luther King was responsible for his own murder and the sorrow of his wife and children. Perhaps Mr McClure will have read the very moving letter from Birmingham jail in your last issue. The responsibility for so much human misery rests with us all in so far as we condone, tolerate or actively assist those whose own inadequacy drives them to deprive others.

Finally, may I ask your readers to consider whether a Christian political opinion must really regard 'the maintenance of our standard of living as a first-class trading nation' as part of a divine plan. I had always supposed that the political implications of Christianity related rather to sharing in poverty, hardship and love – as in the best monastic traditions – than in finding topical formulas which enable us to pretend to serve two masters.

RELIGION!

To the editor,
The *Rhodesia Herald*.   15 Sept. 1966
I see that Mr Smith has declared a public holiday on 11 November in which the people of this country can 'rededicate themselves to those Christian ideals which prompted the Declaration of Independence on 11 November'.

If they are to prepare themselves adequately for such an exercise, it would be helpful to know what those 'Christian ideals' are. What are they?

(signed) **Ida Grant.**

From the *Rhodesia Herald*.   20 Sept. 1966
Mrs Ida Grant
Dear Madam,
We regret the censors would not permit publication of your letter.

The smaller white space on page 5 of our issue today refers.

Yours faithfully,

A vicar promised tonight to apologize for using the word 'wog' in his parish magazine. He said: 'I am sorry I used the word. I did not really mean it to suggest colour prejudice. What I meant to say really was "Continental gentlemen". I intend to apologize in the next issue.

'I always have a go at something during Lent – I just chose football this time. I suppose I was so harsh because I had to give up my pipe for six weeks.' – *The Times*.

Rome, Truth and Relevance   9

ROBERT NOWELL

NEWS FLASH

CHARLES DAVIS: Father Charles Davis, Professor of Theology at Heythrop College and one of the Roman Catholic Church's leading theologians, has left the church because he believes that it does not express concern for truth and concern for people. He will remain a Christian but does not intend to join any other church.

Charles Davis's decision to leave the Roman Catholic Church has come as a shattering blow to Catholics in this country. He was, after all, probably our leading theologian. Nor could he be classed among the wilder extremists of the *avant-garde* who sometimes make one wonder whether sharing the label 'Catholic' is not a simple case of semantic confusion. Although by pre-John xxiii standards he could be dubbed a radical, in the context of Vatican ii he could only be described as conciliar, representing and interpreting the mind of the church as it had discovered itself at this turning point in its history.

There is a danger that Catholics may react by closing their ranks in a defensive withdrawal and refusing to face up to the issues involved in his departure from our communion. The trouble is that the reasons he gave in his statement are all too true, and we can only begin by admitting their truth. There is an increasing number of Catholics who live 'on the fringe of the institutional church and largely ignore it'. They form what might be termed a subversive network. When it comes to pastoral advice and counselling, they rely on each other: they would never dream of approaching their parish clergy, who are regarded simply as mechanical purveyors of the sacraments. True, this underground church is not purely a lay preserve: priests are admitted, but only on the same terms as the laity, on the grounds of their human sympathy and understanding and not in virtue of their ordination.

Such a situation is extremely dangerous for a hierarchical church, but it has come into being because quite ordinary Catholics feel that they will meet with no understanding for their needs and aspirations if these should come into apparent or real conflict with the rigid system of rules and regulations widely accepted among the clergy as the necessary framework for the Christian life. (I am not, of course, suggesting that rules are unnecessary, merely that they exist in order to help people.)

Besides a lack of concern for people Charles Davis also accused the official church of a lack of concern for truth. Both shortcomings were amply evident in the debate over birth-control, when some representatives of the official church gave the impression (I hope unintentionally) that they were concerned merely to uphold the *Casti Connubii* party line and were worried neither by the question of its truth or falsity nor by the effect it had upon people's lives – further (and most damagingly) that they would quite unhesitatingly switch overnight to an equally rigid allegiance to a radically different party line.

This debate also showed a lack of honesty that is all too observable when a serious matter comes up for discussion, the suggestion first of all that no real difficulties are involved but that it is a question of personal sinfulness, followed (when this position becomes untenable) by a retreat to the desire to hush the matter up as soon as possible. Hence the lack of freedom still to be felt within the church – more by the clergy than by the laity, who are not subject to ecclesiastical penalties in the same way and who are relatively unmoved by episcopal displeasure.

Having said all this, one can still be puzzled why Charles Davis should choose to leave the church now, when things are immeasurably better than they were ten or even five years ago. The Council, in fact, could be said to have rescued the church from possibly the most dangerous crisis of its two-thousand-year history, when the gates of hell seemed on the point of prevailing by encouraging it to become more and more irrelevant to the needs and aspirations of the men and women it was founded to serve.

The answer must, I think, lie in the way in which a bad situation, tolerated as long as nothing better seemed possible, suddenly becomes completely intolerable once real hope of improvement appears, especially if this hope is temporarily frustrated. Throughout the church there has been too much dithering and inertia in putting the Council into effect. Thus monks and friars are constrained to continue conducting the most important part of their work – the communal worship of God – in Latin, even though a considerable number would prefer to use their own languages. Thus the instruction on mixed marriages perpetuated the gratuitous insult to other Christian communions whereby marriages involving a Catholic solemnized under their auspices are not recognized as valid (and as a result the Catholic involved can divorce and remarry with the official blessing of the church). Thus, to quote an example Charles Davis has used, we are told on the highest authority that a state of doubt does not exist on the question of birth control, even though doubt is rather a mild word to describe the present confusion among Catholics on this issue. Sometimes, indeed, instead of dragging its feet when moving forwards, the church seems intent on moving backwards, as with the announcement that a revised version of the Vulgate is in active preparation.

Most Catholics, however, find it possible, most of the time, to laugh off the church's absurdities. But it is more than understandable if a Catholic reaches the point when he can no longer laugh the system off and is forced instead to question its necessity. I may be wrong, but I suspect this is basically what happened in Charles Davis's case.

One day, it is to be hoped, we will be able to welcome Charles Davis back into our communion. That will be when the reforms of Vatican II have been fully put into effect and the church is more clearly recognizable as what it claims to be. Yet even then it will still have its defects: it will still be a church riddled with human imperfection and in constant need of reform, while being at the same time the spotless bride of Christ. And the institution will always be necessary. One cannot be a Christian in isolation: community and continuity are both essential for the Christian life. This is why those of us who share Charles Davis's abhorrence of the scandals that disfigure the church cannot follow him in being led on by these to question the validity of the whole institution.

Letters to the Editor

From Mr Neil Middleton, London WC

In your issue of 29 December you comment briefly on the news of Charles Davis's decision to leave the Roman Catholic communion – you remark that the thought of the Roman church without its radicals is very 'uninviting'. Not all those who might lay claim to being considered radicals feel that they must follow Davis's example – but many may well do so if some of the issues he brings to a head are not squarely faced.

A great deal has been said already, and I hope that a great deal more will be said, before this episode passes into history. Most of the comments so far have been in terms of the effect on the Roman church of a radical leader having left us, or of a great mind no longer being here. Indeed, with the Roman communion there is already a strong tendency to talk as if Charles Davis were recently dead; the past participle is frequently used! But he is very much alive and I hope that we shall see him working still as a married radical of enormous theological competence among those concerned to change the face of Christianity. With this in mind we owe it to him to look with some care at our reactions to his decision.

Many of the best comments have talked of the way in which it will be that much harder to carry through reforms within the Roman church without his help on the inside, and this is certainly true. There have been one or two examples of a total missing of points. These are perhaps most easily to be seen in the petulance and poor judgment of Father Brocard Sewell's unfortunate letter to *The Guardian*, or in the more balanced *Catholic Herald* editorial of 30 December. In the latter the editor explained that Davis had lost both '. . . his faith and also much respect by the way in which he exploited his loss'. It is on this reaction to the whole business that I should like to make what seem to me the important points for Romans and possible for other Christians too.

In his original statement to the press Charles Davis began '. . . I remain a Christian . . .', later in his *Observer* article he remarked '. . . I now look for the church in the more informal groupings of Christians, both within and without the institutional church . . .'. There was a time when, for Roman Catholics, leaving the church was equated with loss of faith, but this is surely an old, dead relic of an imperialistic past – certainly this langugage does not sound like that of a man who has lost 'his faith'. The question it does raise for us, and this I take to be the question Davis intended it to raise, is whether the Roman church *in England* can be taken seriously as a Christian institution? In order to get this question through the sense most Roman Catholics have of always being right, it has to be raised as dramatically as possible. It is this that Charles Davis has done in *publicly* proclaiming his conviction that the Roman church here has lost its right to call itself Christian. If we fail to press this question loudly, clearly and publicly now that Davis has made this opportunity for us, then all the so-called 'sympathy' that he has received is so much cant.

We Roman Catholics have to realize what we have done. A man of enormous integrity and of great theological sophistication has been compelled to leave the Roman church. If we content ourselves with merely criticizing, even sympathetically, his reasons for leaving, then we shall be guilty of yet another failure in genuine response. We must, instead, look at the church that *we* have created and ask what is wrong with an organization that can have this effect. We must also ask what sort of mental gymnastics are going to be demanded of the rest of us if we are to remain, and continue to work, in the Roman church. In immediate and practical terms we must make sure that these questions are asked, and that they are asked by all of us. Charles Davis is marrying, and this will be treated by many Roman Catholics as good reason for ignoring the questions altogether. This is a situation with which they feel themselves to be familiar, and will not want to believe that here they are faced with a different case. We must get our heads out of the clouds of incense and see that this public examination of conscience is a necessary first step towards genuinely reforming the church. We must insist that our bishops are involved in this too – not to 'decide' an issue but rather to carry out their responsibilities as representatives of the Roman church. As things stand they are the only people who can get such questioning going. Silence now will not be 'charity'; it will be gross dereliction of Christian duty. On the other hand, if the bishops should move on this, as the late Bishop Bekkers of S'Hertogenbosch moved in similar matters, then we may hope to keep men like Charles Davis in the future. The response to any such move would be terrific. We could all, conservatives and radicals alike, feel that the institutional Church is genuinely human and not just an oracle removed from the world in virtue of its supposedly God-given mandate.

Providential Dilatoriness

ROBERT NOWELL

Many Roman Catholics who have been brought up on an exaggerated interpretation of papal primacy and infallibility are at a loss now that they are left much more to their own devices in the difficult and perhaps turbulent period of transition following the Council, without a clear voice from Rome telling them precisely what they should or should not be doing and saying. Even those of the *avant-garde*, who are wondering how far they can go in the way of interpreting these twin doctrines without actually leaving the church, are concerned at an apparent lack of decisive leadership from Rome in putting the Council into effect.

The picture can, of course, easily be overdrawn. The Pope has lent the prestige of his office to the growing demand for a negotiated settlement in Vietnam. The synod of bishops will meet for the first time this autumn to provide a representative expression of collegiality in the central government of the church. There has been a slow but steady stream of documents from Rome, the latest being the setting up of the lay council and the study-commission for international social justice and development and the reform of indulgences.

But too often the impression has been given of reform waiting upon the outcome of in-fighting in the Curia, and of the Curia and the Pope himself worried and anxious at the stresses and strains inevitably set up within the Catholic Church by the difficulties of long overdue adaptation to the modern world. Too often the Pope has expressed his anxiety at some of the wilder experiments and speculations in extremely vague and general terms, so that his words are mistaken as sorely needed encouragement by the intransigent diehard minority and completely fail to affect the equally intransigent minority at the other end of the ecclesiastical spectrum, while the great majority in the middle remain puzzled and wonder what all the fuss is about.

In addition, perfectly reasonable actions too often tend to get distorted in the Vatican public relations machine. One example is the refusal to allow Professor Chadwick and Fr Lahey to examine the Vatican archives on the Malines conversations of forty-five years ago, when the archives have only just been made available to scholars up to 1878: this was made to look like a clamp-down on the whole project of ecumenical co-operation in this particular field. Another is the warning about the very extreme liturgical experiments carried out by such small groups as the Sjaloom group in the Netherlands: from some of the press reports this sounded like a general ban on celebrating the eucharist in private houses, something which has been found to be of invaluable pastoral help, to say nothing of the impression given of strong disapproval of jazz and other musical experiments in the liturgy.

Finally, when reform does come it tends to be disappointingly half-hearted. The reform of indulgences is a recent example. The first part of the document announcing this is a concise and stimulating exposition of Christian doctrine about the social aspects of sin and reparation for sin: human solidarity on the supernatural plane, in fact, working out the implications of the communion of saints and St Paul's injunction to bear one another's burdens. Then comes the tidying up of the practice of indulgences, whereas many Catholics had hoped that these relaxations of a penitential practice that has long since disappeared would go the same way as the penances they had replaced, especially since fewer and fewer Catholics seem to make use of them or take them at all seriously.

Hence all the murmurings there have been about the character of the present Pope. It does indeed seem to be his character that is responsible – particularly his ability to see and sympathize with at least six sides to any major question and his awareness of his responsibility to all Catholics, not just those who are already looking ahead from Vatican II to Vatican III.

But might not this apparent dithering at the top be providential in the church's present situation? One of the major aspects of the conciliar renewal is an attempt to reverse the process whereby power and authority in the church tended to drain away from the local churches to the centre. This could be done by the centre steadfastly throwing the responsibility for decisions back on to the local churches; but given the inertia of the present system it would need a Curia staffed with Pope Johns to achieve this. At present the decisions are still being taken by the centre, and matters still have to be referred there which could perfectly well be dealt with at a lower level (as for example the question of dispensing with the promise from the non-Catholic partner to bring the children of a mixed marriage up as Catholics), but the decisions are being taken in such a way and with enough publicity to ensure the formation of a public opinion throughout the church and to prepare local churches and individual Christians for the responsibility that will need to be theirs if the *aggiornamento* of Vatican II is to be more than an exercise in public relations.

What would be disastrous in the present situation would be a really determined Pope intent upon pushing the Council reforms through as fast as possible. This would be simply to take the centralized machinery that has grown up over the centuries and put it into reverse with the ever-present danger of this process being put into reverse in its turn. The structural reforms envisaged by Vatican II need to be built up from the bottom, with encouragement from the top; and this is what one hopes is happening, even if some of those at the top do not seem to be very contented with the way things are going.

Letters to the Editor

From Monsignor J. L. Carson, Wimbledon

Robert Nowell's remarks on 'the scandals that disfigure the church' prompt the enquiry whether the least necessary amongst these are not perhaps the writers who manage to portray an image of their church which is unrecognizable to many who are members and/or close observers of it?

Let's face it: some of those whose names appear so regularly in the religious press seem mainly bent on qualifying amongst 'the church's absurdities', to which Nowell rightly refers. As such we can leave them in the Wonderland to which they belong. But other more serious minds – and this is where the scandal comes in – seem at times so obsessed with personal difficulties and with defects, real and imaginary, in the church, that their vision becomes blurred. Not surprisingly their analysis of current problems is unconvincing and their proposed solutions are often irrelevant. Can we afford such luxuries? Jumping through the Looking Glass may be fun, but it is no substitute for taking a hard look at ourselves in the mirror. Can we have more objective criticism and more concern for the whole truth, please?

The McCabe Affair

There is sound and fury on the Roman Catholic front as one of the more important battles gets under way. Bishop Mervyn Stockwood, in a letter to *The Guardian* (16 February), describes what is happening as our 'difficulties'

– some of us are tempted to feel that this ranks as the understatement of the decade. For what is happening in the Roman Church threatens to split it down the middle. It is important to give the story of the immediate cause for battle in order to show just what is going on.

Recently Charles Davis, a well known and very careful theologian, realized that he could no longer stand the official Roman Catholic Church. He occupied an uneasy position in the establishment and felt that the only course open to him was to make a clean break and to look for the form of his Christian commitment elsewhere. Reactions to Mr Davis's position soon divided into two main kinds – there were the denigrators who talked darkly of loss of faith, of defection, or worse, and there were those who tried to see why it was that Davis had to leave the church and why they should or should not follow him.

The finest piece of work to appear in the second group was the editorial in the February issue of *New Blackfriars*. This magazine is sponsored by the Dominican Order in England and has a long tradition of fine radical writing – it was probably the only major Roman Catholic magazine to oppose Franco during the civil war. In recent years at least, although it has been officially the Order's magazine, the editor has been completely independent of any party line pressure.

Fr Herbert McCabe's February editorial took Mr Davis's point that the church is indeed corrupt:

> . . . a Cardinal selects Christmas as the occasion for supporting the murder of Vietnamese civilians; the Pope alleges that the Church is not in doubt about birthcontrol; the Congregation of Rites has just asserted (*The Times* 5 January) that a family communion celebrated in a private home and followed by a meal is a practice 'alien to the Catholic religon'.

All this, and much more, *is* corruption, and, as McCabe continued,

> We have grown accustomed to seeing the Church like this . . . We have lived with this truth so long that we have perhaps forgotten how scandalous and horrible it is: like people who live with racial discrimination and slavery.

But the point McCabe makes is that if this were *all* we could mean by the church, then clearly we should leave it as fast as our disavowals will take us – but it is not. The church is not the bishops, even less is it the Curia – indeed both have put themselves, by their failure to break out of the institutional corruption, on the very fringe of a church which largely ignores them. McCabe makes a profound and forceful case for seeing the church in non-clericalist terms: in terms of the whole People of God. But for Roman Catholics he adds the major point:

> It is because we believe that the hierarchical institutions of the Roman Catholic Church, with all their decadence, their corruption and their sheer silliness, do in fact

link us to areas of Christian truth beyond any experience, that we remain, and see our Christian lives in terms of remaining, members of this Church.

He does not make this point in any empire-building way. It is the reason why we remain Roman Catholics when so often the obvious thing seems to be to leave. It is not given as a reason for converting other Christians to the Roman Church.

In fact Fr McCabe has provided what is probably the only respectable case for both being fairly radical and for staying in the Roman Church. For this the very right-wing Dominican authorities in Rome dismissed Fr McCabe from the editorship of *New Blackfriars*, and suspended him from all his priestly functions. The only conclusion we can draw is that the church would rather not have its radical intellectuals and would prefer to see them go. It is possible for the Dominicans to ignore the great independent history of their magazine and to insist that it is merely the official organ of the Order, but to do so is simply dishonest.

Dreadful as it would have been, McCabe could have been dismissed, even silenced, for misusing the Dominican magazine for his own ends. It would also have been possible to forbid him to write and lecture without first submitting his work for very careful censorship; indeed his written work is already censored as part of the normal practice of the Order. All this would have been bad enough and a gross betrayal of the principle of free speech, but to have suspended him from saying mass and hearing confessions as well was a piece of punitive vindictiveness that was simply disgusting. The withdrawal of the suspension after only seven days indicates how serious a mistake was made.

It is of interest in this connection that the document suspending him was signed by Fr Hilary Carpenter, the English assistant to the Master General. A few years ago Carpenter occupied the position of Provincial, that is head, of the Dominican Order in England, and his reign was remarkable for producing a period of confusing retrogression in the intellectual life of the Order. It was also the period in which McCabe was ordained and in which he began to exercise his special talent for independent and forthright speaking and writing. It is not totally without significance that Carpenter did not approve of many of the ideas which were in their infancy in the Order at the time, and which owe their origin, in part, to the early work of McCabe.

However, it is clear that this is not the only reason for McCabe's present troubles. We have the spectacle of the Apostolic Delegate (Archbishop Cardinale) giving an abusive interview about the editorial to the *Catholic Herald*. We have the silence of the English hierarchy with their pretence that this is simply a matter of Dominican politics. But above all we have a Charles Davis beyond the reach of clerical wrath, and it is impossible to

believe that McCabe has not been made the scapegoat for anger which
would otherwise have been directed at Davis.

Geoffrey Moorhouse, in an excellent article summing up the position in
The Guardian (15 February), also made the very important connection
between this incident and several others. He suggested that it was not
entirely without relevance to recall the virtually enforced resignation of
Desmond Fisher from the editorship of the *Catholic Herald*, and that
similar resignations have been asked for or enforced in the Dutch papers
Nieuwe Linie and *De Bazuin*. In the case of *Nieuwe Linie* the Order concerned was the Jesuits, and the Roman centre of the Order demanded the
closure of the paper. It was only saved by being taken over by laymen.
Three Jesuits who remained on the editorial board were also asked to resign
– one did, the others left the Order. The editors of *De Bazuin*, a very radical
Dominican weekly edited from Amsterdam, have resigned or been dismissed, but the Dutch Provincial, Fr Waesberghe, has so far resisted the
closure of the paper.

Some commentators have seen all this as a concerted effort on the part
of the Roman authorities to crack down on radicalism within the church
and to restore the situation to something like its pre-conciliar days. In
some ways this may be true, but I doubt if it is an organized effort. If it
were, it is unlikely that Archbishop Cardinale would have objected to Fr
McCabe's dismissal (*The Guardian*, 17 February). Certainly no one in
Rome appears to appreciate what it is that they have done.

For once real anger has been generated, and not just in the radical belt.
Catholics of every kind are furious at the high-handedness and the injustice
of the action. A petition of considerable size is being got up, again not
specifically by radicals, demanding Fr McCabe's reinstatement. This is only
a spark on the top of a fire which will not be put down by soothing noises
from the hierarchy. Recently I wrote in these columns of the censorship
problem in the Roman Church: here you see it writ large. The Roman
Catholic Christians of this country are tired of being treated like imbeciles
or infants. If Rome, or the authorities in England, do not make amends for
this action, and that very quickly, they are likely to find that they have
totally lost the sympathy of the people they seek to lead. There will be
nothing dramatic like a mass exodus. All that will happen is that more and
more Christians will feel that their church is merely a fringe organization in
life, and is largely irrelevant. There is, of course, another aspect of this
problem: How can Roman Catholics expect to be taken seriously on the
ecumenical front if this kind of thing goes on? This is the Rome of the 'bad
old days' with a vengeance. Disclaimers from the English bishops will not
be enough, unless they quickly follow the French and Dutch bishops in

their rejection of Roman interference. And unless they take a firm stand on the issue of Fr McCabe, then we may look forward to another century of regression and conservatism.

Freedom in the Church

A front-page article

The dismissal of Father Herbert McCabe from the editorship of *New Blackfriars* has brought to head an issue which is of major importance to all churches. Of the dismissal itself it can only be said that the actions of the Master General of the Dominican Order were clearly conceived in panic and delivered in absurdity. By any kind of reckoning there was no case for suspending Father McCabe from his priestly functions, and the speedy withdrawal of the suspension is an indication of the irresponsible way in which it was first applied.

On the broader front, however, this particularly distressing incident raises the question of freedom in the church and, with it, a key theological judgment about the nature of the Christian community. Of the latter it may be said with confidence that the New Testament and the mainstream of Christian tradition sees the church as a community of love and freedom. Because the individuals who constitute the church have surrendered their lives to Christ, the corporate life of the Christian community reflects something of the quality of life which belongs to the Kingdom of God. This is not to say that the church may gaily abandon all forms of discipline. The institutional aspect of its life demands the cohesion which comes through order and control. But the discipline of the church must be nearer in spirit and application to that of the family than to that of the prison service. The Christian fellowship is a company of mature persons, and not an ecclesiastical remand home in which a group of delinquent adolescents is subject to the will of those who are presumed to be of clearer vision.

This concept of the church has, of course, been one of the fundamental points at issue between Roman and non-Roman Christians for several centuries. Protestant dismay at the impersonal authoritarianism of Rome, often barely distinguishable from that of secular dictatorships, springs from the belief that Roman policy is in many ways a denial of the gospel. The decisions of the second Vatican Council and their consequences have, however, encouraged the view that Rome is at last emerging from its medieval framework and becoming tolerant and free. This may well be true, but if the thoughtful and relatively moderate comments of a Father McCabe can be treated so savagely, it is natural to wonder what the reaction might be to more radical criticisms. And it is important to remember that Father McCabe is not an isolated case. The treatment of the editors of other Roman Catholic journals in this country and in Europe has been equally disturbing, and the dismissal or sending to remote mission stations of critical priests in North America is commonplace. The most charitable interpretation is that these are the growing pains of a great church struggling toward maturity, but it is reasonable to add that unless this church struggles much harder there may not be time to reach maturity since the world cannot be expected to take seriously an institution which is so manifestly lacking in insight.

Here it is necessary to point out that the non-Roman churches have no reason to feel smug. In Britain, Anglicans and Freechurchmen are free to criticize their churches, and some make good use of this freedom. But all too often the attitude of those in authority towards the critic is hardly different from that of the Vatican, and only lack of power prevents reprisals. Those who are dissatisfied with the present condition of the church and have courage enough to say so are considered to be irresponsible or disloyal or betrayers of the gospel. Blame for all manner of problems in the church is laid on their shoulders and, although clerics are not actually dismissed from their present posts, they are frequently left out of consideration when positions appropriate to their gifts and experience need to be filled.

The critics must not, of course, be surprised at this treatment. Few men in authority are great enough to welcome criticism with open arms, and one of the clear lessons of history is that prophets and innovators are rarely honoured during their lifetime. In any case, membership of the church is not intended to be a protection against the tensions and problems which arise from development in human society. The prophets may become martyrs but it is important that they should not feel themselves to be martyrs.

It is, however, legitimate to plead and work for a church which is able to accept criticism more graciously and use it more constructively. And it is necessary to affirm that unless the church is the kind of community in which freedom to criticize is valued and stoutly defended then the church is, as Father McCabe suggested in his editorial, quite corrupt. In this case it ought to be either reformed or abandoned.

The spiritual health of the individual Christian depends to a great extent upon his willingness to examine his life critically and to accept criticism from others. Refusal at this point is rightly seen as a symptom of a fatal disease. It would be surprising if the church as a corporate body could avoid a similar discipline. Without this there can be no future for the church. Here is the case for real concern today.

Letters to the Editor

From Mr John M. Todd, Holcombe, Bath

Would Mgr Carson give a lead to the objectivity he asks for? He refers to names 'that appear so regularly in the religious press' – some 'we can leave in the Wonderland to which they belong', others, more serious, are so obsessed with difficulties and defects that their vision is 'blurred' and their solutions 'irrelevant'. A single objective example, preferably several, would enable one to test the validity of his statements. Without this objective test, his letter can have no effect on the writers he has in mind, and will encourage the complacent to think that all those who are disquieted can be safely ignored. The only effect of the letter is divisive – it can achieve nothing else.

A glance at the pages of the Catholic press during the years 1950–60 might make Mgr Carson very wary of using the word 'irrelevant'. Some of us who became convinced that the ecumenical movement must be taken up by the church and that a liturgy in English was essential for pastoral reasons were treated in just this way at that time. As a result the Roman Catholic Church in this country was taken by surprise when Vatican II committed us all in these directions; we were without the long-term preparation which was essential for the satisfactory achievement of these changes. I suggest a reading of the Old Testament prophets and of the New Testament, not to speak of the whole of human history, will lead to the conclusion that 'crisis' is not an exceptional state!

But let's have a look at the dismal Jimmies that Mgr Carson has in mind.

From Fr Henry St John, OP, St Dominic's Priory, Carisbrooke, Isle of Wight

I would like to congratulate you on your editorial about the McCabe affair. True to its own somewhat radical presuppositions, *New Christian* has yet given its reader a balanced and fair-minded summary of what this incident involves, in its basic implications, not only for the Roman Catholic Church but for all the churches.

The same may be said, with considerably larger reservations, of Neil Middleton's article on the same subject. He says a number of things that are true, some questionable things that should be given a hearing, but it is the way he sometimes says them that alienates sympathy. For, in company with his colleagues in what he himself calls the radical belt, he writes of set purpose in an exaggerated and intemperate tone which tends to make those not already firmly on his side feel that he regards them, if not as plain dishonest, then as entirely pusillanimous.

This approach is intended to stimulate people to genuine criticism and consequent commitment, but in fact it seldom does more than provoke opposition, if only of sheer cussedness. Moreover the radical belt tend to use 'vogue' words, with a meaning different from that in common usage – one of these is 'corrupt' applied to attitudes and ideas in the church, which have been characteristic of dominating authority as opposed to that of service.

Had Fr McCabe used other phraseology than 'corrupt' and similar words to clothe the ideas he was setting out in his editorial comment, they could have been expressed as forcibly and more meaningfully, yet the public press might well have failed to see news in them, and the McCabe affair might never have blown up. It is worth noticing that in 1965, before Fr McCabe became editor, *New Blackfriars* published an article with the title 'How Corrupt is the Church?' Anyone who had read that article and the controversy that followed it, in subsequent numbers, would not have been misled by the special meaning his comment was attaching to the word. Much of what Mr Middleton and the radicals have to say is, in its deeper and more balanced implications, well worth consideration and sometimes of support. Yet there are times in his *New Christian* article when Middleton seems, as McCabe never does, however misleading his language, so to separate the institutional church from Jesus Christ that he speaks of remaining in it or leaving it as a kind of intellectual exercise, in which there is nothing of the givenness of faith, and all is human reasoning; a case to be made out. His words, however, may not fully represent the whole of his awareness.

My further purpose in this letter is to make a point which, up to now, has received scant notice in this affair. It is that this is not a situation about which the English hierarchy has had any official concern up to the present. It is a domestic affair within the Dominican Order itself. Dominicans, together with the other major Orders, are 'exempt' religious, outside the authority of the local hierarchy in all that concerns their domestic affairs; they come under the jurisdiction of the bishops only in pastoral and other matters that affect the faithful parochially.

In the McCabe affair, the removal of an editor of a Dominican journal comes, as his appointment does, under the vow of religious obedience. This is a delicate matter, different from any kind of secular appointment. No bishop would dream of interfering with it officially, since such interference would be quite beyond his authority. No blame can therefore lie on the shoulders of the hierarchy for what happened without their knowledge in an area beyond their competence.

The measures taken against Fr McCabe may well have been an error of justice, even though at times his judgment in what he wrote was at fault. The point is that what was done was done within the family, by the Dominican Order, through the Master General and his Council, whose sole action it was, whether or not unofficial views from the Curia had weight with them. If there was an error of justice, as I think there was, the error has been partially remedied already by those responsible. We may hope that the remedy may be completed generously by Fr McCabe's reinstatement and that he himself may have learned a lesson in communication, a lesson we all need in these days.

From Mgr J. L. Carson, Wimbledon

John Todd has rather surprisingly missed the point of my recent plea for better informed and more objective analyses of church problems. Those who campaigned for Catholic involvement in the ecumenical movement and the introduction of a vernacular liturgy were not generally considered irrelevant in the 1950s. They were unpopular and made many uncomfortable, precisely because their views, though contrary to traditional attitudes, were based on an acute observation of the real church. They were only too relevant, as events have shown. I would be the first to acknowledge and applaud the pioneering work of John Todd in both these fields, if only because I myself was closely associated with another Catholic pioneer of ecumenism, the Revd Charles Boyer, SJ, *in the late 1940s*, besides being one of the not very numerous priest members of the Vernacular Society of Great Britain.

To compare such well-founded pressure for reform to the mixture of shallow theology, unsupported statements, reckless accusations and plain non-facts, often served up at boiling point, which certain clerics and laymen try to pass off today as creative religious writing, is both inaccurate and misleading. The difference between the two attitudes is that the latter writers seem unable, or don't bother, to see the real facts, which were on the other hand the inspiration of the earlier reforming attitude. Todd asks for examples of the lack of accuracy and objectivity. Unfortunately they are not hard to find. Let us take Neil Middleton's article on 'The McCabe Affair' in the 23 February issue of *New Christian*.

First of all, for example, Middleton badly misquotes Father McCabe, OP (whom he is anxious to support) in a crucial passage, stating that Father McCabe wrote in the February *New Blackfriars*, 'the Pope alleges that the church is not in doubt about birth control'; whereas what Father McCabe in fact wrote was, 'the Pope alleges that the church's teaching is not in doubt about birth control'.

'The church' and the 'church's teaching' are not the same thing. The distinction apparently escaped Middleton, but at least he should not ascribe to people words they never wrote. The situation becomes even more nightmarish if we trouble to look at the Pope's actual words when we find that what he spoke about was not 'the church's teaching' (as McCabe, to use his own terminology, alleges) but 'the church's teaching authority'. Again an important distinction is passed over, though Father McCabe at least did not use direct quotation marks and so can perhaps wriggle out of what is, to say the least, an unfortunate and serious inaccuracy.

Father McCabe cannot wriggle out of his very next statement in *New Blackfriars* (which Middleton quotes with approval) namely, that 'the Congregation of Rites has just asserted (*The Times*, 5 January) that a family communion celebrated in a private home and followed by a meal is a practice "alien to the Catholic religion".' In fact the Congregation of Rites has never made any such assertion. What it did say, in a statement issued on 4 January, was that certain what are called *in inverted commas* 'family eucharistic banquets' performed on private initiative are alien to Catholic worship. The reference was to ceremonies portrayed in *Paris Match* on 17 December 1966, copies of which were displayed at the press conference at which the statement was released, a fact noted in *The Guardian* for 5 January. Lest anyone misunderstand this warning as including the increasingly widespread custom of celebrating the eucharist, with due authority, in private homes, the statement concludes: 'It must, moreover, be remembered that it is not lawful to celebrate mass in private homes, except in those cases foreseen and clearly defined by the liturgical legislation.'

In other words, the statement explicitly permits mass in private homes in certain circumstances, which is not surprising since it is signed by one of the best-known liturgical pioneers, Cardinal Lercaro of Bologna. It is clear that there is a contradiction between Father McCabe's description of the Congregation's attitude, which is endorsed by Middleton, and the objective, verifiable facts.

John Todd asks for examples: I have given a few and could give many more. I hope they may help him to understand my plea for more objectivity in current writing on the church's problems. If we don't know what they *really* are, we can never solve them.

From Mr Neil Middleton

Fr Henry St John's letter in your 9 March issue made me re-read the article I wrote for you called 'The McCabe Affair'. I am sorry if my tone seemed exaggerated and intemperate, and I am particularly sorry if it offended men like Fr Henry, who has long been one of the greatest champions of freedom within the church. My anger was due to the injustice done, and the distress caused, to Fr Herbert McCabe.

Fr Henry puts his finger on the main point – can we see Christ manifested in the institutional church? Is there a point where the corruption becomes so extreme that the institutional church is no longer a credible witness? The difficulty in questions of this kind is that 'corruption' is such a loaded word. Let us say that by it we mean a state of affairs within the church's organization, intellectual life, teaching or action, which is so removed from the life of its members in their secular societies that reconciliation of the two becomes difficult or impossible. I am well aware that this is a very imprecise definition, but many of us who use the word do so with something of this sort in mind.

It would take too long to answer Fr Henry's general point, but an illustration of the way in which the church becomes a non-credible witness is provided in the letter from Mgr Carson which you published after Fr Henry's. He seizes on my typing error in order to make what he regards as a serious distinction between the church and the church's teaching, or the church's teaching authority. It is here that the ordinary layman not blessed with a seminary education runs into trouble. Most of us feel that if the church's teaching, or its teaching authority, is not in doubt then to assert that the church *is*, or may be, is to wander into Lewis Carroll country. We are the church (according to many theologians), what we teach is certain, but *we* are doubtful! There may be a world in which it is regarded as moral and not corrupt to teach with certainty what you feel may be in doubt, but it is a world which we cannot reconcile with our secular society. If Mgr Carson really wants to push this distinction, then he simply underlines the point that the church is corrupt.

It is unclear just how wrong Fr McCabe and I were over the question of the 'family eucharistic banquets'; it still does not sound to me as if there is any major difference between Fr McCabe's descriptions and what appears to have been condemned. But even if we were totally wrong about this, several other very different instances of corruption were listed. Why, if Mgr Carson is serious in wanting to refute Fr McCabe, does he not also deal with these?

From Mr John M. Todd

I asked for examples of the 'blurred' visions and 'irrelevant' solutions of those whose names are alleged by Mgr Carson to appear so frequently in the Roman Catholic press. His three examples of careless writing from Fr McCabe and Neil Middleton do not answer very well. Fr McCabe's editorial was very relevant to our problems in the church today. It is significant that no one in authority has yet discussed the central issues raised in it – let alone attended to the continuing argument from twelve months and more back. Careless writing is to be deplored, but castigation of it, and a general indictment of 'irrelevance', is an unworthy way of avoiding discussion of the issues raised.

'Irrelevance' was indeed a charge levelled in this country in the forties and fifties against those who recommended policies now official. 'Lunatic fringe' was a favourite term of approbation. The Vernacular Society, with its minute membership, was dismissed almost without exception by those in authority here with the pained smile reserved for people wanting to alter tradition, crying for the moon.

I deeply regret the generally thoughtless campaign being mounted against the younger writers. They do generate a good deal of heat in order to try to draw attention to problems which, though well-lit, tend to be ignored. But that is common form. Why not look at what they say and reply to it? Correction of careless statements is not an adequate reply.

I would add one word on the birth control issue. It would not be difficult to make out a strong and carefully argued case for saying that 'the church's teaching authority is in doubt about the methods which may be used for birth control' – not least because we are at the moment in the process of trying to re-define in a less autocratic sense what we mean by 'the church's teaching authority' in matters of morals, and because in this age man is trying to understand better the nature of personal relations, and in particular the personal and sexual relationship of marriage.

From June Hurford, Peterborough

Your excellent editorial of February 23 drew a parallel between the spiritual health of the individual Christian and the church; and the self-knowledge that is so necessary to the person and the institution. Perhaps one could go further and say that by reason of our pride it is first necessary that we are brought to our knees to cry 'My God, my God, why hast thou forsaken me?' before a renewal of faith is possible.

For the Catholic Church it *does* mean a renewal of faith. It means a paring away of all that which has grown up within the church, layer upon layer of it, which conceals the essential and simple truth the 'I and Thou' of Christian living.

The unyielding spiritual imperialism of Catholicism restricts individual thought and conscience to such an extent that those who remain within simply because they feel – so they tell me – that they 'have a job of work to do' must be in a state of perpetual inner conflict. They would say, perhaps, that it is easier to step outside the church in search of freedom as I, a former Catholic and now an Anglican, have done. But in the freedom I have been given I have begun to know the meaning of faith.

Whatever one's allegiance, the conflict and the acceptance must at some point be personal, if faith is to mean anything at all, and from this point we 'grow'. The question is, is it possible to go on 'growing' in the Catholic Church, where rules of life, and thought, are so dogmatic? Or are there better ways?

From Mr Dennis Northfield, Cambridge

Is not the flood of moral indignation over the case of Fr McCabe somewhat overdone? Surely even a cursory knowledge of the history of the Roman Church during the last two centuries would suffice to mitigate it. The marvel is that a growing number of people, including many laymen, are beginning to claim that freedom of conscience which that church has never granted, either implicitly or overtly. The great mass of dogma which has been proclaimed *de fide* since Trent must now be thought out afresh, and a new Reformation inaugurated, the course of which must necessarily be painful, even agonizing. We outsiders must honour the pioneers, not forgetting their precursors, the Modernists of half a century ago. As one who has found it necessary to abandon not a few beliefs firmly held in youth, I would advocate prayerful compassion for all such, whether or not they find themselves compelled to abandon the church of their upbringing. Perhaps for all of us the time for a true Reformation is short, but at least a start has been made, and, miracle of miracles, we are beginning to love one another.

The Church and the Churches
CHARLES DAVIS

In dicussing the church, much confusion is caused by the failure to distinguish two different kinds of statement. There are, first, theological statements about the church as the community of Christ: that community which is the body of Christ and the fellowship of the Holy Spirit, a community not devised by men but gathered by God through the Lord Jesus by the power of the Spirit. These theological statements are grounded upon the teaching of the New Testament; they are put forward as interpretations of God's Word made known in Christ; the criteria for judging their truth or falsity are theological criteria.

By all this I do not mean that theological statements refer to the church only as an invisible, spiritual community. On the contrary, the New Testament makes it clear that the community of Christ's disciples is a social reality visibly present in the world. But theological statements are those that formulate what is permanent and essential to the church as the community of Christ, setting forth its mysterious nature as built upon the risen Christ by the action of the Spirit, and that do this through a believing reflection upon the revealed Word of God.

The second kind of statement about the church or, as I should say here, the churches, is sociological. Sociological statements refer to the churches insofar as they are social institutions subject to empirical investigation according to principles and methods of sociology. The criteria for judging the truth or falsity of such statements are the criteria of empirical verification as practised by sociologists.

It seems to me that much present discussion about the church does not rise intellectually above the level of the pious uncritical use of the Bible; indeed, some talk about the church is about as intellectually respectable as the biblical interpretations of the Jehovah's Witnesses. What we need is a detached, rigorously conducted sociological investigation, so that we can perceive the actual social reality and social function of the present Christian churches without illusion or pious rationalization. We have next to evaluate that reality in the light of a doctrine of the church, formulated with theological rigour and ecumenical impartiality. Then perhaps we might achieve some advance in understanding and avoid both outbursts of masochistic self-criticism and defensive rationalizations of the *status quo*.

While most of this work remains to be done, it is necessary to act upon provisional conclusions. My own assessment of the present situation of the church of Christ includes these points:

First, it is ecclesiastical fundamentalism, the parallel here to biblical fundamentalism, to identify the social reality of the church of Christ with any of the existing Christian denominations or even with all of them put together. As a social reality the church of Christ is not primarily a society or group of societies; it is primarily a movement within the human community, uniting men by adherence to a common set of meanings and values and in action based upon those meanings and values. Its fundamental social form is not that of a clearly defined social group with a determinate membership, but that of a movement of thought and action where no clear boundaries can be drawn between those who do and those who do not belong to the community of meaning and action; there are many varieties of participation.

The Christian church as a movement within the human community does form more precisely defined social groups, such as the present denominations. But in relation to the church of Christ these are secondary social formations, derived from and dependent upon its fundamental communal existence as a movement. They never succeed in embracing or institutionalizing the total social reality of the Christian church. They are transitory and take their structural forms from the surrounding culture. They should come and go, but unfortunately, with the inertia of social institutions here increased by religious conservatism, they remain well beyond their useful span of life. However, to hold, for example, that the threefold ministry of bishop, priest and deacon is *the* Christian ministry for all ages is the equivalent in ecclesiology to maintaining that the world was created in six days – indeed, it has far less biblical warrant.

Second, since the present Christian denominations are all more or less obsolete, derived from a past historical situation and redolent of a past culture, it has become increasingly difficult for the Christian movement, namely the social reality of Christ's church, to find embodiment and expression in them. Hence they have undergone a gradual secularization. By this, I mean they have to a greater and greater extent become merely natural, human groupings, Christian in name but not in substance, manifestations of ordinary human togetherness, following the usual social patterns of race and class. Their ethos does not rise above that of the surrounding culture; they merely supply for some what the country club or political association provide socially for others.

Christian truth disturbs and arouses opposition; the average church congregation provides social adjustment into the world, the values and the social class of the neighbourhood. For that reason, the present denominations frequently function as anti-Christian institutions. By this I mean that their political, social and cultural impact reinforces values and activities that contradict Christian teaching and values. I do not have in mind here simply the glaring instances where the Christian churches have supported, and still do support, iniquitous political and social orders. But there are the more hidden ways in which the effect of existing denominational institutions is anti-Christian. In *The Noise of Solemn Assemblies*, Peter Berger shows how the social function of the Protestant churches in the United States is to provide a symbolic integration of the present values of American society, values such as success through competitive struggle, activism, and so on, which are not those of Christ. The churches are emphatically reinforcing social and political values alien to Christianity.

Third, while the social reality of Christ's church still largely exists within the framwork of the Christian denominations, this is becoming less and less true. The Christian movement is increasingly found in people and in groups that either have nothing to do with present church institutions or exist on their fringes with a nominal link for old times' sake. The Christian church is in fact becoming institutionally less specialized. In other words, less and less exclusively is it embodied in precisely defined Christian institutions marked off from the general social institutions. The Christian movement is more and more diffused throughout society in individuals and fluid, varied social groups.

Or look at this in another way: modern industrial society is pluralist in regard to all ultimate or religious questions, which means that there is no longer an official world-view supported by the public institutions generally and mediated to society by specialized institutions of a public nature. Even though the major Christian churches keep the trappings of their former public position and function, in reality they are institutions functioning in the private sphere of society in competition with many less exalted contenders for the adherence of people to a particular world-view.

Ultimate or religious questions, that is, questions about a comprehensive universe of meaning or total world-view, are no longer in our society the prerogative of specialized public institutions. They are matters of personal choice and are found in the variegated social life, without any firm institutional specialization, of that sphere of modern society called private, as distinct from public.

At the present time the Christian denominations have a double character. On the one hand, they are survivals of the past social form of religion, retaining the institutional set-up appropriate to their past role as specialized public religious institutions, now lingering on the periphery of the public life of modern industrial societies, providing ceremony and rhetoric rather than exercising an effective function.

On the other hand, they are the framework for some of the manifestations of newly emerging fluid non-specialized social forms. In serving as a framework for what are, in effect, radically new social forms, they are useful in helping to preserve a continuity between new and old. But they need to recognize that the new social manifestations of the Christian movement are increasingly extending beyond their institutional boundaries and that the changes that are taking place will eventually dissolve their present institutional structures or leave them behind as useless fossils.

I am now ready to answer the question why I have not become an Anglican. I begin by acknowledging, and I do so with sincere conviction, that the reality of the church of Christ, the Christian *koinonia*, is indeed found within the Anglican church and among Anglicans. But I cannot identify the Anglican church as a social institution with the church of Christ. As a social institution it is for me a human institution only partly of Christian meaning and largely determined by national and social factors. I admit that many Christians may find in the Anglican church a useful environment in which they join themselves to the reality of Christ's church and exercise their Christian mission. I cannot do so because as a social institution it is out of keeping with my social background and intellectual formation.

My social background is industrial working-class, and in England the religious affiliation corresponding to my social class is chapel, not church. Not surprisingly, then, my grandfather and my father, as a boy, were converts to the Roman church from non-conformity. My political and social convictions, or prejudices, if you like, still bear the marks of my social origins. I would not by an inverted snobbery make too much of class. After all, an intellectual like myself is always *déclassé*. I simply wish to point out that the dominant social ethos of Anglicanism is alien to me and would not correspond to my personal identity and social background.

Intellectually my formation as a theologian of the genus Roman Catholics call dogmatic, which roughly corresponds to what is more generally called systematic, was Scholastic. In other words, I was trained in a theology conceptualized through the instrumentality of metaphysics, a theology rigorously logical and highly articulated in its speculative complexity. Even though I have altered my convictions in my intellectual development, I still remain of a systematic cast of mind, seeking consistency in my thinking, desirous of proceeding according to precise method and criteria and finding satisfaction in theoretical elaboration.

But if the Anglican church is rich in biblical and historical theologians, systematic theology is poorly represented within it. More than that, I think that the systematic pattern of thought is foreign to the particular genius of Anglicanism. In Great Britain, I had more in common with theologians of the Church of Scotland than with Anglican thinkers. Intellectually I should not be at home in the Anglican church.

The final and principal reason why I could not join the Anglican church is that in leaving the Roman church, I wanted to bear witness to what I regarded as the truth in regard to the church of Christ. This was that the social reality of Christ's church as the visible and active embodiment of Christian faith, hope and love could be identified with the present denominations and that these with their obsolete structures were often hindering and destroying rather than promoting the work of Christ.

I should have falsified that witness, had I sought a haven in the Anglican church, even though I recognize that had I been an Anglican, I might have remained so and yet bore a similar witness. A change of denominational allegiance is irrelevant in the present situation. I remain a Christian of Roman Catholic background who refuses the institutional claims of that church and protests against the anti-Christian elements in its structure, attitudes and actions, but sees no reason to deny or jettison the positive elements in the tradition he has inherited.

This stand leaves me comparatively isolated as a Christian. I say, comparatively, because besides the agreement and support of my wife – a fact of great importance to myself as a person – I am in touch with a sufficient number of Christians in various parts, who are in sympathy with my position, even if with qualifications, for me to know that I am on to something true.

Anyone who pursues the truth with passion and without conscious compromise must be prepared to be alone. He has sometimes to forego, at least in part, the comfort and security of human togetherness. But the Christian community is grounded upon truth. It is founded upon that truth which can divide 'father against son and son against father, mother against daughter and daughter against her mother' (Luke 12.53). The search for Christian community should not be confused with the desire for human togetherness, with the pull this exercises upon men to conform to the tribal mythology without questioning.

I do not want to end on a negative note. I would not give the impression that nothing is to be gained by working for the reform of the existing churches. I should regard it as historically and sociologically absurd to suppose that the present institutions are to disappear without trace and entirely new social forms to arise without connection with the past. What is new will come chiefly from change and break-up of the present churches. Any genuine reform of these is, therefore, to be welcomed.

However, the question arises, 'What makes a reform genuine?' I think this question can be answered from a general perspective and then from a specifically Christian point of view.

From a general perspective a reform is genuine when it is inspired and directed by an ardent, unremitting quest for truth, a quest that constantly strives to overcome individual and group bias and to get beyond the restrictions of a single, limited viewpoint. Human authenticity depends upon a disinterested pursuit of truth. Love itself cannot avoid a narcissistic self-deception and self-seeking, unless it finds objectivity by a respect for truth. And church reform is particularly endangered by an indifference to or fear of truth, leading to a biased defence of cherished convictions and institutions.

Much that goes under the name of church renewal or of ecumenical advance is simply a bureaucratic tidying-up of ecclesiastical administration. I say this because it rests upon unexamined assumptions. The bureaucrat typically does not question the presuppositions of the system for which he is working. He takes these presuppositions for granted and, within the framework they create, he efficiently orders everything according to a rational functionality.

The ecclesiastical set-up is in many respects inefficient, and the divisions between some closely related churches are financially wasteful and harmful for public relations. Hence the ecclesiastical bureaucrats are busy introducing a more rational order into church affairs. Their work has a limited value, but it does not deserve the name of church reform, because it is not governed by a disinterested and unrestricted search for truth.

A problem becomes a problem only from a particular perspective. Many of the so-called problems worrying church people and incessantly discussed by them are only problems in the sense that things are not working in the way they are officially supposed to work. Outside the narrow presuppositions of churchmen they are not problems at all, but merely the inevitable sequel of present conditions. For example, how far is the problem of vocations a problem outside the unquestioned but questionable assumption that a numerous full-time ministry is a desideratum for Christ's church?

The general test, therefore, of a genuine reform is whether the reformers are seeking the truth without reserve even to the upsetting of established assumptions. Bureaucrats have their place, but a subordinate one, because typically they seek order and efficiency, not truth. Truth is often administratively most inconvenient.

From a specifically Christian point of view, only to a limited extent is it possible to plan a genuine reform. The reason is that the source of authentic renewal is the Holy Spirit, and the Holy Spirit is a gift. God's gift cannot be measured by human expectations. It upsets man's anticipations. It surprises and disconcerts. Whether we consider biblical history or the history of the church, we find that the achievements of genuine reform has never been neatly according to human planning. Reform has been brought about at unexpected times and places and by unexpected persons. Typically, too, it has come out of seeming disaster. The central act of renewal for the human race is the death of its Saviour – a fact that fails to disconcert only because it is now so familiar.

A Christian, then, who is working for renewal, has to be open to the unexpected form of God's gift. He has to be prepared to see his best-laid plans shattered and for reform eventually to come through the destruction of all he has worked for. He has to be ready to see the hand of God in the most unlikely places and people. God will not allow us to claim his gifts as our own achievement. But if the experience of genuine renewal is always humbling, it is because the gift we receive is transcendent. We are humbled in order to be exalted.

Include Me Out!

10

TREVOR BEESON

A discussion of Colin Morris, Include Me Out!, *Epworth Press, published in March 1968*

Colin Morris, President of the United Church of Zambia and a close friend of Kenneth Kaunda, is a very remarkable man and he has just written a very remarkable book. It came into the office unheralded and outrageously close to its actual publication day; a modest offering of 99 pages with a pleasant picture of its author on the front cover. Having now read the book a couple of times, or rather been possessed by it, I can do no other than demand that review space be found in our first available issue so that readers of *New Christian* can obtain a copy before the first edition is sold out.

This is undoubtedly the most significant book to have appeared since *Honest to God* and, in many ways, it is I believe more important than *Honest to God*. Sub-titled 'Confessions of an Ecclesiastical Coward', the book was provoked by the death through hunger of a Zambian whose body was found a few yards from Colin Morris's front door. He had seen emaciated bodies before, but in this particular death he saw, as in a vision, the utter futility of virtually every aspect of the contemporary church's life: 'There is barely a single one of those great questions at present convulsing the church that is worth fighting over. So I shall capitulate without a struggle.'

But he certainly does not capitulate quietly. There follows the most devastating examination of the church's life, and as scathing a denunciation of its corruption as can be found anywhere outside the Old Testament. There is in fact a markedly prophetic feeling about the whole book; in its startling epigrams and passages of pure poetry. Unless the Christian community bends all its efforts in the direction of the world's 'little people' it becomes obscene.

Of the current Anglican/Methodist conversations, he says, 'Either side can buy my vote for a quid's donation to Oxfam'. Much theological writing he believes to be 'a highly elaborate conspiracy against that little man with the shrunken belly and his skeletal brethren', and he adds, 'I honestly believe we can get by with a lot less theology provided the little we need is all used up.'

Turning to worship, he complains not so much about the liturgical forms as about the spirit and attitudes which inform too much worship – if Christians were spending themselves in compassionate action, worship would have an air more of desperation than formality – and goes on: 'All the architectural glories of Christendom are not worth the life of a single child.' Prayer he sees not as talking to a God who stands by the hungry man, but as the total response to the God who is materialized in the hungry man.

Is all this but a destructive and negative approach to the church and the Christian tradition? I think not. Beneath all the fiery denunciation there is a glowing Christian charity and a desperate concern for humanity in all its strengths and weaknesses. I find here not the death of theology, but its rebirth; not the death of worship and prayer, but the recovery of true devotion; not the end of the church, but the way to its resurrection. For this I can only be grateful.

Is Colin Morris a Nazirite?

KENNETH SLACK

There was nothing for it after reading the *New Christian* of 7 April but to make a hot-foot detour to Foyles *en route* to the editorial board to get hold of *Include Me Out!* According to Trevor Beeson it was 'in many ways more important than *Honest to God*'. Colin Morris's bombshell had not yet arrived on the Charing Cross Road. Work taking me Westminsterwards after the board, I tried the bookshop shrewdly attached to the west wall of the Abbey. With wise prudence they were not stocking dynamite in that proximity. However, I got hold of it in a day or two, and feel warm gratitude to the editor for drawing our attention to this superb piece of Christian pamphleteering.

And yet . . . and yet . . . as the weeks have gone by I have found myself worried about this book. Well, you may say, what in heaven's name did I expect to be? Wasn't the whole searing purpose of Colin Morris to make complacent ecclesiastics like me unable to sleep in our beds at night? Wasn't this a twentieth-century Amos stamping in, with Zambia as his Tekoa, with a word of the Lord that would shatter the irrelevant hypo-crisies of the shrine and the cruel injustices of a well-fed society?

Certainly; and I do not relish seeming to play Amaziah to Colin Morris's Amos. But my worry is not that he disturbs me profoundly (although I must admit that he may be disturbing me more than my conscious mind is ready to face); my fear is that we may make enthusiastic verbal response to his superbly written book, but that this response is bound to be only with the mind and not with the will. Nothing could be more hateful to Colin Morris. His whole message is that it is in *doing* the truth that we shall know it, and that obedience to present insight regarding our duty to our neigh-bour is worth endless tomes of intellectual reflection. But I think he has brought it on himself. His whole argument seems to me vitiated by that nostalgia for a less complex world which has always tempted the earnest Christian.

He quotes Lenny Bruce, 'I know in my heart, by pure logic, that any man who claims to be a leader of the church is a hustler if he has two suits in a world in which most people have none'. Then Colin Morris adds, 'Anyone in the house care to argue?' I boldly say 'Yes' to that challenge. When he goes on, 'Can we see that what he was describing is a greater obscenity than all the filth that poured from his mouth?' I say 'No' as firmly. Is it really an *obscenity* for a Christian leader to own two suits? For, say, William Temple, who, unless he did his Lakeland walking in episcopal gaiters, must have had a couple at least? For Colin Morris? Has he really only one suit? Was Jesus a hustler with his seamless robe when Lazarus was in rags?

Now what *would* be obscene, if we must use this somewhat imprecise word, in such a context, would be if a Christian with two suits were cheek by jowl in the same situation with a naked man and refused to part with one. Possibly Colin Morris would say that if we had enough imagination we would see that to be our real situation today. Our 'one world' has brought us into a neighbour relationship with our needy brother across the globe. I agree as to the relationship; but is it capable of solution in such individualistic terms? There must be a costly individual Christian response to human need, but there is great danger in believing that individual action can deal with world hunger. It is the constant problem of the relief agencies to secure support without implying that voluntary action can do more than

show that the problem can be tackled. Only massive political action can
finally cope.

Colin Morris's nostalgia for simplicity appears particularly strongly in relation to the church. Here he is a modern Nazirite. The Nazirite, it will be recalled, did not drink wine because he believed that the religious man must be a nomad. He must not settle anywhere long enough for the vine to mature. God was only the God of the desert, not of the land flowing with milk and honey. Colin Morris is his blood brother.

He writes, 'It would be silly to suggest that any continuing form of human co-operation can get along without a structure of some kind . . . But when that organization is the church, she ought never to forget the judgment implied in the need for a structure. It is a material sign of our lack of faith, our reliance upon the principles of administration and good business instead of looking solely to Jesus to keep our heads above water.' It appears that God can be the God of total uncomplication, but when serving him in his little ones caught, say, in a famine in India, or a tidal wave in Chile, or an earthquake in Yugoslavia, involves the churches in 'administration and good business' in terms of offices, cables, telephone appeals for supplies, well-designed appeal publicity, and all the rest, we have somehow stopped 'looking solely to Jesus'. The plain fact is that if the church is to be relevant to the world of today it has often to be complex in its structure and administration, and not to pine for the simpler day when a Christian could, St Martin-like, divide his cloak and give half to a beggar.

Again, Colin Morris makes a slashing attack on the complexities of the theologians, and the tentative nature of their work in such a volume as *Soundings*. He reasonably asks how the wayfaring Christian is to cope with life whilst the perplexities of doubt are resolved. I warm a great deal to his general line; but is he fair to the theologians? Barth may forbiddingly have piled up volume upon volume, but did any man do more to inspire the Confessing Church in its heroic witness in Nazi Germany? Didn't the inspiration of Dietrich Bonhoeffer, which is writ large in all the chapters of *Include Me Out!*, come from a most profound hammering out of a Christian faith which is intellectually honest in the modern world? A prophet like Colin Morris is more indebted to the theologians than he admits. Moreover, when he himself tackles – as he does courageously and profoundly in his sixth chapter – the issue of prayer today, he becomes, wholly understandably, much more difficult to read. Even a simple sentence like 'The test of truly secular prayer is the willingness to abandon any address to an invisible Third Party', makes us ask whether the whole concept of a transcendent God can be so cavalierly dismissed? Is Colin Morris's simple Christian trying to 'do the truth' able to make this dismissal without a great deal of wrestling?

I have left to the end of this article one of my biggest causes for disquiet arising from reflection on this book. Starkly, chapter after chapter, the author makes us face the shrivelled body of the Zambian who dropped dead a hundred yards from his door. His only possessions were a pair of shorts, a ragged shirt and an empty Biro pen. That figure brought to mind words of D. R. Davies quoted in *New Christian* last year, 'To say that man lives by bread alone is a monstrous satanic lie; but when a man has no bread that lie becomes true.' Much of this book is a salutary commentary on that; but the author leaves me with the impression that Jesus would have done well to have yielded to the first temptation and turned stones into bread for a desperately hungry world.

In fact man lives by every word that comes out of the mouth of God, and God speaks to us in a very rich vocabulary. Among his words are compassion and justice – without them such men as that Zambian will never have their bread. I entered Calcutta in January 1944 at the tail-end of the Bengal famine. They picked up corpses by the dozen every morning from the pavements outside the well-stocked shops on Chowringee. To natural disaster had been added appalling cupidity and greed, with godowns of rice stacked to the roof as thousands died and the price went remorselessly up. There was no compassion. And there was a failure in administration, too. Decently conducted business, sound administration, wise and discerning government – these are some of the words that proceed from the mouth of God and that we have to hear if his children are not to starve today.

But another of God's words is beauty. A wise Frenchman said that civilization is the art of the superfluous. Colin Morris writes as if in a hungry world all that does not put literal bread in a man's mouth is sinful waste of effort and the earth's resources. To restore York Minster is wrong; 'For all the architectural glories of Christendom are not worth the life of a single child.' This means that Bach and Beethoven as they wrote their music when there was poverty to be tackled in Leipzig and Vienna were sinful triflers; that Shakespeare should have been redeeming the slums of Southwark instead of writing plays for the Globe there; and that Rembrandt should have abandoned palette and paintbrush and tackled the social injustices of Leyden. All creation of beauty, not just that devoted to the church, stands condemned if all that matters is bread.

I wonder if Colin Morris, after he wrote his book, found himself reflecting on that one mass-produced artefact the dead man had – the pathetic evidence that he too wanted some of the fruits of civilization and not only bread? I wonder what he had written to empty his Biro?

Faster with a Vengeance

STEPHEN WHITTLE

An interview with Merfyn Temple, a tireless crusader for the world's poor, who has worked in Zambia for the past twenty-five years as a Methodist missionary.

In many ways Merfyn Temple has the touch of traditional Methodism. A streak of restlessness, a tanned and craggy exterior bear testimony to a life lived in the open in the tradition of the travelling Wesleys; he has a highly developed social conscience; and he is much happier about smoking when away from his wife than when in her company. But he is, too, an intuitive radical and in part his restlessness derives from his search for what 'the New Testament seems to want me to do'. He claims to be no theologian. 'Colin Morris,' he says, 'articulates my thinking for me; my concern is not with the "death of God" but how to become the new form of the living church in the world.'

Born in 1919, the son of a Methodist missionary in China, Merfyn Temple was ordained in 1942 and has spent the past twenty-five years following in his father's footsteps, working as a missionary in Zambia. During the early part of his ministry there, in what was then Northern Rhodesia, he was very much the Wesleyan figure. As a travelling evangelist he toured the rural areas preaching salvation and applying what he describes as 'Bible grease'. Today, his dog-collar replaced by a turtle-neck sweater, he stumps the country preaching rural development and, as one of the few Europeans to talk of Zambia as 'our country', is a trusted friend of Kenneth Kaunda. His ability to move a meeting and his record as an untiring architect of development proved invaluable when he was released from Zambian government service to spearhead the World Poverty campaign meetings for Christian Aid. With characteristic energy he has returned to his 'evangelistic' ministry to plead the cause of the world's poor.

Temple cuts a striking figure. Tall and good looking, he combines an impressive presence with great strength of character, and his laconic manner does not conceal his deep sensitivity to the needs of others. Not least among his achievements is the ability to analyse his own actions rigorously. His life has been marked by 'reckless obedience' to his intuition.

His early success as an evangelist embarrassed him; he found preaching the gospel and piling up the conversions too easy, to the point where it became meaningless. It was doing nothing to alleviate conditions in the rural areas, nor could he even claim to be building up a solid Christian community; the drift to the towns was taking its toll. About this time, when he was feeling some doubt about the point of his ministry, he was forced by family circumstances to join the drift to the towns himself. He took a job in publishing with the United Society for Christian Literature and moved into the 'copper belt'. Here he was confronted with the colour bar.

For the first time he became aware of the nature of the society the European settlers had constructed. At first, influenced by his Methodist upbringing, he looked on the colour bar as a 'social evil, as wicked as the problem of drink'. He worked, in what he describes with some irony as 'my liberal phase', to form the multi-racial Constitutional Party. 'How the Africans must have laughed', is his comment on that episode. His work as a publisher brought him into contact with Kenneth Kaunda, at that time the much feared African nationalist leader, and Colin Morris. *Black Government* ensued, a book which was to mark a turning point. For Temple, it meant a break with comfortable liberalism and a recourse to civil disobedience. He made his stand with the African.

What decided him upon this course of action? First, he was greatly impressed by the warmth and humanity of Kaunda. But, secondly, he was staggered by the reaction of the European community to the book. A plan to place Kaunda's portrait on the cover of the book was considered subversive. Temple's secretary resigned. Having decided to make his stand, he was thoroughgoing in his execution of it. He joined the African party and campaigned for election. But his fate was sealed as far as the Europeans were concerned by his refusal, when commanded to do so by the law, to join the 'European Riot Squad' – intended to act as a European army should the Africans riot. It was a stand his friends and family found hard to understand; they regarded it as 'a concession to extreme nationalism', but they stood by him. He was expecting arrest when the Federation broke up and Zambia was born.

As the country becomes more and more independent, Temple is struck by the fact that the church in Zambia is becoming more and more dependent on the church overseas. 'The only hope for the church,' it seems to him, 'is to identify with the people in the villages as closely as possible. Only then can the church begin to talk about Christianity. The only viable pattern for the ministry in this situation is the tent-making variety.'

Temple has found the outlet for his talents at the Land Settlement Board. From the beginning he had been obsessed with the importance of

rural development and the need to 'demonstrate how a rural community 140
can live a healthy life and earn a similar income to the workers in the
towns'. At the Board he has helped to co-ordinate development at the grass
roots. He went to live in a village with the peasants to share their life of
poverty. But if Zambia is to succeed she requires the rich countries to make
available the skilled middle level personnel who can help to make it happen.
Temple's current crusade is to make sure the rich countries produce the
people. Britain has so far been slow to respond but there is now a Dutch
team at work.

I asked him how the churches could help the poor countries. His answer
was quick: 'Obviously, as a signatory to *The Haslemere Declaration*, I am
committed to a political solution, but the churches must make the eradication of poverty a much higher priority. They must examine their wealth and
their use of available resources and give. But when the money comes, it
should not go to church projects – too many church and World Council
projects are used for the training of the élite. The money should be used to
send Christians to work on governmental development projects, especially
at the middle level of technology in the rural districts.'

Next week Merfyn Temple begins a fast in Westminster Abbey, despite
the reluctance of the Dean and Chapter to afford any assistance, in an
attempt to confront the British churches with their wealth and misuse of
resources as against the needs of the world. It would be an ironic proof of
his prophetic role if his plea were to be unheeded.

Letters to the Editor

From Mr R. Graham Carter, Newcastle-upon-Tyne
I would like to thank Kenneth Slack for his
counterbalancing article on Colin Morris's
Include Me Out! Like many others, I have been
profoundly moved by Colin Morris, but I could
not see how following his ideas to the letter
could, in the modern world, efficiently present
Christ to the world. I now value Morris's book
even more; not as a blueprint for modern
Christianity, but as a much needed word of
prophecy to the modern church.

Prophecy has always over-simplified; it has
done so to make the situation so obvious that
response is necessary. An accurate description
of a need or a way forward may be so blurred
by detail that the 'hearers' are so confused that
they cannot become 'doers'. Christ himself
drew many black and white pictures where in
fact there were many shades of grey. How
many of us would dream of following to the
letter Christ's words that 'If anyone comes to
me and does not hate his own father and
mother and wife and children and brothers and
sisters, he cannot be my disciple'?

We need prophets to shock us into seeing the
situation as it is, so that we can spend less time
and energy on the less vitally important aspects
of our discipleship. Colin Morris is a true

prophet in our day. Let us respect him as such. I hope no one will spend time in pointing out details of discipleship so that they become greater than the overriding goal of loving the world with the love of Christ. Let us not be found guilty of smothering God's prophetic word.

From Eileen Mable, London N

'God speaks in a very rich vocabulary' and 'another of God's words is beauty', writes Kenneth Slack in his criticism of *Include Me Out!* True enough. But I find his reasoning strange.

For what good is beauty to a starving man, and how shall he hear the words of that 'very rich vocabulary' when he is dead for want of bread? Physical life is the first condition for hearing God's words; without that they fall upon empty air. Civilization and all the abundance of the human spirit are fine for us who have enough to eat; they are no good to a man who is starving to death. First of all, you've got to feed him – to keep him alive – and only then can he take an interest in all that will enrich and deepen his life. But until you feed him, beauty is no good to him; he cannot eat it. It is as simple as that.

Colin Morris does not condemn beauty or creativity. He asks questions about priorities and has the uncomfortable ability of enabling us to look at our concerns through a dead man's eyes. He shows us how utterly irrelevant most of them are to his problem of how to get enough food to keep himself alive.

Our Lord had a word, surely, for this situation – 'What man is there of you, whom if his son ask bread, will he give him a stone?' Stones are no good for food – not even the stones of York Minster.

From Mr R. F. Raine, Brighton

I would not quarrel with any of Kenneth Slack's criticisms of Colin Morris' *Include Me Out!* – except one. The reference to what the hungry Zambian had written with his empty Biro was a debating point, and not a good one either, in view of the fact that the vast majority of poor péople of Africa and Asia cannot write

at all. The terribly poor will collect anything, whether useful or not, in order to have something to call their very own. If Kenneth Slack sees a tramp wearing a cast-off dinner jacket, does he assume that the man has just had dinner at Buckingham Palace?

Every possible criticism can be levelled at *Include Me Out!*, but one fact for me outweighs the lot. It is moving, not in the emotional but in the action-impelling sense. My family's reading of it has led to the reorganization of our family budget, has my two teen-age children, whose cynicism was driving my wife and me to distraction, offering for work camps overseas and has injected new life into our virtually moribund church fellowship. Of how many religious books of our day can it be claimed that they shake the average layman out of his lethargy and get him *doing* something?

I agree absolutely with Trevor Beeson's estimate of the book as being 'in many ways more significant than *Honest to God*'. *Honest to God* got our church group arguing interminably. *Include Me Out!*, after almost blowing the group sky-high, has driven us out of church premises and into the local welfare centre – not to talk but to help.

From the Rev. Alan A. Brash, Director of Christian Aid

Merfyn Temple's suggestions as to how resources given for the eradication of poverty should be handled call for a reply.

He says that money 'should go not to church projects – too many church and World Council projects are used for the training of the élite. The money should be used to send Christians to work on governmental development projects . . .'

Obviously the high moral motivation of a dramatic fast in Westminster Abbey does not save one from ignorance about the actual programme of the World Council of Churches and its member churches, nor from attitudes that are essentially paternalistic. How can one of such experience suggest that the training of even a minority of people in the developing countries should be rejected in favour of sending hosts of young 'Christians' from the West?

Obviously some qualified personnel are required and are requested from outside, and the vast majority of them are for work in governmental programmes. The churches in the WCC are persistent in responding to such requests. But the essential basis of the selection of all WCC projects is an initiative and a judgment about priorities by the local churches in the countries concerned.

I share the gratitude of many people in this country to Merfyn for his challenge to our complacency, and to our fixed assumptions about our rights to affluence. But I must reject absolutely his suggestion that our contribution to developing countries could be improved by the sending of more and more personnel, and place on record the fact (which a glance at the WCC annual project list would establish) that the world-wide programme currently supported is on the whole competently assembled, efficiently administered, and substantially integrated into the governments' overall development programmes. Obviously there are exceptions, and perhaps some of them are to be found in the particular country in Africa which is Merfyn's special care. But that does not justify a sweeping generalization which is grossly untrue and could do more to dry up the springs of generosity than a protest fast will achieve in releasing them.

From Mr John S. Cox, Birmingham
At the west end of Liverpool Cathedral a monumental stone front is to be the alternative to the brick wall. Were the wall to remain it would, in the words of the chairmen of the 'Finish the Cathedral' appeal (*The Times*, 6 May), 'proclaim to all comers the failure of a generation.'

For my part it would be the stone front that would proclaim a failure. Certainly it might do all that the chairmen mentioned – tell of the glory of God, of faith and courage. That these elements are in the Christian message, I accept, but it also speaks of brokenness, of man's need and of sacrifice. And that is what the brick wall could do. Let it be the monument – not to failure of a finishing campaign but to the courage *not* to finish, the courage to find another

priority. Let us be willing to sacrifice that stone front and in its place launch an appeal to fill empty bellies, house the homeless, rehabilitate the outcast. In such a project let the cathedral finds its completion.

We are told that while people will donate for a cathedral they will not give for such other projects. If that is the case, *that* is this generation's failure. But has it been tried?

The Bishop of Liverpool has written recently in the diocesan leaflet of a 'Sermon in Stone'. A completed cathedral, it is argued, would proclaim God's glory and sovereignty. I cannot help feeling that with a brick wall the sermon would have much more impact and be theologically richer.

RELIGION!

The Church of St Michael, Paternoster Royal, which stands in the city of London and was shattered by flying bombs in 1944, is to be restored by London diocesan authorities at a cost of about £150,000.

Work will begin before the end of the year, and, when it is complete, the church will become the headquarters for the London diocesan stewardship movement. – *Church Times*.

Last year, Pope Paul abolished the ostrich plume fans which customarily followed him about. Now his court is instructed to turn up for a papal mass simply dressed, as if they were merely on their way to a society ball. – *The Guardian*.

For 140 years St James Church, Shirley, has faced west, probably because of a mistake when the foundations were laid. Now there are plans for an estimated £8,000 to be spent to turn the interior round – so that it faces east, as most churches do. – *Birmingham Evening Mail*.

Had Herod applied the funds he lavished on the erection of the Temple to the relief of poverty and distress, no doubt the local poor would have benefited. But what then would have become of all the craftsmen who earned their wages by the exercise of their various skills in the erection of that magnificent edifice? Might not they thereby have been reduced to something like poverty and distress? – *Letter in the Church Times.*

During July and August when the warm weather seems to make everyone lethargic, it might appear that Cathedral activities – apart from the regular Services – are in the doldrums too. But far from it! Plans are fermenting for the Jumble Sale in September, the purpose of which is to provide basic finances for the Bring and Buy Sale in December. – *Church News for all Denominations: Malta.*

I wish to protest against the suggestion that our harvest festivals should display pictures of starving children. I find such pictures extremely distressing. – *Letter in Methodist Recorder.*

11   Out of the Wreckage

Front-page article on the Papal Encyclical Humanae Vitae, *8 August 1968*

There is little point in adding to the comprehensive criticism which has, from almost every quarter, been levelled at the Pope's disastrous encyclical. After ten days of continuous bombardment the time has come to consider what might be saved from the wreckage.

Two inter-related matters cry out for immediate action if the Roman Catholic Church is to survive as a credible expression of the Christian gospel. First comes the cruel dilemma in which Catholics who are unable to accept the Pope's reasoning and conclusions now find themselves, and this is swiftly followed by the basic theological issue which lies at the heart of the crisis. Here it is necessary to emphasize that Christians of other communions cannot watch the salvage operation simply as disinterested spectators, for the encyclical raises issues which remain to be resolved in nearly every part of the church.

What, then, is the line of action to be pursued by the Catholic who is utterly convinced that the Pope's ruling is wrong? He has little choice. He must disregard the ruling insofar as it relates to his own conduct and do everything possible to assist the church in its task of formulating new proposals which are nearer the mind of Christ and therefore better able to serve the needs of humanity. In short, he must as an individual, and in company with his fellow Catholics, do all in his power to expose the inadequacy of the encyclical and point to a more excellent way.

This will not be easy for the layman; it may call for heartbreaking sacrifice from the priest. Some of those who have been called as 'shepherds' will accuse him of disloyalty and suggest that he is placing private opinion before the mind of the church. Others will accuse him of compromising with the worldliness of the present age and thus betraying his Lord. But none of these charges can relieve a man of the duty to follow the leadings of his own conscience. Christian obedience demands much more than strict observance of ecclesiastical regulations and, though a conscientious man

will think many times before rejecting the advice of the leaders of the
Christian community, there is in the present circumstances a clear case for opposing both the encyclical and the bishops' pastoral letters which have followed it. In taking this costly step the Catholic will be fortified by the companionship of Christians, past and present, whose consciences have led them in a similar direction. He may also find it helpful to reflect upon the fact that when Peter made a mistake about the extremely serious matter of the conditions under which Gentiles were to be admitted to the Christian fellowship, Paul 'opposed him to his face, because he stood condemned' (Galatians 3.11).

Beyond the proximate issue facing the individual Catholic there is, however, a vast theological question which has been lurking about for some time and which can be dodged no longer by those who are concerned with the continuing expression of the Christian revelation: what is the nature and character of the church? Pope Paul's apparent lack of insight and sensitivity must not become a scapegoat for a fundamental weakness in the life of the Catholic church as a whole. It is now necessary to ask by what canon of Christian community life an individual leader is entitled to make a statement lacking that *consensus fidelium* which alone can give it authenticity. Furthermore, it must be asked what fault in the church's institutional life is revealed by the fact that a single pronouncement by one man can throw the whole community into disarray.

The sad truth is, of course, that contemporary Catholicism is finding it desperately difficult to struggle free from the monarchical structure which it inherited from sixteenth-century absolutism. This is not altogether surprising. Historical trends are not easily changed and the movement from an élitist to a fully corporate society has rarely, if ever, been achieved without a bloody revolution. But this is the task which now faces the Catholic church and it remains to be seen whether violence can be avoided. Certainly the decrees of Vatican II can be regarded as no more than tentative first steps – the crucial Constitution of the Church was in relation to the need essentially conservative – and the events of the past few days have shown clearly how little they have influenced the basic structure of the church.

On the other hand, the fierce opposition to the encyclical and to the system which gave it birth is a significant pointer to the size of the forces which are massing in support of change. Similar forces are needed in every other part of the Christian church where freedom from the papal pyramid has led only to the creation of other power pyramids in which the corporate character of the Christian community is almost equally denied. This suggests again that the major theological issues of the day can only be considered adequately in an ecumenical context.

And the aim of all this? Simply that the church may become a more adequate embodiment of the gospel and a clearer sign of the kingdom. This means a society in which fear is replaced by trust, hatred by love, strife by peace, disorder by self-control; above all a society in which men and women find through the service of Christ perfect freedom and the realization of their full humanity. Seen against this background, the importance of the present salvage operation cannot be exaggerated.

An Archbishop's Verdict

On the day following the publication of the papal encyclical *Humanae Vitae* Trevor Beeson discussed the situation with Archbishop T. D. Roberts, S.J.

T.B.   After your efforts over the past four years to get the church to take a more liberal attitude to birth control, Pope Paul's encyclical must have come as a great shock to you?

T.D.R.   Yes and no. Some people thought that the Pope would not make a statement and simply allow matters to drift, but he was in fact so far committed to the making of a pronouncement that it was bound to come sooner or later and, since Pope Paul sees himself as continuing the work of Pius XII, the chances always were that he would be conservative.

T.B.   Do you think the encyclical is the work of a strong man who, in spite of the known difficulties about birth control, is determined to do the right thing as he sees it, or is it the work of a weak and uncertain man who has yielded to the pressures of the reactionary men around him?

T.D.R.   I think it is a little of both. There is no doubt that Pope Paul is surrounded by conservatives who subject him to a great deal of pressure. You will remember that an attempt was made by a group at Vatican II to commit the Council to the conservative view on birth control, and the situation was only saved by the intervention of Cardinal Leger of Montreal, who stated quite bluntly that such a standpoint will be a disaster to the church.

T.B.   Do you think that part of the genius of Pope John lay in his ability to resist these conservative pressures?

T.D.R.   Pope John had the great gift of a sense of humour. This enabled him to see things in their right proportions.

T.B.   According to the encyclical the Pope has based his decision on 'all the moral, natural and evangelic laws'. Do you know of any such laws that would rule out absolutely the use of all contraceptives?

T.D.R.   This is really the kernel of the whole thing. The basis of natural law is that it derives from the reasoning and insights of rational men and is not subject to external revelation or authority. The Pope now claims to be the arbiter of what is reasonable, and has allowed authority to invade the sphere of human conscience. This is the fundamental weakness of the position taken in the encyclical.

T.B.   Many people will wonder whether the Pope's decision is not based on the view which regards the physical elements in a sexual relationship as something intrinsically evil and not therefore to be indulged more than is absolutely necessary for the continuation of the human race.

T.D.R.   There is, I think, no doubt that much of the Pope's thinking is derived from St Augustine, who saw the sexual act as only tolerable for the sake of procreation.

T.B.   The Vatican II decree *Gaudium et Spes* stated that 'marriage is certainly not instituted solely for procreation'. Yet in his encyclical the Pope says that 'Union and procreation are inseparable'. There seems to be a contradiction here. Does this mean that the Pope is not ready to carry forward the thinking of the Council?

T.D.R.   Evidence is not wanting that Pope Paul is going behind the Council to the teaching of Pius XII and his predecessors, and to this extent I think we can conclude that he is ignoring the Council.

T.B.   The Pope seems to be particularly anxious about the abuses which might arise from contraception: he mentioned marital infidelity, lack of respect for women and government interference in private matters. Do you feel this to be a valid reason for condemning contraception?

T.D.R.   No. When God gave man free will he ran the risk that man would abuse his freedom. The value of anything is to be judged not by its abuse but by its right use. I regard many motorists as highly dangerous, but I do not think that motor cars should be banished from the roads.

T.B.   Do you think that a distinction should have been drawn between a couple who wish to avoid parental responsibility altogether and those who desire to have no more children than they can bring up with reasonable care?

T.D.R.   Yes. It is the strength of the pronouncements of the Lambeth

Conferences on birth control that it has made this distinction, and I deeply regret that Anglican thinking on this subject has not been given far more serious consideration in Rome.

T.B.   Would you want to distinguish between the pill and mechanical contraceptives?

T.D.R.   No. One aspect of the encyclical which I am very pleased about is that the Pope did not make any distinction here. I am sure that the question of contraception must be treated as a whole and without differentiation in the matter of techniques.

T.B.   How important are encyclical letters and what degree of authority is to be attached to them?

T.D.R.   The years between Vatican I and Vatican II were years of papal fundamentalism and overwhelming weight was given to the Pope's writings and utterances. Much of this remains, and rightly so, for the Pope is the captain of the ship. But the Pope must remember that he is not the owner of the ship, and that he needs the assistance of a pilot when navigating difficult waters. The disturbing factor in the present situation is that the Pope took on a pilot, i.e. the commission of experts, and then disregarded the advice offered.

T.B.   Do you think that part of the Roman Catholic Church's problem when dealing with family matters is that there is in the ranks of its decision-makers no first hand experience of marriage?

T.D.R.   Yes, this is, I believe, a serious problem, for there are so many things one can learn only by experience. It is therefore of the greatest importance that the church should consult its married members when family affairs are being discussed. Over birth control this was the first time in history, or at least recent history, that the advice of people involved in a problem was sought. It is therefore all the more disappointing that their advice was not taken.

T.B.   Many bishops in Holland and Germany have already instructed the parish priests to take a less rigorous line over birth control when hearing confessions and giving pastoral advice. Do you think they will now be obliged to reverse these instructions?

T.D.R.   I think the bishops will try to avoid divisions in the church and will therefore speak quietly and confidentially to their priests about this matter.

T.B.   What instruction would you give if you still had diocesan responsibilities in Bombay?

T.D.R.   It is always difficult to answer hypothetical questions, but I certainly would not make any public statements on the subject and would prefer to speak personally to the priests.

T.B. To what extent are Roman Catholics prepared to obey Papal instructions in this essentially personal matter?

T.D.R. It is difficult to generalize here, but you will have noticed that the size of Roman Catholic families is not significantly larger than that of other families, and we must therefore conclude that a large number of Roman Catholics follow their own conscience in this matter. There is, I think, a tacit understanding that the subject of birth control is no longer discussed between priests and people – in or out of the confessional.

T.B. Do you think that the overall effect of the encyclical will be to undermine papal authority?

T.D.R. In the long term the answer is yes. One very good thing about the letter is that it has raised in the clearest possible way the place of authority in the church and in the Christian conscience. I am sure that we cannot avoid this issue any longer and it is of the greatest importance that it should be resolved satisfactorily.

T.B. You must, however, agree that this clarity is being purchased at the price of untold human suffering. May this not be too heavy a price to pay?

T.D.R. Yes, it is a heavy price, but I do not think the decision will affect those who have been taught to think for themselves. Those who will suffer most are the people who absolutely identify the voice of the Pope and the voice of the Holy Spirit.

T.B. Will there not be additional suffering for people who decide to use contraceptives but have a bad conscience as a result of the Pope's statement?

T.D.R. Yes, and I think this may result in many thoughtful people leaving the church. It is difficult for them to contemplate the possibility of spending their lives without the sacraments, and they are faced with additional difficulties when their children ask them why they do not receive Holy Communion.

T.B. Do you think that many priests will leave the church?

T.D.R. Your guess is as good as mine. Priests have already started leaving the church because they have difficulty in equating the pastoral advice they give with the moral theology which they were taught in the seminaries. It is also difficult to find priests who are prepared to teach moral theology in the seminaries along the official lines. The Pope's decision will not make this situation any easier, and I think that those priests who are unhappy about the present place of authority in the church may now feel driven to leave its ranks.

T.B. More serious, of course, than the undermining of papal authority would be the undermining of the credibility of the church and the gospel. Is it not going to be much more difficult now to persuade non-Christians that the church is really concerned about the needs of humanity?

T.D.R.   Yes. It is also bound to deepen the gap between Catholics and
non-Catholics. I would certainly now advise most strongly against mixed
marriages. In the present circumstances a mixed marriage is virtually the
same as an attempt to bring together two separate civilizations. This is
impossibly difficult and highly dangerous, and remember, we are dealing
with the nerve centre of marriage.

T.B.   How do you see the position developing? Will the encyclical be
repudiated one day?

T.D.R.   I do not think we shall see any change of attitude during the reign
of the present Pope, but there are rumours in Rome that he might retire
fairly soon. I think the matter will resolve itself in the same way that the
Galileo crisis was resolved. Although Galileo was condemned for stating,
on the best scientific evidence, that the earth moved round the sun, this
condemnation was conveniently forgotten and the scientific view prevailed.
The birth control encyclical will not be repudiated but forgotten. The
important lesson which the church still has to learn is that the obedience
of an individual is worth little unless his intelligence enters into it; otherwise a man's obedience is no different from a dog's.

Outside the Farmyard
PRUDENCE TUNNADINE

A consultant in psycho-sexual problems to the Family Planning
Association on the nature of human sexuality.

On the papal encyclical, an English bishop of the Roman Catholic Church
said on TV, with evident sincerity, how good it was that in these materialistic
days, the Holy Father could stand firm and say, 'This is not the farmyard'.
To me – a family planning doctor concerned less with the physical tech-
nicalities than with the human personalities involved – the ruling suggested
precisely the opposite. Rome seemed to say 'Sexuality – in man as in animals
– is merely a biological necessity, designed solely for the procreation of the
species.' What is this but the farmyard? It is perhaps here then that the

ways truly part; not on the practical issues of contraception but on the fundamental nature of human sexuality.

It is often argued that scientific revelation, enabling us over the centuries to control both death and birth, is God's gift and that this in itself justifies contraception. I would go deeper and suggest that God has given man the potential of a sexuality which is in itself different from animal sexuality, and that it is on this fact that all our decisions on sexual morality must be based. Animals have only unknowing seasonal desire, chemical lust, that their species may continue.

Human sexuality in contrast is capable of love as well as lust, of emotional and spiritual commitment as well as physical pleasure, of the free-will choice between selfish exploitation and the gift of the whole self to another on a given occasion; the potential, in short, of holiness. Do we not believe that human sexuality, unlike animal sexuality, is an essential and integral part of spiritual love, and that spiritual love is an essential and integral part of it? I submit this is scientifically proven.

Any young profligate caught in the disappointment of purely physical experiment knows instinctively that the essence – the intention, the meaning, the love – was missing. We fail to understand the 'new morality' of the young if we ignore this. Many of them know that to be ready physically for sex is not to be ready emotionally for love and marriage. These, contrary to the assumptions of traditional moralists, they regard as far too important to be based on desire alone. Many commit themselves to marriage as soon as the deeper emotional union has entered their physical relationship. Others who wait for marriage, regarding the act as purely physical, find their loving a failure in human terms.

At the other end of the scale, those who can – who dare to – give themselves totally to each other in intercourse for intercourse's sake, as the deepest and most intimate communication God has given us, know that there is a 'plus' quality in the relationship – greater than the sum of the parts, outside and above themselves – which they may call divine. This happens to the fortunate, marriage or no marriage, procreation or no procreation, and they know in it right from wrong. To such fortunates the stark concept of 'abstinence from the conjugal act' as a graceful discipline makes no more moral sense than would abstinence from Holy Communion to the pious. Each daily act of tenderness is to them a sacrament in as deep and fundamental a sense as any hopeful but hazily understood promise.

Many youngsters who reject outright the prohibitive 'thou shalt not' can accept gladly the concept of intercourse as 'nothing but the best'. Many married couples are learning the difference between dutiful and passionate marriage. Indeed if Christian marriage appears to hold duty rather than passion as its ideal, there will be few of the next generation who want any part of it. They have seen the sad results of duty; they know better about passion.

Can we not, then, turn finally and positively away from the view that in humans, as in animals, sexuality is a necessary biological evil to be suppressed when possible; that the Creator was mistaken in making it potentially beautiful in itself? Can we not say instead, 'A Christian must make love for fully human reasons, as well as possible, totally and joyfully for the comfort of each unto other, and to the glory of God'?

Letters to the Editor

From Mr M. Grannell, London

The most puzzling part of the Pope's statement on contraception is that its use will cause the wife to lose the respect of her husband, who will abandon his regard for her physical and mental health and come to regard her as an instrument of his selfish pleasure.

This seems to me a complete travesty of the facts. By the use of contraceptives the woman has been given a dignity and freedom hitherto unknown. Conjugal love is enjoyed without constant anxiety; and from being a mere instrument for breeding purposes the woman has gained in self-respect, and in the respect of her husband.

The considerate husband appreciates the newer freedom and well-being that his companion has. Hitherto, such a man had to have recourse to the unnatural practice of celibacy, harmful to both, and fraught with the danger of temptations to infidelity. The woman overburdened with unwanted pregnancies, and with the care of more children than her physique or her nervous stamina can cope with, is not likely to be a pleasant companion.

The kindest comment one can make about the statement referred to is that it arises from ignorance of the marital situation. The alternative would be a charge of hypocrisy. Neither is a qualification for the making of authoritarian pronouncements.

From Mr Neil Middleton, Wedhurst, Sussex

There can be very few, if any, Catholic theologians of any stature in recent years who have not expressed the view that the traditional Roman objection to birth control is unscriptural, theologically bad and philosophically absurd. It is also a matter of common knowledge that many Catholics use forms of 'artificial' birth control and that the confessional practice of many priests has been to advise them to follow their consciences in the matter.

The Pope's own commission is known to have advised him to rescind the ban, and his delay in pronouncing on the matter has led many to believe that the question was virtually decided in favour of a more reasonable approach. In view of all this it is impossible to see the Pope's pronouncement as anything other than totally dishonest and completely irresponsible.

So far I have only been able to see newspaper reports of the encyclical, but from these it seems to me clear that one or two points should be made. First, a morality which depends upon the strict linking of what are called 'conjugal rights' and procreatory purpose is biologically weird and sexually sub-human; it betrays an extraordinary blindness towards the realities of married life and the part that sex plays in it. Second, the Pope's affirmation that 'No one of the faith will deny also that the interpretation of the natural moral law is the competency of the *magisterium* of the church' simply ignores the generally accepted view that this 'natural law' is founded on a debased and discredited neo-Thomism (for an excellent account of the arguments behind this see *Birth Regulation and Catholic Belief* by G. Egner). Third, the notion that seems to have been expressed that contraceptives open the way to marital infidelity, loss of respect for women and unscrupulous political behaviour on the part of public authorities, betrays a curiously Victorian account of the world. One in which all men are prevented from leaping into bed with the first available woman only by fear of the consequences; in which women are seen as the retiring creatures of nineteenth-century popular fiction whose home is in the kitchen or who spend their lives embroidering samplers; a world in which governments care about the thunderings of the church.

It is probable that many, if not most middle-class and well-educated Catholics will ignore the pronouncement. The people who will be hurt, as always, are those who have never had the opportunity to learn how to criticize and assess the value of ecclesiastical pronouncements, those, in fact, that cardinals and bishops are so fond of calling the 'simple faithful'. I hope that as many of my fellow Catholic laymen as possible will not only ignore the ban, but make their protests loud and clear to their bishops, their clergy and their fellow lay Christians. The ban must be rejected both as an affront to our consciences and as a scandal to our fellows.

Clearing up the Mess

Now that with his encyclical on birth control the Pope has undermined his own authority by creating a situation in which he is not speaking for the whole church in communion with Rome but merely for one section of it, the church as a whole is left with the immensely difficult and dangerous problem of clearing up the mess he has thus caused.

First, it needs to be stressed that this is not something we can simply close our eyes to in the hope that it will go away. It is no use suggesting, as Archbishop Roberts did in the last issue of *New Christian*, that the encyclical should just be forgotten. What it has to say about the morality of artificial contraception needs to be repudiated, perhaps by means of an equally public, solemn and authoritative statement, once the church as a whole has been able to sort out what it really does believe on this question. The encyclical itself has taken a first step towards this by quietly scrapping

the old formulation about the primary end of marriage being the procreation and education of children. Having babies is now seen as one of the
four integral aspects of married love, and it is mentioned last of the four.

Second, we have to learn to live with the dissension created by the
encyclical. To put it mildly, this is not going to be easy. What would be
dangerous here would be if the dissension were allowed to go underground
– if a situation were to arise where public statements by English Roman
Catholics officially supported the papal 'line', but it was common knowledge that this was widely ignored in practice. This may seem far-fetched as
far as English Roman Catholic lay-people are concerned, but there is a risk
of something like this happening with the clergy: all the bishops to have
spoken out so far have come down in favour of the encyclical, and it is
doubtful how long they will tolerate open dissent among their priests. It
would, I think, be fair to say that our bishops are prepared to tolerate some
limited dissent as an initial reaction to the encyclical, a reaction having its
roots in what they regard as the confusion of the last four years, but that
they expect clerical unanimity once this transitional phase is over. This
does not, of course, apply to Archbishop Cowderoy of Southwark, who is
treating the whole matter as one of simple obedience to papal authority.

Third, there is thus a risk of the impression being given of an illusory
consensus on this question among the clergy: hence the offer a group of us
made to enable priests to express their dissent anonymously but publicly
without fear of finding themselves suspended. There is also a risk of an
illusory consensus being created among the laity through sheer boredom:
those of us who dissent must continue to make our opposition clear without becoming obsessive about the whole thing.

Fourth, it would be disastrous to look for loopholes or casuistical ways
out. These cover quite a spectrum from a 'soft' line in the confessional (on
the grounds that the poor dears are too weak to resist the temptation offered
by contraceptives) to acceptance of the encyclical coupled with vague mention of previous papal blunders. Honesty demands that if we disagree with
the encyclical we must say so, politely but firmly; and this goes not just for
lay-people but perhaps especially for bishops. Withstanding Peter to his
face does, after all, enjoy excellent apostolic authority.

Fifth, we have to remember that some Catholics are utterly convinced
that the Pope is quite right, and sincerely welcome his reaffirmation of what
they genuinely regard as the authentic teaching of the church. We have to
respect their sincerity while refusing to allow them to impose their beliefs
on the rest of us.

Sixth, it is as well to recall how limited the actual area of disagreement is.
We are all agreed that sex in marriage is something good in itself; that

having babies is part of married love; that Christian couples have a duty of responsible parenthood; that forms of birth control like abortion and infanticide are completely ruled out. Where we disagree is over the admissibility of means of birth control other than the safe period. And we should all remember how far we have travelled from the suspicious attitude to sex of a St Augustine or a St Gregory the Great. Both would have been horrified at the idea of the safe period as a licit means of birth control.

Seventh, it looks as if we have an ecclesiological revolution on our hands. It is in this field of how the church should operate that the more important questions are raised by the encyclical. How should the Christian community articulate its beliefs? Which are the beliefs and patterns of behaviour that are essentially involved in membership of the Christian community? How do we reconcile the demands of continuity with the fact of change? Granted that the papacy is essential to the church as the focus of unity, how should this ministry of unity be exercised, and what is the relation between it and the entire community it is called upon to serve?

Finally, the whole sad episode has emphasized once again how deficient are the means and structures of communication within the church. The encyclical will have done good if the debate it has aroused helps by its very momentum towards creating these structures of communication that we need. Here, perhaps, the first essential is the habit of honesty in expression. In the past a dangerous gap has been allowed to grow between dogmatic formulae, to which all proclaim assent, and how they actually work these beliefs out in practice. This has meant it has been all too possible for an illusory consensus to appear, and not just on matters like birth control (remembering all those of an earlier generation who deduced that, since the church condemned artificial contraceptives, it must approve of *coitus interruptus*). One example is the way all Roman Catholics will agree that Jesus was true God and true man while many of them will boggle at the idea of regarding him as a man. And the only way we can sort out this kind of difficulty is by being able to know what we are all really thinking.

The Agonized Revolt

Catholic laity challenge bishops over the suspension of priests

Last weekend saw an unprecedented reaction against authority on the part of many Roman Catholic laity in Britain. Over 400 attended the mid-day Mass in Westminster cathedral on Saturday to pray for those who are being victimized for their opposition to the papal encyclical and for those anguished by the Pope's ruling. In almost every Roman Catholic cathedral in the country, groups gathered for prayer, and attendance was greatest in places like Cardiff and Southwark, where episcopal authority has been most unbending. On Sunday afternoon 150 parishioners of St Cecilia's, North Cheam, marched from Westminster cathedral to Southwark cathedral in protest against the suspension of their assistant priest.

Although much of the reaction is spontaneous and organized locally, a small *ad hoc* committee is meeting regularly at 10/4 Stanhope Road, London, N 6, to undertake elementary co-ordination and offer suggestions to those who are looking for the most effective forms of protest. 2,500 copies of a petition are now in circulation and it is expected that some hundreds of thousands of signatures will be collected.

Efforts are also being made to raise funds for the support of priests who are suspended and left without accommodation or allowances. It is suggested that lay people should reduce the amount of money given to their local churches, devote the balance to the support of suspended priests, and place a slip of paper in the collection plate explaining their actions. The setting up of a national fund for this purpose is expected shortly.

One significant development is the emergence of lay groups in various parts of the country. The London *ad hoc* committee is encouraging these groups to bring their local clergy into the discussions and to send their conclusions to the local Press.

The position regarding discipline is still somewhat confused. In some dioceses priests face suspension if they speak in public against the encyclical whereas other dioceses appear to be allowing a certain amount of freedom or simply arranging for the rebels to go on 'holiday'. The absence of many bishops and priests on real holiday also makes it difficult to assess the reactions of the clergy as a whole. There is, however, a broad impression that the hierarchy met shortly before the publication of the encyclical and agreed that priests should be allowed to make a single statement of dissent and be disciplined if they continued to protest.

Misleading the silly sheep

Next time a bishop or church leader stands up as the protector of 'the simple faithful' against the onslaughts of those who dare to have a new thought or refuse to toe the traditional line, I shall have to resort to violence There seems to be no other way of dealing with this kind of dishonest nonsense. Whenever a thoughtful man suggests some new way of interpreting the Christian faith in lecture, broadcast, paperback or sermon you may be sure that he will be attacked, not on the grounds that his ideas are untenable, but because they may lead astray all those silly sheep who occupy church pews on Sunday and cannot distinguish truth from error or right from wrong. This is, I believe, not only a flagrant insult to the laity but a dishonest way of concealing the fears and insecurity of the 'shepherd'. Why on earth doesn't he admit that 'this idea is thoroughly objectionable because it upsets some of my own ideas and preconceptions and will lead me to re-think the grounds of my belief in . . .'?

It is, I am sure, high time that the laity kicked against this. Imagine yourself at Mass in a Catholic church in the Archdiocese of Southwark a couple of Sundays ago. The people of God have assembled to offer their lives to God and to be renewed for their mission in the world. And what do they hear in the pastoral letter from Archbishop Cowderoy which is read to them? This: 'Some of our poor, simple people have been misled by disobedient priests who did not heed the command of the Holy Father . . They, like other priests were told not to confuse their people . . . it is not to be wondered at that simple people . . . are now very disappointed.'

I find this kind of approach to adult human beings far more offensive than anything in the encyclical – and that, believe me, is saying something.

ARCHWAY

RELIGION!

But who can blame us when others of greater erudition and theological learning than we possessed seemed to falter. If this encyclical has proved anything, it has proved in these matters of interpreting the natural law that all honesty, all compassion, all erudition, all theological acumen is of little account. – *Archbishop Murphy in Catholic Herald.*

'Continence is the answer,' said Archbishop Ruiz Solorzano of Yucatan. – *The Universe.*

Mgr Ferdinando Lambruschini, in presenting the encyclical, explained that it was not infallible (although it could have been had the Pope wanted it to be). – *The Guardian.*

Archbishop Cooke recommended that married couples 'receive the sacraments often' to help them conform to the church's teaching. – *The Universe.*

No one in this archdiocese has any authority to teach other than what the Pope and I teach. – *Archbishop Cahill of Canberra-Goulburn, Sydney Daily Mirror.*

Letters to the Editor

From Mr Anthony Holden, Accrington

Whatever other issues are raised by the papal encyclical on human life, two are central. The attitude towards contraception gives a partial and fragmented view of family life in general and of the purpose of marriage in particular.

To isolate this one issue of contraception as having a detrimental effect upon the family unit is to fail to consider what is creative and life-enhancing for the members of the family in the totality of their lives. This one problem cannot be judged in legalistic terms of right and wrong without taking into account the rights and wrongs of the whole family situation. The issue turns on the fact that without contraceptives families become too large and consequently, in a majority of cases, poor. From this there is the whole effect of environment upon the home – and this is spelt out in terms of lack of educational opportunity and, more widely, lack of the necessary care and security which leads to personal development and maturity. A more positive understanding of the end of man is needed: one which views the dignity of man in terms of the whole man.

In the same way contraception is isolated from marriage as a whole. The purpose of marriage is understood in the encyclical as being 'the most serious duty of transmitting human life' – that is, procreation. There seems little concern about sexual relationships as being creative, enjoyable and relational (will it ever be admitted that sex is good?). There seems to be little understanding of love-making as an expression of so many emotions ranging from tenderness through laughter to passion. Sex is not only either procreation or pleasure (unless the word pleasure is used in a wider sense than usual). It is an expression of the whole man and woman. At times it is the truest expression of a marriage; at others the reconciling factor in a marriage; at others, the only total way of self giving. Whatever the problems and abuses of sex (as with every aspect of human relationships) it provides an opportunity for treating another person in a personal and human way.

Sex is concerned with far more than procreation. Sex cannot be isolated in this way – it is a particular expression of the whole life of a man and woman together (laughter and tears – the mundane and the memorable). This requires a more positive attitude towards marriage than one which simply condemns certain forms of contraception: it requires a more positive attitude to the purpose of marriage than one which debases it to 'the responsibility to transmit life'.

From Mr Peter Mackie, Bingley, Yorks

It seems to me that you have missed the point of the birth control controversy, which is merely a part of a much greater question.

The issue that faces Christians today is whether on the one hand we continue to support traditional morality and the religious teachings out of which it springs, or whether we shall support relative moral standards and the new theology in whole or in part.

If we are to make a decision on these matters I would suggest that the following two points be considered:

1. Is it not reasonable to start from the proposition that His Holiness the Pope is more likely to be right than wrong? Your correspondents seem to take it as self-evident that the Pope has made a wrong decision, although he has taken almost four years to make up his mind after much research and prayer. It seems to me, whatever theology about the Papacy may be adopted, that the Holy Spirit is likely to have guided the head of the largest group of Christians into truth rather than error.

2. On the other hand, consider the disarray manifested by the varied views of all the minor self-appointed popes, who are ready to pontificate on any religious or moral topic and are united only in their almost universal surrender to the attractions of affluence and lust.

The powers of entrenched evil surround the Christian camp today on a scale never before imagined. We need think only of such recent events as Katyn Wood, Belsen, Czechoslovakia

159 (twice in thirty years), Vietnam, coupled with apartheid, factory farming and germ warfare, to mention but a few modern horrors. Do you suppose that the reversal of evil on such a scale will be brought about by a Christianity dedicated to easy living? It will in fact need faith and virtue on such an heroic scale as would make celibacy in marriage, where necessary, a very little thing.

I daresay you will find this letter quaint and emotional, but the most fundamental issues of principle are currently at stake and I see so little evidence in your columns of anything indicating other than a stampede to modernity, that I would like to suggest other answers do exist. Obviously, there can be no easy solution, but these issues are not going to be decided satisfactorily, as you suggest, by general councils of church people who by and large, are already so hopelessly riddled with the lead shot of materialism that they can see nothing straight.

It is easier to go on discussing one reform after another than actually living a religious life. The modern Christian, after spending a lifetime in these pursuits, may well hear a sentence of doom pronounced hereafter, and perhaps he will then suggest to God that he runs the world on a power pyramid, headed by the Holy Trinity, and that what he really requires is a new heavenly constitution written out by every condemned sinner.

Unless traditional Christians quickly awaken from their slumber and tell the world of the power and purity of the gospel and how it can still change men's lives today, there will soon be no church left, and the world will be enveloped by the unbridled forces of pleasure seeking and self-satisfaction. In fact, my only regret about the papal pronouncement, coupled with the earlier re-statement of traditional beliefs, is that I fear these have already come too late to stem a tide that appears to be almost irreversible.

From Mr Frank O'Hara, Tolworth, Surrey

We face today a crisis of authority in the church which needs to be seen against the background of changing social institutions and discontent with society as a whole.

Those who are seeking to reverse the recent papal decision about birth control are no doubt engaged in a noble task. One must wish them well (though without much hope). But there are long term issues here about the structure of authority in the church which we shall neglect at our peril.

In the Roman Catholic Church bishops are appointed by Rome to carry out Rome's policy. They in turn exercise an almost absolute economic dictatorship over their clergy. In the face of the hierarchy and the Vatican, only the laity are economically free. This freedom is limited, as the church has vast capital resources; but real, as the church depends on contributions from the laity.

On the other hand the laity are less well educated in theology than the clergy. This is rapidly changing, but remains true. It follows that most theology is written by people whose bread and butter depends on the 'orthodoxy' of their views. One does not impugn their sincerity. One simply notes the fact.

Again, the laity have been drilled in the past to regard themselves as 'second class members' of the church, as belonging to the church almost as associate members, co-opted into union with the hierarchy, the successors of the apostles. It follows that the laity have been very reluctant to take any initiative in church matters. This again is rapidly changing.

In all the circumstances, it seems to me that we need a Union of Catholic Laity or better still perhaps, a Union of Christian Laity prepared, as a last resort, to use economic sanctions against bishops. Positive aims of such a Union would clearly be greater participation of the laity in church government, education of the laity in theology, discretion of the laity in the choice of ministers.

Anyone interested in such a Union is asked to write to me.

From Mr J. R. Pilkington, Newhaven

In your leading article on the Pope's encyclical, you write:

'It is now necessary to ask by what canon of Christian community life an individual leader is entitled to make a statement lacking that *consensus fidelium* which alone can give it authenticity. Furthermore, it must be asked what fault in the church's institutional life is revealed by the fact that a single pronouncement by one man can throw the whole community into disarray.'

Before we get down to answering your questions, may I ask if it is really true that no statements can be regarded as authentic unless they have the *consensus fidelium*; and that a fault is necessarily revealed in the church's institutional life if a single pronouncement by one man can throw the whole community into disarray?

I am not writing in support either of the encyclical or of the method of government operative in the Roman Catholic Church. But I do wonder whether the nature of authority may merit consideration at greater depth than it is at present receiving by radicals. As was said in a recent article in NC, it is the role of leadership to be creative as well as representative.

various parish priests up and down the country who have objected to the restrained editorial line (especially when contrasted with *The Tablet*) the paper took on the papal encyclical. Apparently these priests feel that nothing short of total obedience would do and there have been many reports of sales being stopped at the church door. One priest in the South of England went so far as to destroy the offending issue except for the page on which the encyclical was printed in full. This sort of pressure is a heavy one for any editor to bear and, as the *Herald* still relies on church door sales, will no doubt continue to be a burden, unless the self-appointed guardians of the public good wake up to the fact that free debate is essential within the church if it is to be true to its calling.

As Desmond Albrow, the editor of the *Catholic Herald*, writes in an article defending the paper's freedom to publish all news and views, if discussion is stifled the tremors which are shaking the church could erupt into an earthquake with disastrous consequences for all concerned.

Publish and be damned

ARCHWAY

I was not surprised to learn that the *Catholic Herald* is again suffering from censorship by

---

Views on that Encyclical

The reactions of some European bishops to the Pope's ruling.

Both the German and the Belgian hierarchies have held special meetings to discuss the papal encyclical *Humanae Vitae*. After the meeting of the German bishops, a statement was issued which declared that the emphasis of the encyclical was in accordance with views expressed at the Vatican Council but the teaching with regard to methods of birth control was not infallible. The statement recognized that many conscientious Roman Catholics, both priests and laymen, had reached a conclusion different from that of the encyclical and were asking how it should affect their personal attitude. Recalling a previous statement, the bishops declared that 'a responsible decision on the matter that is dictated by one's conscience should be treated with respect by all concerned'. The principles to be applied were that everyone should consider seriously and sympathetically what the encyclical had to say and that, in the administration of the sacraments, pastors must respect the responsible decisions of conscience made by the faithful.

The bishops continued their statement with an appeal for discussion of the important moral issues raised by marriage by all Catholic Christians. Their appeal was taken up the following week in Essen at the biennial congress of German Catholics. After a two day debate on marriage and the family, a resolution was passed by 3,000 votes to 90, with 58 abstentions, calling on the Pope to revise the passages in the encyclical dealing with artificial contraception. The resolution declared that the great majority of German Catholics could not in 'judgment and conscience' obey the Pope's ruling.

The Belgian bishops address themselves to the same question: to what extent are the faithful bound to accept and observe the directives given by the Pope? First, they say, every doctrinal declaration of the church should be received with the respect and spirit of docility which the teaching authority established by Christ can legitimately demand. Second, the faithful must adhere to a statement made *ex cathedra* or by the Pope and bishops in unison. But 'if we do not find ourselves considering a statement which is infallible and therefore unchangeable – generally an encyclical is not infallible and furthermore *Humanae Vitae* does not claim to be such – we are not bound to an unconditional and absolute adherence such as is demanded for a dogmatic definition . . . Someone who is competent in the matter under consideration and capable of forming a personal and well-founded judgment – which necessarily presupposes a sufficient amount of knowledge – may, after a serious examination before God, come to other conclusions on certain points. In such a case he has the right to follow his conviction.'

What L'OSSERVATORE Saw

PETER HEPPLETHWAITE

The two qualities which *L'Osservatore Romano* most prizes are 'serenity' and 'objectivity'. This can be deduced from the fact that its adversaries, who are legion, are invariably said to lack them. Has *L'Osservatore* itself given proof of serenity and objectivity in the last few weeks? The question is worth asking. It was a constant tactic of the minority during the Council to suggest that attacks on the Roman Curia were attacks on the Pope himself. But we learned to distinguish. And we can also distinguish between the Pope and *L'Osservatore Romano* and enquire about the tactics of the paper without in any way discrediting the Pontiff.

There is a preliminary difficulty. It is sometimes hard to see what *L'Osservatore* is driving at. Its anonymous contributors all use the same orotund circumlocutions. Here is how one of them answered the suggestion that 'Vatican circles' has been taken by surprise by world reactions to the encyclical: 'As far as we are concerned, we believe that this suggestion is a hypothesis far removed from reality.' That is how *L'Osservatore* says: 'Far from it'.

But the message comes through loud and clear. The paper has daily given long lists of telegrams received commending the encyclical and praising the Pope's courage. 'Hundred and hundreds' have several times been mentioned. Staggering under this *embarras de richesses*, the paper has reported a message from a Norwegian Protestant family of fourteen and an anonymous telegram from Boulogne-Billancourt. The principle of selection is obscure. But some piquant details emerge. Thus one learns from Cardinal Tisserant's letter that he has 189 nephews, nieces, grand-nephews, grand-nieces, great-grand-nephews and great-grand-nieces, on all of whom he calls down the pontifical blessing.

But we live in an imperfect world and there are trouble-makers about. *L'Osservatore* knows all about them. They are moved by a frantic desire to be 'up-to-date'. They seek after 'novelty for novelty's sake'. They have read the encyclical only partially and interpret it tendentiously. They positively enjoy disagreeing, since '*contestation* has become a fashionable literary form for all those who wish to be *à la page*'. If the cap fits, wear it.

In dealing with these malcontents, the tactics of *L'Osservatore* vary from the bland to the no-holds-barred. An example of the bland, *suaviter in modo, firmiter in re*, can be found in the treatment given to the resolution of the Lambeth Conference on the subject. The text of the resolution is given in full. Then follows the cool comment: 'The encyclical *Humanae Vitae*, in reality, says nothing different.' This baffling judgment suggests some ghastly error of transmission, but read on: 'The point of disagreement lies in the use of contraceptives which, evidently, the Lambeth Conference approves of.' One is left to ponder the exact significance of the *evidentemente*.

Catholics do not get off so lightly. 'A noted German theologian' rashly hinted at a comparison with the Galileo case. A whole article refutes him. It begins with the rumble of heavy irony: 'If this comparison were found in a sensational Parisian newspaper from the pen of some unfortunate hack who has to write about everything and *de quibusdam aliis*, it would still not be justified, but at least we could explain it and certainly understand it. But when it is attributed to a noted German theologian, then one has the right to ask whether words and concepts have not lost their meaning.' Out of delicacy, *L'Osservatore* does not give names, but on the next page of the same edition one can find the name of the incautious theologian: Hans Küng. Bad luck that he is Swiss. In any case the *locus classicus* is Cardinal Suenens, who said at the third session of the Council: 'I beg of you, my brother bishops, let us avoid a new "Galileo affair". One is enough for the church.' *L'Osservatore* has no difficulty in showing the invalidity of the comparison, if taken narrowly, but the whole business seems like an irrelevant smoke-screen.

Indeed, a reluctance to discuss the question directly has been a feature of *L'Osservatore's* treatment. One persistent theme has been the courage, sincerity and painstaking hard work of Pope Paul. These are admirable qualities, but no one has really seriously suggested that the Pope has been cowardly or insincere or lazy. The Pope's moral qualities would be relevant if *L'Osservatore* were defending some sort of 'morality of intention', but this, of course, it does not do, for then we would be out of the 'objective order' altogether.

Another tactic of the paper is to pose false dilemmas: do you think that the church should be democratically ruled and that decisions should be reached by majority vote? If so, 'those who have short memories' – a favourite phrase – are reminded that the Nazis attained power through elections, as though this somehow discredited all majority decisions. And the only alternative to democracy which *L'Osservatore* can imagine is monarchy.

The Pope prayed for those who disagreed with his encyclical: *L'Osservatore* tries to discredit them. The Nazis, nasty crew, come in handily here. An editorial in *The Economist* is compared to the prose of *Angriff* or *Schwarze Korps*, organ of the ss. The editorial was certainly intemperately written and substituted epigram for argument. *L'Osservatore* gives it the full treatment in a special article called *Misura*, 'Balance'. Knowing little about the briskly controversial temper of our weekly press and thinking of the English in terms of the stereotype of 'the gentleman', it rubs its eyes in astonishment at the style, accuses *The Economist* of materialism and recommends the writer to read Chesterton, where he will discover the chaos to which Protestantism inevitably leads.

One sympathizes with the stakhanovites of *L'Osservatore Romano*, placed at the centre of what must appear like a daily hurricane of comment and cross-fire. They keep up a brave front and remain optimistic. But the paper has become an organ of combat rather than communication. It is tending to over-react. I do not think that it is lacking in 'serenity' and 'objectivity' to suggest that bad arguments and dubious methods do not help a good cause.

Letters to the Editor

From Mrs Pauline A. Mills, Leicester

Your letters supporting the Pope's encyclical are all from men. Mr Wright may be a 'veteran of the bed', but it would be a miracle if he were a veteran of even one pregnancy! I have three small boys, two born to me and one who is adopted. It seems that those who speak loudest and longest about the evils of contraception are those who know nothing at first hand about pregnancy and child-rearing. I am not writing from the quiet comfort of a book-lined study. Whilst I write this the washing-up waits and the children consume illicit sweets and beat each other up. I suspect this is why so few mothers have contributed to the acres of print on this subject. *We* are on the battlefield, *we* have the sleepless nights and the long hours of often back-breaking work. I am in a relatively privileged position. I can feel only deep compassion for the mothers who have broken under the strain.

As a Christian I feel no sense of guilt in making use of contraception. I consider that its proper use in the context of a stable, happy marriage is one of God's gifts to us as responsible human beings. If priests like Fr Flanagan had even one child to care for full time, I suspect that all this marvellous theological claptrap about the magisterium, etc., would begin to sound very hollow, even to them. His letter makes my blood boil, as does a great deal of the unrealistic nonsense written by men who lack charity because they never experienced real life, only a shadow cast on the wall of the seminary. For God's sake, listen to the voices of those who *know* something about all this. Believe us when we say that without contraception we should go under. My children are happy, healthy and nourished in body and mind; they would suffer from the advent of others. I thank God with all my heart for giving us the power to control our destiny to this extent. Finally, if any priest is wondering how a mere *mother* is qualified to speak on this highly theological subject, may I add that I also have a degree in theology.

From Mr James M. Finnerty, Gateshead

Fr John Flanagan claims that the Papal Commission on birth control was 'divided on this vital issue' and therefore the problem was 'naturally insoluble'. But he cannot deny that the Papal Commission gave an unmistakable verdict.

After two years of careful study, the Commission's bishops were unanimously in favour of modern contraception. The medical experts were without exception of the same opinion. Not one of the married members dissented from the majority verdict. An overwhelming majority of the theologians supported the introduction of modern techniques in addition to the dangerous and unreliable rhythm method of contraception. Out of seventy members only four opposed the majority report, and even the four dissenting theologians could not defend the *status quo* on scriptural or rational grounds. They discounted any appeal to natural law, the professed basis of *Humanae Vitae*. Their sole objection to change was the fear that papal authority would be diminished if the Pope were to admit that previous papal teaching had been wrong.

The same anxiety to save face even at the expense of truth brought about the tragic conviction of Galileo in 1632. Galileo was punished for heresy because his theory that the earth is in orbit round the sun threatened the fundamentalist interpretation of scripture taught by the Catholic Church at that time. *Humanae Vitae* rejects the new sexual insights accepted by the Papal Commission because they threaten a fundamentalist interpretation of papal authority.

Fear begets intolerance. Galileo was under house arrest for the last ten years of his life. Priests opposed to *Humanae Vitae* have been evicted, and the encyclical urges Catholic governments to impose the Pope's views by law on all their citizens.

It can be said of the Galileo case and of *Humanae Vitae* that the judgment was in 'conformity with the traditional teaching of the Catholic Church' and 'a re-affirmation of the universal teaching of the church, known as its magisterium'. But Galileo taught us that we must not attribute infallibility to the magisterium, or attempt to subject human reason to human authority. Tradition must not exclude development. St Augustine would have been horrified at the suggestion that contraception by the rhythm method was licit, and one medieval pundit had the comical notion that sexual intercourse was grievously sinful unless the lady adopted the supine position.

If Fr Flanagan believes that sexual intercourse with modern contraceptive methods is 'mutual masturbation' then he must take the same view of post-menopausal relations, or use of the rhythm method. The use of such a phrase suggests an ignorance of the relationship of married people unusual even among lifelong celibates. How can a Christian believe that the only effective methods of population control approved by God are puerperal hazards, kwashiorkor, famine, and just wars with support of the hierarchies on both sides?

From Mary Hills, London W

In all the controversy about Pope Paul's encyclical, one point seems to have been either entirely overlooked, or much neglected. To my mind it is of the utmost importance, and it is 'Intention'. Surely what a person intends by his action governs to a great extent that action. If a dangerous criminal goes for me with a weapon, I not only am right to defend myself, even if I happen to cause his death and, of course, instinctively, I shall defend myself. But if, having known and feared this criminal for years, I seize this opportunity, in defending myself, to kill him, then have I not, in fact, committed murder although I am comfortably aware that I shall not be charged with my crime? Surely, by the same reasoning, if husband and wife deliberately wait for the safe period before having intercourse, with the intention of preventing ovulation, they are practising birth-control just as much as if they practise some artificial method?

I really cannot see why the pill is all wrong, but some pill to make the safe period even safer is all right. I would very much like enlightenment on this question.

From Mr Bruce Stewart
...Father Flanagan of CEPHAS, criticizing Archbishop Roberts, fails to pay enough attention to the fact that *Humanae Vitae* reasserts authoritatively the old notion that contraception is evil *because it is against the natural law*. But the natural law, it is agreed by theologians, is derived from reason. How then is there 'matter' here for an authoritative pronouncement? Archbishop Roberts is quite right to say the Pope 'claims to be the arbiter of what is reasonable'. The various other truths of religion don't come into it, as they are either directly revealed or logically derived from revelation. This one isn't – as the complete absence of any attempt at the discredited 'Onan' and 'Thou shalt not kill' theologies in the encyclical shows – and that is what makes it odd. I should also like, in charity, to warn Father Flanagan against any further use of that glib expression 'mutual masturbation'. Fifteen years of marriage and the fathering of six children have convinced me it can have little meaning in the Christian context. It fits in no doubt with the (magisterial?) teaching of a Pope like St Gregory the Great on the general sinfulness of sex even within marriage, but in the modern day, especially coming from a celibate, it sounds more like the (regrettable?) dirty talk for which an irreligious Pope like Julius II was renowned.

From the Rev. J. Jackson Stevenson, Clogher, Co. Tyrone
I wish to write about Lance Wright's statement that 'once it (the sexual act) is established as an act of no consequence our ideas about it will change very rapidly'. As a married priest I could never subscribe to the view that the thought of procreation must always be present when intercourse takes place. This is a spontaneous act expressing the mutual love of husband and wife, and can be among the most enriching, beautiful, peace-giving, renewing experiences of life. As a Christian wife recently expressed it, 'at its climax I feel my husband's semen as an injection of Divine grace'. Is it to be considered a satisfactory position when a Roman Catholic mother has twenty-one children, as is the case in a family here in Co. Tyrone? Can parents adequately supply the varied needs of this size of family?

As Christians I believe we have a duty to give adequate teaching to those about to be married so that they can make their informed decisions in this important aspect of married life. Contraception is here to stay, whatever we may feel about it. Having prayed sincerely and asked for the Holy Spirit's guidance, I fail to see how condemnation can be levelled at any couple using the method they feel to be most suitable for them. Love took the place of Law: that in a nutshell is what the New Testament says to the Old.

From Mr Robert Sencourt, London SW
I would like to add a word to those of my old friend Lance Wright on the Pope's encyclical. Indeed, there are within it noble words on the dignity of marriage and the value of life. What I find disgusting in the encyclical is the proffering of the safe period as the sole method of contraception. It is well known that this is the period when the wife is least attracted towards intimacy with her husband. What the Pope is counselling is that, instead of honouring his wife as a partner in love, the husband should put her in the position of a prostitute, to satisfy what the Prayer Book rightly calls 'his carnal lusts and appetites'.

It is often said that since the Pope took four years to reach his conclusions we should consider them for four years before we voice disagreement. But what are the facts? The Pope overruled a practically unanimous decision of lay specialists and advisers and went against the majority of bishops. Why? Because after the Council had dispersed, the old Italian die-hards who live in one of the most immoral towns in the world – a town despised all over Italy for its appalling standards of behaviour – decided that they must keep up the old façade which hid the depravity around them, and, in spite of the vehement protests from Cardinals in Northern Europe, the Pope went back to the mentality of the worse kind of curial official.

I write as one who has not only written on *The Genius of the Vatican* but who in a course of lectures given in America during the Council defended Pope Paul at every turn. When, however, I came back to see the Council end, and saw how Pope Paul was tinkering with the conscience of the laity and subjecting it to clerical *mores* I came to the conclusion that I had been deceiving the people who had been paying me in America.

I believe that the encyclical may do great good – in making it clear that though the Pope has a unique position, he can say things which are absolutely unreliable.

From Mr G. F. Pollard, Paignton

It is ironical that *L'Osservatore Romano*, in its issue dated 2 September 1968, should accuse those who disagree with the ruling of *Humanae Vitae* of 'putting the fallible light of human science and the divine light of . . . the Holy Spirit on the same level'. For this is precisely the error of those scholastic theologians who composed the encyclical. For they have made their decision on birth control, not in the light of that divine element in man which the Greek Fathers term the 'spiritual intellect', but rather on the basis of a set of abstract principles which Thomas Aquinas chose to term the 'natural law': but which, in fact, are simply formulations of the fallible human intellect divorced from the deep operation of the Spirit acting through man's existential environment. The ancient Pharisees likewise quenched the light of the Spirit beneath a slag-heap of legalistic formulations, thereby drawing from the divine Master the caustic comment that 'if the blind lead the blind both fall into the ditch'. Perhaps this is what the Roman bureaucrats mean by the phrase: 'to die in the last ditch'. Let them do so, by all means; but let them, of their charity, at least refrain from taking the poor and uninstructed faithful with them. This is assuming, of course, that their theory of knowledge permits them the luxury of any natural human feeling and compassion. Fr Martin D'Arcy has warned us that in Thomas Aquinas 'we must expect to meet one who is coldly indifferent to the world of emotions and imagination'. Alas! how can we expect the disciples to be above their master?

Truth and Love at Stake

A leading article

The sight of the Roman Catholic hierarchy of England and Wales playing ecclesiastical politics while crucial matters of Christian truth and love are at stake is not edifying. Last week's tortuous statement from Westminster on *Humanae Vitae* served only to show that Cardinal Heenan and his colleagues have not really begun to understand what all the fuss is about

and why so many loyal Catholics are determined to withstand the teaching
of Pope Paul's encyclical.

The debate has, of course, long since moved from the initial question of
birth control, though the bishops are apparently unaware of this. Their
attempts to deal with the crisis simply by appealing to papal authority or
by assuring the 'sinner' (who is acknowledged to have the duty to 'be true
to conscience') that he is still within the ambit of the church's pastoral
concern, do not come anywhere near to meeting the objections of those
who see in the publication of the encyclical a threat to the church's credibility as an instrument and expression of the gospel. When the bishops
produce for serious consideration a document which asserts: 'It is against
the plan of God to take positive steps to destroy the possibility of the transmission of life. The use of marriage during infertile periods, on the other
hand, does not destroy the act's "openness to the transmission of life" ',
there seems no alternative to the conclusion that they are either incompetent or dishonest.

Two fundamental questions are at stake: Is the view of marriage
expounded in the encyclical Christian? Is the church the kind of society in
which belief and behaviour are controlled by the insights of one man? The
theological grounds for returning a negative answer in both cases are so
strong, and so widely held by Christians of every tradition, that it is impossible for the questions to be regarded as open or even as matters for further
investigation.

This being the case, loyal Catholics just cannot be expected to remain
silent or submissive. They are not here dealing with a peripheral issue. They
are handling a central tenet of their faith since the church is intended to be
a zone of God's truth and love. If truth is displaced by error and love by
authoritarianism (no matter how paternally exercised), the question arises
as to whether the church can any longer claim the allegiance of responsible
men and women. In this situation episcopal wriggling of the kind displayed
in last week's statement is bound to undermine confidence even further.

At this point the non-Roman churches have an interest to declare. It is
a welcome indication of the present ecumenical climate that none of these
churches has attempted to make capital out of the Roman Catholic embarrassment. They have naturally made their own position clear but have hardly
breathed a word of criticism or fallen for the 'we told you so' temptation.

But the fact remains that the current activities of the Roman Catholic
hierarchy are bringing the entire Christian body into disrepute and making
it more difficult for everyone to present the church and the gospel as
reasonable options for intelligent human beings. The whole basis of the
encyclical must be destroyed quickly.

Papal Encyclicals of the Past
LANCELOT SHEPPARD

If we are to believe some of the Roman Catholic advocates (official and unofficial) of blind obedience to *Humanae Vitae*, papal encyclicals not only ought to be so obeyed but always have been. Yet looking back over the past thousand years or so, one can think of more than one example of an alteration in moral practice due to changed economic or social conditions. It would probably be unfair to instance the toleration, to put it no stronger, of the castration of boys to preserve their voices for singing in the papal choirs, yet it has to be borne in mind that in the eighteenth century the popes were the civil as well as the religious rulers of the Papal States.

A clearer case is that of torture. Gregory IX (Pope 1227–41) established the Inquisition, inserting in the papal registers the constitution promulgated by the Emperor Frederick in Lombardy in 1224 imposing the death penalty for heresy. Death was by burning. Innocent IV (1243–54) allowed torture to be introduced into trials for heresy, though it was not allowed to cause the loss of a limb or death (decree *Ad extirpanda*, 15 May 1252). This was confirmed by Alexander IV and Clement IV. But there was one inconvenience about this. Clergy (and the Inquisitors were in this category) taking part in the taking of evidence or the extortion of a confession in this way incurred the canonical penalty of irregularity, rendering them incapable of exercising their orders. To keep the proceedings in clerical hands Urban IV (1261–4) allowed Inquisitors and their companions to grant each other absolution from this canonical penalty.

If torture seems too much of a thing of the past to be relevant to the present controversy there are other moral pronouncements of a later date which can be instanced. Gregory XVI (1831–46) rejected railways and gas lighting for the city of Rome as contrary to the natural law. Then there is the question of lending money at interest. Certain early canons of councils, Carthage (345) and Aachen (789), prohibited the taking of interest for all, and several councils (Arles and Nicaea, for example) were especially strict on clerics who indulged in the practice. In the Middle Ages the third Lateran council (1179) and the second council of Lyons (1274) repeated the injunction as applying to all. The second council of Vienne (1311) laid down that if anyone maintained that there was no sin in demanding interest for money lent he was to be punished as a heretic. All down the Middle Ages the teaching is the same, in Thomas Aquinas, Scotus and others; in the sixteenth and seventeenth centuries it is repeated by the post-Tridentine Jesuit theologians, Lessius, de Lugo and Molina. In the eighteenth century it was solemnly reaffirmed by Benedict XIV in his famous encyclical *Vix pervenit* (1745). Benedict himself believed in the existence of a patristic tradition which regarded the prohibitory passages of the Bible (Exod. 22.25 and Deut. 23.19, 20) as of universal application. Benedict's encyclical was occasioned by certain Italian cities raising municipal loans at interest, and because the letter was addressed only to the Italian bishops some thought that it was not of universal application. It was not intended as an infallible statement, but it was a dogmatic judgment on a point of morality, and in July 1836 the Holy Office issued an official statement that the encyclical applied to the whole church. The change that has occurred in the course of the last hundred years is significant. Nowadays, of course, the Vatican puts money out at interest and requires church authorities to do the same. And the reason for the change was the alteration in the prevailing economic conditions.

Not very much more than a hundred years ago Pius IX issued an official statement in solemn form. This was the Bull *Quanta cura* (1864), to which was attached the celebrated Syllabus of Errors. Both documents repay perusal. In the Bull we can read, for example, that liberty of conscience and of worship are to be condemned as 'an insanity'. The Syllabus of Errors, besides condemning once again freedom of worship and of conscience, concluded with rejection of the idea that 'the Roman Pontiff can, and ought to, reconcile himself to and agree with progress, liberalism and modern civilization'. Running all through these documents is the thought of the threat to the temporal power of the Pope: thus proposition 76 condemned as false that 'the abolition of the temporal power of which the Apostolic See is possessed would contribute in the greatest degree to the liberty and prosperity of the church'. And a note is added referring to other documents issued during the previous fifteen years in favour of 'the certain doctrine which all Catholics are bound most firmly to hold touching the temporal sovereignty of the Roman Pontiff'.

We have only to read the controversy aroused by the issue of the Syllabus to realize that it was not received by Catholics everywhere with the submission that was expected of them, though it was welcomed, of course, by men like W. G. Ward who would have liked an infallible statement every morning with *The Times* on his breakfast table.

Leo XIII, known among Catholics as the pope of the 'great social encyclicals', certainly had plenty of constructive suggestions to make, but still he reflected the prevailing conservatism of his days in his attitude to nationalization and the state's taking of private property which he roundly condemned. Presumably his encyclicals are still binding today (if the official line on encyclicals means anything), though it has not been unknown for the Roman Catholic authorities in this country to resort, through the local education authority, to the compulsory purchase of land for the erection of a Catholic secondary modern school. Leo XIII condemned freedom of worship as 'opposed to the virtue of religion' and laid down that it is 'quite unlawful to demand, to defend, or to grant unconditional freedom of thought, of speech, of writing, or of worship as if these were so many rights given by nature to man'.

All these instances are examples of the solemn statements of Popes in the past which, it must be admitted, are hardly followed by Roman Catholics as their rule of conduct at the present time. And then, too, except in recent years, encyclicals have usually been followed by controversy, have often been dead letters almost at once on publication, and have frequently been disregarded by convinced and sincere Catholics. The uproar consequent on *Humanae Vitae* is really not quite so unusual as some think it to be: certainly two hundred years ago, when the Pope was secure in the possession of the papal states, Benedict XIV had cause to lament the reception of one of his pronouncements. 'The Pope orders,' he complained, 'the cardinals do not obey, and the people do as they please.'

Letters to the Editor

From Mr Lance Wright, Pangbourne

I share Trevor Beeson's distress ('A suicidal teach-in') at our apparent inability to get discussion on the pill off the ground. Some of the fault for this lies on my side, on that of the anti-pill men: we thunder forth on the issue of authority when we would do much better to draw on the wealth of fact and probability which tells against contraception and which rises from common experience.

But I suggest that much fault lies also at the door of the pro-pill lobby. For it has always seemed to me that this is much too anxious to narrow discussion to the case of the weak-willed, sickly but very fecund wife who is married to a compulsive copulator . . . Alright. She exists and calls for our compassion; but it would be dotty to tailor the law to meet her case. For hard cases, as we know so well, make bad law.

Outside of this, the pro-pill case seems to rest almost exclusively on the testimony of those who say: 'I-and-my-husband-have-been-using-contraception-for-25-years-and-think-it-so-right.' A sense of chivalry compels me to grant the last word in this class of testimony to the lady reported by your correspondent, J. Jackson Stevenson, as saying that she felt her husband's semen as the injection of Divine grace.

Confronted with this self-approving testimony I am tempted to call it sanctimonious. People accord themselves a licence: they enjoy it (good luck to them): and then they seek to apply the seal of God's approval to what they have done. 'Sanctimonious' is not the right word in many cases; but this testimony suggests strongly that those who make it lack knowledge of the human heart, of their own and of other people's. Good 'new Christians' see contraception in the context of their own more or less dedicated lives. Even so, they could be mistaken; for how easy it is to underestimate the distorting influence upon us of the remorseless sex propaganda which our society has generated.

But to see this matter clearly we must look to the general effect of contraception on the world at large.

The trouble seems to be that by according a much more important role to sex stimulation in marriage than Christians traditionally admit, contraception has made marriage itself much more brittle. People who learn to depend on frequent sexual intercourse tend to tire of one another more quickly, and to want the stimulus of a new partner.

Margaret Mead the anthropologist, in a recent issue of *Life*, outlined how marriage is likely to be modified to meet the different approach to sex which contraception has engendered. She thought that the average man and woman would seek three or four different partners in the course of a lifetime. This is not an out-of-the-way prophecy, since it is happening already in some strata of American society.

Fortunately or unfortunately Our Lord was very strict on sex and we must accept, surely, that this new concept of marriage is incompatible with Christian teaching. Is it not likely that contraception, which is playing so large a part in ushering it in, is incompatible too?

From Dr W. Juchnowicz, Birmingham

I am a general medical practitioner, with a practice in a working district of Birmingham. About 30 per cent of my patients are Roman Catholics (like myself), mostly Irish and Polish.

Pope Paul's *Humanae Vitae* does not in practice alter much, since my Catholic patients have been practising contraception of some kind for many years. How otherwise could anybody explain an average Polish family in Birmingham of two to three children? An average Irish family for the time being is three to four children, with occasionally five to six. Taking into account that they are healthy specimens of humanity, were they not practising any kind of contraception they should have at least ten children.

Many of these young couples are on the pill. For the last two months since *Roma locuta* I have not noticed any less demand for contraception prescriptions; if anything, more, though it is just my impression, as I do not keep any statistics on how many prescriptions for the pill I give in one week.

So as far as I can see, we are where we were before Vatican II. Some will consider it a sin, will go to confession, get absolution and as soon as they go to bed start all over again. Some, such as myself, will not consider it a sin and will not confess it. This I suppose will be the position until it will please Almighty God to give us another Pontifex Maximus, when the discussion will start again.

One Parish and the Pope
DAVID WOODARD

The parish of Our Lady of Peace, Burnham, is on the edge of Slough. It is an ordinary working-class parish with 4,500 Catholic parishioners of whom three are priests. And I should like to relate not what we in the parish imagine to be possible but what we have proved to be possible since the publication of *Humanae Vitae*.

We priests had three days to prepare a joint statement which we preached and published on the 'Sunday within the Octave of the Encyclical'. We meant to reassure the people that there would be no change in our customary attitude to contraception: in and out of the confessional we sympathize and advise on moral problems but take up neither a lax nor a rigorous position. On that Sunday we could not do better than quote the Holy Father's paragraph 25 on the use of the sacrament of penance. The sermon was received with approval in the parish and outside. But something more had to be done urgently to demonstrate to people, both priests and laity, that there was some light coming up over the very black horizon. So we decided to read the encyclical together.

On three Sunday afternoons we read it, discussed it, and attempted to frame in intelligent and dispassionate language the questions that we were all asking in one form or another at home and in the factories. These questions we sent to the diocesan theological commission. Then a small group continued the debate: they undertook to give the Parish Instruction on Sunday for a term's course on marriage; they split into smaller groups with the intention of reporting back and providing enough spokesmen by 1 November to preach that day on the sanctity and blessedness of married love. However, the Bishop has refused permission for laymen to preach. The group undertook to accept introductions to people intending to be married so that they will supplement the help already given by the Catholic Marriage Advisory Council and the clergy in marriage preparation. They also promised to edit and publish anonymous statements or interviews that married people might be induced to contribute, relating their own insights into the meaning of married love.

All this has been most satisfactory. The debate has been intelligent, respectful to authority and far from 'niggling'. We appealed to those who came for the reading to steer clear of the question that was at the heart of the matter – authority – and to concentrate on moral problems that arise in marriage.

What next? What's going to happen now? We four and a half thousand clearly have very little influence beyond the parish boundaries. Within these boundaries we want to find an effective forum for the laity so that the statement of truth on moral issues as it is perceived by individuals during their living of the Christian life can readily be shared by all.

So what do we hope for? The laity's most natural forum seems to me to be in the streets and factories and offices. There is hardly a road in the parish that has not got its prophetic example of Christian married love. And if that is one of the laity's vocations, I wish we priests could think that we, the celibates, were proclaiming with equal effectiveness our celibate prophetic witness, which I take to be an un-attachment to the things of this world, instead of finding heaven, as some of us do, in a passing bird! In the ecclesiastical sphere, though, are we content with the forum that the laity seems to be getting for itself? It is a voice at the present which is exercised through their own professional skills, in writing books, in the press, radio and television, drama, lecture and discussion associations; and recently on commissions, national, diocesan and parochial.

Unlike the laity, the *magisterium* has a most effective system of communication downwards: to reach the laity the *magisterium* uses not only all the best means of modern communication but the most effective Christian means of all, pastorals and sermons during the Liturgy of the Word. The *sensus fidelium* must find its voice and become articulate so that in time the *magisterium* will express, on these personal moral issues, something more realistically sympathetic to the laity's problems. The clergy have a forum at Mass. Therefore I hope that the expounding of the Word will not just be left to the clergy. The most authentic occasion for the expression of anyone's inspirations is at the end of the Liturgy of the Word: and in small group Masses on weekdays, in homes, in classrooms, in Mass centres and even, I believe, in the Sunday assembly. It is both desirable and practicable for the homily to extend into a sharing of the truth by whoever perceives it, and to cease to be a monologue by the representative of the *magisterium*.

In time the celebrant should be seen more clearly to be what in fact he is: the controller of the assembly and the preserver of the unity that exists amongst God's people. The traditional function of celebrant or bishop would in no way be jeopardized by this, because, after all, his chief function is to foster the life of the Spirit by preserving the unity. When the bishop and his own people celebrate the eucharist, the *magisterium* will in this way be granted a ready means of discovering the *sensus fidelium*.

Letter to the Editor

From Mrs Pauline A. Mills, Leicester

Lance Wright's imagination is beginning to get out of hand. He has managed to turn most responsible, hard-working young parents into sanctimonious sex-maniacs with a stroke of the pen. Among my numerous acquaintance of new, old and non-Christians most love the children they have, work until all hours on their behalf and, contrary to Mr Wright's assumption, worry about overpopulation and starving children in Africa. Most would not have any more children if you paid them, and fail to see how having more would solve the problems of the starving and homeless. Tell us, Mr Wright, what is our problem. Are we over- or under-dedicated, or just plain damned?

Meanwhile, Back in Rome
ROBERT NOWELL

Although the Vatican did not expect *Humanae Vitae* to have an easy passage, the evidence here in Rome suggests that the strength of the reaction within the church came as a surprise to the Roman Curia. From the Curial point of view, the main cause of distress is not so much that hierarchies such as the Belgian and German should have contested the encyclical but that even the Italian bishops should, despite representations from the Secretariat of State, have offered an interpretation of the Pope's teaching which goes some way towards robbing it of its sting. And perhaps it is not too cynical to see in the appointment as Archbishop of Perugia of Mgr Ferdinando Lambruschini, who presented the encyclical to the press in Rome, a measure of the Curia's anxiety at finding that all theologians of any note view the document with at least very considerable reserve.

In other words, the Curia would now seem to be rattled. Defying the
Pope is no longer something confined to a handful of North Europeans.
And the Curia is itself to some extent divided. If it was ever the monolithic
power-structure which it appears from the other side of the Alps, it is
becoming less so now that it is faced with a situation that from its point of
view is out of hand.

This is probably the explanation of the disputed rumours now circulating
to the effect that the Pope is preparing an encyclical or some other document on authority which would deal with the Petrine office in the church
and its relations with the episcopate. That such a document is in preparation I have been assured by friends whose judgment and knowledge I trust.
Other equally trustworthy sources, however, have assured me that they
regard rumours to this effect as lacking all foundation. Of course, if the
Pope should speak out on authority in the church, the tone of his remarks
can be deduced in advance; and if he does issue an encyclical on authority
the resulting theological explosion will make the present uproar in the
church seem as decorous as a vicarage tea.

Meanwhile, the clearest indication of Curial anxiety over the independent-
mindedness shown by certain episcopates (the Canadian bishops being most
outspoken) is given by the curious case of Fr Edward Schillebeeckx. Apart
from the fact that the former Holy Office contradicted its own regulations
by not informing Schillebeeckx himself or Cardinal Alfrink that proceedings were under way, it does not make sense for it to pick on the one
theologian who, however radical his conclusions, is most thoroughly
soaked in theological tradition, and especially in the thought of St Thomas
Aquinas.

It seems unlikely that a general attack is being mounted on theologians
as a class, even though such an explanation would more easily fit the
nomination of Fr Karl Rahner to defend Schillebeeckx on the grounds that
this would be an attempt to implicate him as well. It seems more likely that
what is involved is an attack on the Dutch hierarchy through their most
brilliant theologian. And in this context it should be noted that Dutch
bishops wisely refrained from issuing any immediate collective statement
on the encyclical, but instead decided to wait until they had been able to
consult the Dutch church as a whole. This means that when they do speak
out – and they are hardly likely even to give a qualified welcome to
Humanae Vitae – they will have the whole Dutch church province behind
them, and it will be that much more difficult for the Curia to act against
them.

A further factor in the situation is the blockage of information, especially
the way in which the Pope is liable to receive a one-sided picture of what is

going on in the church. There is, admittedly, an innocent aspect to this, in that those who write to the Pope and to the Curia in general about what is going on in the church are more often those who are profoundly distressed by what is happening. Thus the views of the conservative minority are given undue importance.

But there is also evidence that information reaching the Pope is filtered so as to present a biased picture. One theologian, I understand, felt that if the Pope was to learn his views he would have to speak out publicly on the encyclical: for if he were to write privately the Pope would be unlikely to receive his letter. For both these reasons we have to realize we are dealing with a Pope who is habitually badly informed. Moreover, he is influenced by the fact that the theological idols of his youth – Journet, Maritain, Congar, De Lubac – on the whole have taken a pessimistic view of the post-conciliar situation. If such voices cry out that the faith is in danger, the Pope (who does not regard himself as a professional theologian) cannot but take alarm.

Finally, what really makes the situation more complex and painful than it need be is the habit of secrecy. The church as a whole is not informed about what is going on – as, for example, with the preparation of *Humanae Vitae* and this rumoured statement on authority. The trouble is that in the Curia it is not considered the business of the church as a whole to know what is going on before it happens. At its most extreme, the view is that it is for the Pope to speak and for the rest of the church to listen and obey. In other words, what we are faced with here is the clash of two conflicting ecclesiologies, one with an exaggerated emphasis on the papal primacy and the other stressing the primary role of the Christian community. Resolving this conflict will hardly be easy.

RELIGION!

England's newly elected Orthodox Chief Rabbi Immanuel Jakobovits recently got around the traditional Orthodox opposition to birth control by ruling that the biblical injunction, 'Be fruitful and multiply,' was addressed to men only – and that women are therefore free to use contraceptive devices to limit births. – *Time.*

Venezuelan women must either give up miniskirts or be 'condemned to hell', according to the Roman Catholic Church in Caracas. Father Alfredo Laboren, of Caracas Cathedral, said miniskirts were condemned by the Roman Catholic Church and whoever 'wore such attire would go to hell'. About 70 per cent of young women in Caracas wear miniskirts. – Reuter. – *Daily Telegraph.*

Bishop Muldoon said last night he was certain Cardinal Gilroy would wish to be addressed simply as His Eminence, Norman Thomas Cardinal Gilroy, KBE. 'His Eminence is the most humble and modest of men,' he said. – *Sydney Daily Telegraph.*

Act of God Surprise Pack

Copy out on back of postcards, shuffle and lay face downwards on table.

1 You have changed your sex and, strangely, have an urge to consult a Methodist Minister. Move at once to the *Methodist Recorder*. If you pass 'Let Us Begin' collect 200 Talents.

2 Patience Strong has a crush on you. Keep calm and apply to join the Cerne Abbas friars as a lay brother. Pay 50 Talents to each player and miss a turn in penance and terror.

3 A hurricane has removed your neighbour's dustbin lids and smashed them into your TV aerial on the night you are doing the Epilogue. Repairs cost 150 Talents. Go to Hell for one turn.

4 The Archbishop of Canterbury has appointed you Vicar of St Mary's, Woolwich. Explain the position to Nicolas Stacey quietly over the telephone and report back to fellow players.

5 Neil Middleton asks you to advise him on publicity matters: you rename *Slant* for him anagrammatically as *Stalin*. You are, not surprisingly, fired. Pay 200 Talents to the Director of *Parish & People*.

6 Dr Ved Mehta, the noted Indian mystic, has asked you to write your spiritual biography for serialization in the *New Yorker*. Your vanity overcomes you. Pay 2,000 Talents penance money to each curate player and proceed direct to Hell.

7 The Bishop of Bath and Wells has resigned to take the job of foreman in a Nottingham shoe factory. You are appointed in his place. Take 1,000 Talents and enjoy yourself.

8 The Archbishop of York calls upon you as Archbishop of Canterbury to give him and all other young persons 'clear moral guidance'. Tell them it's wicked. Advance to 'Let Us Begin'.

9 Billy Graham's toupé fell off at a crusade rally last night. Explain, as his barber, to your fellow-players how this happened. If they are not convinced, go to Hell.

10 Malcolm Muggeridge has revealed that for the last three years he has been surreptitiously ordained through the Southwark ordination scheme. You sell the story to the *New Statesman* for 1,000 Talents.

11 Your doctoral thesis on the biblical basis of Roman Catholic football pools has led to your appointment as General Secretary of the Evangelical Alliance. Move to the *Methodist Recorder* as racing correspondent.

12 You are praised by your local bishop for your 'tremendously worthwhile' views. Move to the mission field as male nurse in Lusaka. Do not pass 'Let Us Begin'. Pay 200 Talents penance for your spiritual pride.

13 You have been asked by the General Assembly of the Church of Scotland to publish its new report which suggests that marriage is one of the remnants of a decayed English capitalism and must be replaced by free love. Order a kilt and advance immediately to 'Moderator'.

14 You have doubts on a number of religious issues. Try harder. Think about it in Hell. Go Direct to Hell. Do not pass 'Let Us Begin' Do not collect 200 Talents.

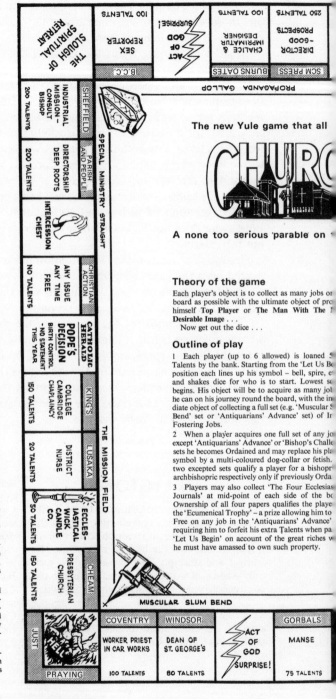

The new Yule game that all

CHURC

A none too serious 'parable on

Theory of the game

Each player's object is to collect as many jobs or board as possible with the ultimate object of pro himself **Top Player** or **The Man With The** **Desirable Image** . . .

Now get out the dice . . .

Outline of play

1 Each player (up to 6 allowed) is loaned S Talents by the bank. Starting from the 'Let Us Be position each lines up his symbol – bell, spire, e and shakes dice for who is to start. Lowest so begins. His object will be to acquire as many job he can on his journey round the board, with the im diate object of collecting a full set (e.g. 'Muscular S Bend' set or 'Antiquarians' Advance' set) of In Fostering Jobs.

2 When a player acquires one full set of any jo except 'Antiquarians' Advance' or 'Bishop's Challe sets he becomes Ordained and may replace his pla symbol by a multi-coloured dog-collar or fetish. two excepted sets qualify a player for a bishopri archbishopric respectively only if previously Orda

3 Players may also collect 'The Four Ecclesias Journals' at mid-point of each side of the bo Ownership of all four papers qualifies the playe the 'Ecumenical Trophy' – a prize allowing him to Free on any job in the 'Antiquarians' Advance' requiring him to forfeit his extra Talents when pa 'Let Us Begin' on account of the great riches w he must have amassed to own such property.

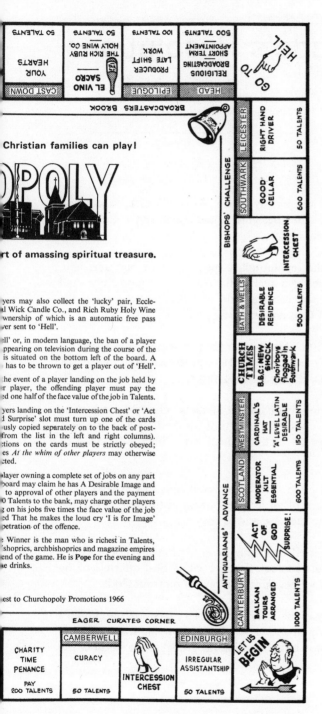

Christian families can play!

...OPOLY

...rt of amassing spiritual treasure.

...yers may also collect the 'lucky' pair, Eccle-
...al Wick Candle Co., and Rich Ruby Holy Wine
...wnership of which is an automatic free pass
...ver sent to 'Hell'.

...ell' or, in modern language, the ban of a player
...ppearing on television during the course of the
... is situated on the bottom left of the board. A
... has to be thrown to get a player out of 'Hell'.

...he event of a player landing on the job held by
... player, the offending player must pay the
...ed one half of the face value of the job in Talents.

...yers landing on the 'Intercession Chest' or 'Act
...d Surprise' slot must turn up one of the cards
...usly copied separately on to the back of post-
...from the list in the left and right columns).
...ctions on the cards must be strictly obeyed;
...es *At the whim of other players* may otherwise
...cted.

...player owning a complete set of jobs on any part
...board may claim he has A Desirable Image and
... to approval of other players and the payment
...0 Talents to the bank, may charge other players
...g on his jobs five times the face value of the job
...ed That he makes the loud cry 'I is for Image'
...petration of the offence.

...e Winner is the man who is richest in Talents,
...shoprics, archbishoprics and magazine empires
...end of the game. He is **Pope** for the evening and
...e drinks.

...est to Churchopoly Promotions 1966

Intercession Chest Cards

Copy out on back of postcards, shuffle, and lay face downwards in middle of board.

1 The Revd Stephan Hopkinson has launched an appeal for starving ex-stars of ATV epilogues. You are moved to tears at his entreaties. Pay 200 Talents to all ordained players and start campaigning for the social morality council.

2 You have won a beauty contest organized by Messrs Wippell & Co.; dress up in a cassock and jump up and down for a while.

3 Your latest best-seller, *Dialogue in Ecumenical Honesty, a Moral Approach*, has been burned by the Irish Customs. Go back three spaces.

4 You have been appointed Vice-Provost of Leicester Cathedral and decide to substitute readings from *New Christian* for the normal Epistles and Gospels. The Bishop and the Revd Timothy Beaumont are delighted. Move to Leicester or *New Christian* immediately.

5 The Revd Simon Phipps has had a vision of God on Sunday. The Bishop of Southwark, much moved at a report of this miraculous visitation in today's *Daily Mirror*, has sent you and his favourite countess up to celebrate with him over a case of gin. Pay 100 Talents to his Lordship's cellarman.

6 Your profession of teenage love for Sir Cyril Black on Twenty Four Hours last night has brought you a strange gift of 1,000 Talents from the Moral Rearmament organization via your bank.

7 Monica Furlong has written of your beautiful nature in the *Daily Mail* today. You feel a million. Give each player 200 Talents to celebrate.

8 You have been elected New Christian of the year by a team of judges including Trevor Beeson, Marghanita Laski, Dame Sybil Thorndike, Mrs Margaret Knight and Mr David Frost. At your ton-up cycle outdoors eucharist in Stepney you are concussed in a gang fight. Miss three turns.

9 Your recent articles in *The Observer* on the significance of the Dead Sea Scrolls qualify you for appointment to the new Chair of Religious Journalism at Lancaster. Take this job quickly before anyone notices your inconsistencies and, if challenged, point out that you always feel obliged to honour a deadline. Do not pass 'Let Us Begin'. Do not collect 200 Talents.

10 The President of the Methodist Conference has indicated that your ideas on the coming non-church have solved all the outstanding issues in the Anglican/Methodist Conversations. Take 700 Talents.

11 Cardinal Heenan has appointed you to be his personal representative to the Dominican Order and the Newman Society. Your main task is to encourage more radical thought in both bodies and if successful you will be appointed Editor of the *Catholic Herald*. Move to *Catholic Herald* in anticipation.

12 Your new revised Quaker report on preteen sexuality passes unnoticed in the Press. Resign any job you hold forthwith and pay 100 Talents to the curate in Camberwell.

13 You have lost your faith. Well done. Take 500 Talents.

New Decade's Resolutions

25 December 1969

We shall try to discern more clearly God's activities in the world and encourage and support all efforts designed to assist men and women in the expression of their full humanity.

We shall take seriously the revolutionary movements of our time and, while never failing to judge them against the truth of the gospel, we shall recall that Jesus came to set men free and that the implications of the concept of the kingdom of God are primarily political.

We shall expose all simplistic solutions to the problem of world poverty and devote a major part of our intellect and energy to assisting in the search for the most just and effective way to end hunger.

We shall listen to the opinions of people of races other than our own, remembering that they have waited a long time for their say and recognizing that God normally speaks to us through that which is puzzling or apparently outrageous.

We shall remember more often that our commitment to Christ is to be expressed not in the defence of an ideology or an institution, but in the acceptance of people where they are and as they are.

We shall refuse to be diverted from our main work as agents of God's reconciling love by ancient theological and ecclesiastical quarrels or by modern urges to accept every new idea as a revelation from God.

We shall recognize the provisional character of every aspect of the church's institutional life and gladly abandon any building, committee, office or wealth that stands in the way of incarnating the gospel in the world of the 1970s.

We shall remember that women, as well as men, are 'in Christ' and that their gifts may properly be exercised through any office or function in the church.

We shall cease being anxious about the size of our congregations or pleased with the length of our reports, recognizing that we shall be judged by our service of the kingdom and not by our ability as recruiting agents or as devourers of paper.

We shall not despise those who are concerned with the re-shaping of the church's institutional life for we recognize that the gospel is either commended or denied by the corporate life of the church at every level, but we hope that they will not find it necessary to discuss everything five times before reaching a decision.

We shall recognize that Christians of other churches and traditions have apprehensions of truth that we urgently need to share, and we shall steadfastly refuse to regard any Christian as outside the church's fellowship.

We shall remember that in 1964 representatives of the churches meeting in Nottingham 'dared to hope' that their parent bodies would have found a way to unity by Easter Day, 1980.